'GIVE US GOOD MEASURE'

ARTHUR J. RAY is a member of the Department of Geography at York University. He is author of *Indians in the Fur Trade* and co-author of *Early Fur Trades*.

DONALD B. FREEMAN is with the York-Kenya Project in Nairobi.

Throughout most of the pre-confederation period the fur trade dominated the life of Indians and Europeans alike. Arthur Ray's earlier book, *Indians in the Fur Trade*, studied the role of the Indians as they responded to the changing environmental and economic conditions between 1660 and 1870. *'Give Us Good Measure'* concentrates on the early contact between the Indians and the Hudson's Bay Company. It offers a path-breaking analysis of the differing European and Indian economic customs and the ways in which the two cultural groups accommodated their differences in order to establish a long-lasting partnership. The authors also examine the way in which the partnership responded to changing economic conditions around Hudson Bay.

The book's approach is innovative in several ways. Extensive use is made of Hudson's Bay Company business records, little-studied sources which have proved to be highly illuminating. The data have been subjected to a variety of statistical treatments in an effort to obtain new understandings of the economic behaviour of European and Indian traders alike. In assessing their findings, the authors consider whether models drawn from comparative economics, economic anthropology, and economic geography provide any new and useful insights into trading relations that developed between Europeans and Indians before 1763.

The book's clear focus and wide-ranging perspective result in a fresh and important reassessment of early Canadian history.

'Give us good measure' was a phrase often used by Indian leaders in trading speeches, according to James Isham, a factor at Hudson Bay.

ARTHUR J. RAY and
DONALD B. FREEMAN

'Give Us Good Measure': an economic analysis of relations between the Indians and the Hudson's Bay Company before 1763

UNIVERSITY OF TORONTO PRESS

Toronto Buffalo London

© University of Toronto Press 1978
Toronto   Buffalo   London
Printed in Canada

Canadian Cataloguing in Publication Data
Ray, Arthur J., 1941–
   "Give us good measure"

   Bibliography: p.
   Includes index.
   ISBN 0-8020-5418-8 bd.   ISBN 0-8020-6334-9 pa.

   1. Hudson's Bay Company – History.   2. Fur trade
   – Canada – History.   3. Indians of North America
   – Canada.   I. Freeman, Donald B., 1942–
   II. Title.

   FC3207.R39   971.01   C78-001152-X
   F1060.R39

To Irene M. Spry
friend, inspiration, stimulating colleague, and valued critic

Contents

PREFACE / XV

PART ONE: THE DEVELOPMENT OF THE HUDSON'S BAY COMPANY FUR TRADE

1
Fur trade history / 3

2
European and Indian cultures at the time of contact / 10

3
The fur trade before 1670 / 19

4
The struggle between the English and the French for the Hudson Bay fur trade / 27

PART TWO: THE SPATIAL AND INSTITUTIONAL STRUCTURE OF
THE HUDSON'S BAY COMPANY TRADING NETWORK

5
The inland trading network of the Hudson's Bay Company / 39

6
Fur trading institutions / 53

7
The factor and the trading captain / 63

PART THREE: THE ECONOMIC STRUCTURE OF THE FUR TRADE SYSTEM:
A QUANTITATIVE ANALYSIS

8
Analytical objectives and approach / 79

9
The early Hudson's Bay Company account books / 81

10
Variables and methods of analysis / 120

11
The terms of trade / 125

12
Variations in exchange rates and levels of competition / 163

13
Trade expenses, factors' gains, and competition / 198

14
The Indians' responses / 218

PART FOUR: EMPIRICAL EVIDENCE AND COMPARATIVE ECONOMIC THEORY:
SOME IMPLICATIONS OF THIS STUDY

15
Trade and politics: a reinterpretation / 231

16
Economic dimensions of the trade / 237

17
The Hudson Bay fur trade as a spatial system: conclusions, and
implications for comparative economic geography / 246

APPENDIX / 261

NOTES / 273

BIBLIOGRAPHY / 289

INDEX / 295

Illustrations

1 Balance remaining inventory, Prince of Wales Fort (Fort Churchill), 1724–5 / 84
2 Shipping invoice, Prince of Wales Fort (Fort Churchill), 1727–8 / 86
3 Men's debts, York Factory, 1723–4 / 88
4 Expenses, Prince of Wales Fort (Fort Churchill), 1724–5 / 90
5 Goods traded, Prince of Wales Fort (Fort Churchill), 1724–5 / 92
6 Furs received in trade, Prince of Wales Fort (Fort Churchill), 1724–5 / 94
7 Index to the ledger, Prince of Wales Fort (Fort Churchill), 1724–5 / 96
8 Reconciliation of the general charge, debit entries, Prince of Wales Fort (Fort Churchill), 1724–5 / 98
9 Reconciliation of the general charge, credit entries, Prince of Wales Fort (Fort Churchill), 1724–5 / 99
10 Reconciliation of bead, kettle, and gunpowder accounts, debit entries, Prince of Wales Fort (Fort Churchill), 1724–5 / 104
11 Reconciliation of bead, kettle, and gunpowder accounts, credit entries, Prince of Wales Fort (Fort Churchill), 1724–5 / 105

Figures

1 Distribution of Indian groups, ca. 1720 / 16
2 Cartogram of major fur trade routes / 26
3 Major fur trade routes / 28
4 Furs traded at Hudson's Bay Company posts, 1695–1770 / 34
5 Canadian physiographic and vegetation zones / 40
6 York Factory canoe departure dates in relation to freeze-up dates / 46
7 Zonal model of the Hudson's Bay Company fur trade, ca. 1670–1763 / 48
8 Mean annual volume of exchange in MB at Hudson's Bay Company posts, 1695–1770 / 50
9 Flows of furs and goods in the Hudson's Bay Company trading system / 52
10 Phases of the trading ceremony / 74
11 Fort Albany: brandy traded / 135
12 Fort Albany: brandy used / 136
13 Moose Factory: brandy traded / 137
14 Moose Factory: brandy used / 138
15 Fort Churchill: brandy traded / 139
16 Fort Churchill: brandy used / 140
17 York Factory: brandy traded / 141
18 York Factory: brandy used / 142
19 Estimate of York Factory overplus derived from the brandy trade / 143
20 Estimated percentage of total York Factory overplus consisting of brandy overplus / 144
21 Fort Albany: overplus trade / 145
22 Fort Churchill: overplus trade / 146

23 Moose Factory: overplus trade / 147

24 York Factory: overplus trade / 148

25 Fort Albany: index of actual price variation / 149

26 Fort Churchill: index of actual price variation / 150

27 Moose Factory: index of actual price variation / 151

28 York Factory: index of actual price variation / 152

29 Eastmain: index of actual price variation / 152

30 Fort Severn: index of actual price variation / 153

31 Fort Albany: actual price variation in relation to fur receipts in made beaver, 1695–1770 / 154

32 Fort Churchill: actual price variation in relation to fur receipts in made beaver, 1695–1770 / 156

33 Moose Factory: actual price variation in relation to fur receipts in made beaver, 1695–1770 / 157

34 York Factory: actual price variation in relation to fur receipts in made beaver, 1695–1770 / 158

35 Eastmain: actual price variation in relation to fur receipts in made beaver, 1695–1770 / 160

36 Regional variations in trade good prices, 1695–1770 / 164

37 Fort Albany: total value of furs traded / 166

38 Eastmain: total value of furs traded / 175

39 Fort Churchill: total value of furs traded / 176

40 York Factory: total value of furs traded / 180

41 Moose Factory: total value of furs traded / 184

42 Fort Albany: expenses / 202

43 Fort Churchill: expenses / 203

44 Moose Factory: expenses / 204

45 York Factory: expenses / 205

46 Fort Albany: average factors' expenses per made beaver / 206

47 Fort Churchill: average factors' expenses per made beaver / 207

48 Moose Factory: average factors' expenses per made beaver / 208

49 York Factory: average factors' expenses per made beaver / 209

50 Fort Albany: factors' net returns in relation to official standards / 210

51 Fort Churchill: factors' net returns in relation to official standards / 212

52 Moose Factory: factors' net returns in relation to official standards / 213

53 York Factory: factors' net returns in relation to official standards / 214

54 Eastmain: factors' net returns in relation to official standards / 216

Tables

1 A comparison of the official standards of trade at Fort Albany and York Factory, 1710–60 / 64–5
2 Account book outline / 82
3 Reconciliation of the general charge, Fort Churchill, 1724–5 / 100
4 Reconciliation of the trading account for beads, Fort Churchill, 1724–5 / 102
5 Reconciliation of the beaver account, Fort Churchill, 1724–5 / 103
6 Reconciliation of the men's debts account, Fort Churchill, 1724–5 / 106
7 Reconciliation of the expenses account, Fort Churchill, 1724–5 / 108
8 Reconciliation of profit and loss, Fort Churchill, 1724–5 / 109
9 Reconciliation of balance remaining account, Fort Churchill, 1724–5 / 110
10 Reconciliation of factory use account, Fort Churchill, 1724–5 / 111
11 Fort Churchill schedule of accounts, 1718 / 112
12 Reconciliation of the general charge, Fort Churchill, 1718 / 113
13 'The Acct of the Several Skins & Furs Valued into Beaver as pr ye Comparative Trade wch is the Product of ys Years Trade Commencing from July ye 14th to July ye 16th 1718,' Fort Churchill, 1718 / 114
14 Reconciliation of the beaver account, Fort Churchill, 1718 / 115
15 Profit and loss, Fort Churchill, 1718 / 116
16 'An account of how and in what manner the factors are capable to give the company the overplus trade' / 130–1
17 Gallons of brandy traded and expended / 132–4
18 Beaver and marten returns, Hudson's Bay Company posts, 1701–63 / 168–74

19 A comparison of French and Hudson's Bay Company prices in the Fort Albany hinterland / 188

20 Hudson's Bay Company and peddler prices in the York Factory hinterland, 1769–70 / 196

21 Fort Churchill: expenses and overplus / 211

22 Relationships between factors' returns, expenses, and trade good prices / 219

23 The lagged effect of trade good price changes on the total furs traded / 220

24 The standards of trade at Fort Albany, 1715 / 262–3

25 Goods traded at Fort Albany, 1715 / 264–5

26 'Furrs and other Commodities Received In ye Trade of Ye aforesaid Goods' / 266

27 Fort Albany, 1715: the official comparative standard and Richard Staunton's standard / 267

28 Fort Albany, 1715: the official standard and Richard Staunton's standard / 268–70

29 Fort Albany, 1715: sources of overplus / 271

Preface

Although there have been many studies of the fur trade, relatively few have considered it explicitly as an economic system having geographic expression as well as historical and anthropological ramifications. Even fewer have focused on the Indians' role in the economics of the trade. This case study of the Hudson's Bay Company fur trade in its first century of operation explores in detail these important aspects of Indian–European exchange. It is based on quantitative data of trade at six 'factories' or trading posts, collated from meticulously kept company account books, as well as from the more conventional non-statistical sources used by previous researchers.

This study examines the system of institutions, relationships, and processes which permitted two highly dissimilar cultural groups, the Indian and the European, to maintain continuous trade over an extended period of time. It explores the nature of the trading system – a set of institutions which developed as a compromise between the customs and norms of traditional Indian exchange and those of European market trade. It takes account of evolutionary trends in exchange practices and motivations, in addition to spatial variations in trade, creating a sense of time and place. The influence of European competition for furs and the transitional nature of Indian band society at this period are shown to be pertinent in the analysis of trading patterns.

The analysis of statistical data in this study, and the examination of ancillary accounts of the trade, lead the authors to call into question previous assessments of the economic and political significance of the trade, as well as their implications for comparative economic theory. The interpretation of the trade by some earlier scholars as being primarily a ceremonial reaffirmation of political alliances is refuted by the data presented in this book. So, too, are the notions of fixed pricing systems for furs and goods, and alleged non-economic behaviour of the Indians. The key elements underlying the specific interpretations in this study are the behaviour of the Indians in the face of French–English rivalry for their furs and the existence of an unofficial traders' profit called the *overplus*, which enables us to measure competition among the traders and variations in the Indians' responses.

It is emphasized that this example of trade between people from a commercially oriented, politically complex state society (the Europeans) and those from a traditional and later a transitional band society (the Indians) does not fit neatly into previous theoretical categories of trade and exchange. The implications of this fact for comparative economic theory are discussed, leading to a search for a more satisfactory theoretical framework. By extending the discussion to geographical aspects of the trade, we can assess the applicability of current theoretical constructs of economic geography to the analysis of the spatial and ecological characteristics of dissimilar economic or cultural systems.

The authors would like to thank the Hudson's Bay Company for granting them permission to consult and quote from the company's microfilm collection on deposit in the Public Archives of Canada, Ottawa. We would like to express our appreciation for the help that the staff of the Public Archives, especially Peter Bower and Garry Maunder, have given to us over the past five years, and we would like to extend a special note of thanks to Mrs Shirlee Anne Smith, Hudson's Bay Company Archivist, Provincial Archives of Manitoba, for her assistance and valuable commentary on sections of the manuscript. We appreciate the assistance that Kathy Frawley, Charles Mathews, Arthur Roberts, and Joan Yasui provided us in the collection and analysis of the accounting data used in this study. We would like to thank Conrad Heidenreich and Carol Judd for their many helpful comments and incisive criticisms of the manuscript. The authors, of course, are solely responsible for the interpretations offered. The efforts and patience of the Cartographic Office, Department of Geography, York University, have also been greatly appreciated. Finally, we would like to thank the Canada Council for the financial assistance that was provided to support archival research in Ottawa.

This book has been published with the help of grants from the Social Science Federation of Canada, using funds provided by the Canada Council, and from the Publications Fund of the University of Toronto Press.

PART ONE

THE DEVELOPMENT OF THE HUDSON'S BAY COMPANY FUR TRADE

1
Fur trade history

Although there is an extensive literature dealing with the North American fur trade, relatively few studies have considered the trade explicitly as a system of economic interaction. Most scholars have concentrated on providing detailed accountings and interpretations of events and the evolution of trading empires,[1] biographical narratives of key figures,[2] histories of the major companies,[3] and analyses of the influence of the fur trade on the political development of the continent.[4]

The comparatively small number of studies that have examined the fur trade as the meeting point of two dissimilar economic systems have, nonetheless, raised some interesting questions and theoretical issues about the significance of trade institutions and the applicability of various explanatory economic concepts. In doing so, these studies highlight problems that have hitherto not been fully resolved in the fur trade literature. These questions relate to the nature of the exchange as a mixture of economic, political, and social relationships; the role of exchange as an acculturation process; and the significance of fur trade studies for broader theoretical issues concerning comparative economic analysis. These questions will be taken up in the present study.

THE EARLY HUDSON'S BAY COMPANY FUR TRADE

The trading activities of the Hudson's Bay Company are particularly attractive for the above lines of research because records of the company extend back to the early post-contact period. This enables us to obtain a glimpse of English and Indian trading practices before they were modified as a consequence of prolonged intercourse. Furthermore, since the company had a highly centralized system of control and accounting, nearly all of the early business records have survived. These records are a rich source of quantitative data dealing with various aspects of the trade. This information supplements contemporary journals, letters, diaries, and books written by the fur traders themselves. These latter sources are frequently the only ones available to historians studying other companies, such as the North West Company, because these other enterprises frequently lacked a strong centralized administration.[5] Their business records are, for the most part scattered and fragmentary, making meaningful statistical analyses of the surviving business data nearly impossible.

Studies of the Hudson's Bay Company fur trade are numerous. It is not our intention to provide an exhaustive review of them, particularly those of a biographical or historical–descriptive nature. Rather, consideration will be given to a few notable works that treat the Hudson's Bay Company fur trade from an explicitly economic or political viewpoint, and that serve to illustrate general theoretical concepts or principles. Attention will also be directed to those studies that focus on the geographic aspects of the exchange network. These studies will serve as important points of departure for the present work.

The classic study of the Canadian fur trade is Harold Innis' *The Fur Trade In Canada.*[6] Innis subtitled the book 'An Introduction to Canadian Economic History,' reflecting his effort to portray the role of the fur trade in Canada's fledgling economy. He dealt both with institutions and processes operating generally throughout Canada and, in addition, examined the details of the trade on a regional basis.

Innis' careful observations of the fur trade culminated in the well-known staple thesis, which provided an explanation of the pattern of development of resource-rich lands newly opened to exploitation in what is now Canada and, by extension, in other parts of the new world. In the conclusion to his study, Innis states: 'The importance of staple exports to Canadian economic development began with the fishing industry but more conspicuously on the continent with the fur trade. The present boundaries were a result of the dominance of furs ... The geographic unity of Canada which resulted from the fur trade became less noticeable with the introduction of capitalism and the railroads. Her economic development has been one of gradual adjustment of machine industry to the framework incidental to the fur trade.'[7]

In its broad design, if not always in its detailed interpretation of the trade, Innis' study is primarily economically oriented. It emphasizes the

European side of the trade, being 'interested ... primarily in the effects of a vast new land on European civilization.'[8] While considerable attention is given to Indian participation in the trade, it is concerned more with the explanation of European trade behaviour than with a detailed understanding of the Indian role in the system per se, or with the specific effects which participation in trade had wrought on traditional Indian cultures and livelihoods. The activities of the Hudson's Bay Company were viewed by Innis as simply part of a much broader arena of the North American fur trade.

E.E. Rich, who has spent a lifetime studying the Hudson's Bay Company fur trade, paid more attention to cultural adaptation stimulated by Indian–European trade contacts. However, he was also strongly interested in the participation of Europeans in the system. In particular, Rich viewed the fur trade as an important aspect of British imperial history.

Yet, apart from this interest, Rich has been concerned with the economic issues raised by the fur trade. His work is notable for its assertion that there was an important connection between the trade and the quasi-political alliances that were a feature of Indian social linkages before and after the initiation of European trade. This was most clearly evident in the case of the St Lawrence–Great Lakes trade. In this area, traditional rivalries between the Huron and their allies and the Iroquois were carried over into trade pacts with the British, Dutch, and French, whose commercial rivalries in North America were thereby given a new dimension.[9]

In an important article entitled 'Trade Habits and Economic Motivation Among the Indians of North America,' Rich raised the significant question of the degree to which the economic motivations of the Indians differed from those of the European traders. Rich asserted that the Indians did not act as 'economic men' in the sense of trading to maximize the economic return for status enhancement. Rather, he contended that the Indians bartered with the Europeans solely to satisfy their immediate needs, to maintain their political alliances, and to gain access to reliable sources of European arms.[10] Rich emphasized the manner in which the Indian motivations for trade influenced the evolution of the trading system. Particular attention was given to the ceremonial exchange of gifts and the elaborate system of standards which became an integral part of the Hudson's Bay Company trading operation.[11] The functions which these institutions served and the manner in which they operated will be treated in detail below.

Rich's ideas were later developed by the economist A. Rotstein, who put forward the thesis that the fur trade was primarily an institutional extension of the Indian alliance system. Rotstein states that 'the fur trade bore a striking similarity to [Indian] institutional procedures, suggesting that the fur trade was closely embedded in the intertribal political process.'[12]

In his dissertation entitled 'Fur Trade and Empire,' Rotstein pays more attention than have most previous historians of the fur trade to the effect of pre-contact Indian traditions on the subsequent development and structure of fur trade exchange institutions. Thus, intertribal wars, territoriality (hunting rights and access routes), formal treaties (councils and alliances), and gift-giving ceremonies are considered to have an important bearing on the way in which the European–Indian trade evolved. In stressing that trade was closely linked with, or embedded in, the political sphere of Indian life, Rotstein questioned whether concepts of the market, price, and supply-and-demand drawn from formal economic theory were appropriate analytical devices to apply to the fur trade. Rather, he proposes that the concepts of the 'substantivist' economists should be employed, particularly the notion of administered or treaty trade.[13] According to this concept, rather than being governed by price-making markets that are regulated by supply-and-demand pressures, exchange is assumed to be largely regulated by other institutional elements such as kinship obligations and ceremonial requirements.[14]

Rotstein contends that the advantage of this approach is that a wide variety of 'non-economic' factors which influenced trade are considered, freeing analyses and interpretations from the theoretical preconceptions of the market framework. Although Rotstein demonstrates that political, kinship, and other non-economic factors did play a role in the fur trade, in our opinion, he does not give adequate consideration to the market aspects of exchange. It is assumed at the outset of his study that market institutions did not play a central role in the fur trade.[15] Thus, in effect, we believe Rotstein substituted a theoretical framework based on the notion of treaty trade in place of one based on the market mechanism. It is our opinion that before such conclusions can be drawn, more research should be done to determine both the degree to which market and non-market institutions may have played a role in exchange as well as the extent to which these sets of institutions may have changed in relative importance over time and space.

In this context, the recent studies of C. Heidenreich, C.A. Bishop, and A. Ray warrant attention. Heidenreich's exhaustive study of the history and geography of the Huron Indians in the early seventeenth century devotes a great deal of attention to politics and trade, and clearly demonstrates that the two were intricately interwoven.[16] The connection between exchange and the social system is also thoroughly explored, as is the motivation for trade. Regarding the latter, Heidenreich points out that the Huron engaged in the fur trade in part to accumulate goods to give away in a variety of ceremonial exchanges. The more an individual gave away, the greater his status enhancement, since liberality was regarded as a quality that a leader should exhibit.[17] However, Heidenreich also points out that there were economic motives for participation in the fur trade besides those of a social and political nature. French goods were prized because of their technological superiority over many traditional Indian utilitarian items.[18]

In his discussion of the historical evolution of Huron trading patterns, Heidenreich points out that the French expansion up the St Lawrence Valley into the Huron area significantly altered pre-contact and early contact trade relationships. Prior to the arrival of the French, it appears that the Huron traded mostly with their northern Algonkin neighbours, the Nipissing, exchanging corn, corn meal, wampum, and fishing nets for skins and fish.[19] As will be discussed in greater detail subsequently, the development of the French trading network led to a reorientation of Huron trade eastward to the St Lawrence River, via the Ottawa River. At the same time, Huron exchange with their western neighbours, the Petun and Neutral, as well as some Georgian Bay Ottawa, increased.[20] For the above developments to take place, a whole series of adjustments of inter-tribal relationships had to be worked out. Ultimately, the New York Iroquois set out to destroy the trading system that evolved during the historical period and this led to the eventual destruction of the Huron. Thus, Heidenreich's study gives careful attention to the effects of the fur trade on the social, political, and economic spheres of Indian life, making it clear that the trade brought about rapid and extensive changes. Although Heidenreich's study does not involve the Hudson's Bay Company fur trade, it is important for an understanding of that trade since the French–Huron network was one of the precursors to the Hudson's Bay Company system. Also, some of the trading conventions worked out between the French and the Indians were carried over into the English trade.

In his *Northern Ojibwa and the Fur Trade*, Bishop examines socio-economic change among the Ojibwa of northern Ontario from their initial contacts with Europeans to 1967.[21] Bishop's study complements that of Heidenreich, from the perspective of Indian fur trade history, in that it deals with a group who lived to the north and west of the Huron and who assumed a central role in the French fur trade shortly after the Huron passed from the scene. Eventually, they became important participants in the Hudson Bay fur trade as well.

Of significance to the present study, Bishop discusses the effects of the fur trade on the migrations of the Ojibwa. Bishop points out that their involvement in the trade in the seventeenth and eighteenth centuries as middlemen and trappers led them to expand northwesterly from their original homelands in the vicinity of Sault Ste Marie into northern Ontario.[22] This movement necessitated a variety of socio-economic changes, since the Ojibwa had to adapt to an environment which was quite different from that of the Sault Ste Marie area. He further suggests that the French–English rivalries served to heighten, if not initiate, warfare between the Ojibwa and other tribal groups. Also, Bishop demonstrates that the fur trade brought about a major change in the aboriginal land tenure systems of the subarctic region. Over time, the flexible hunting range scheme was replaced by the family territory system, and a strong notion of trespass began to develop among Indian bands.[23]

To the west and southwest of the Ojibwa were the Cree and Assiniboine. The participation of these groups in the fur trade has been examined in Ray's book, *Indians in the Fur Trade*.[24] While Ray considers many of the same topics as does Bishop, he devotes less attention to the effect of the trade on Indian social systems and gives somewhat greater regard to the changing nature of trading institutions under differing economic conditions. Ray points out that although the English adopted certain Indian trading conventions such as the ceremonial gift exchange, they modified and manipulated these institutions to serve their own ends.[25]

Collectively, these three studies make it very clear that Indian societies differed considerably at the time of European contact. In each case it is shown that the nature of the fur trade changed substantially over time and had a wide range of effects on Indian life. Therefore, to deal adequately with the issues raised by Rich and Rotstein, the temporal and spatial aspects of the trade have to be carefully managed. To accomplish this objective, Part One of this book provides a discussion of European and Indian socio-economic systems at the time of contact as a prelude to an analysis of the early Hudson's Bay Company fur trade. This is followed by a brief survey of the evolution of the fur trade in Canada up to the time of the founding of the Hudson's Bay Company in 1670. Again, this survey is not intended to be exhaustive, but it draws attention to salient features and events which have bearing on subsequent discussion in this book. In

Part Two, the geography, ecology, and institutional aspects of the Hudson's Bay Company fur trade are considered. Part Three is devoted to a thorough temporal and spatial analysis of the company's account-book data with the objective of determining how the system operated. The concluding chapters in Part Four address the theoretical implications of the study for comparative economic analysis. Consideration is also given to the insights that this approach might offer to studies of the diffusion and culture change of North American Indians.

2
European and Indian cultures
at the time of contact

The early Hudson's Bay Company fur trade brought together two distinctly different cultural groups, the European and the Indian. Vast differences in social values and political structures, in technological sophistication, and in the means of producing and distributing goods marked the disparity between the two groups.

THE EUROPEAN TRADERS

After a protracted struggle with the French for control of Hudson Bay during the late seventeenth and early eighteenth centuries, the English emerged as the dominant European group involved in the fur trade of central and western Canada. As subsequent discussion will show, although the French continued their opposition in the interior by establishing an extensive inland trading network oriented to the St Lawrence River, the English merchants of the Hudson's Bay Company managed to obtain the major portion of the trade throughout the period before 1763. In the latter year the Treaty of Paris extinguished French claims in Canada and left the fur trade entirely in British hands.

The British traders came from a society with well-developed hierarchies in social and political institutions. Theirs was also a society in which there were marked divisions of socio-economic status or class. The British economic system at that time was still strongly 'embedded' in the socio-political system, in the sense that social relationships and political authority had a dominant role in economic decision-making. Although the 'laissez-faire' form of market economy had not yet developed by the mid-seventeenth century,[1] commercial activity was assuming an increasingly important place in English society, as well as in other European countries. Complex trading and financial relationships and institutions were being established at this time for overseas trade.

The precise time at which extensive involvement of British merchants in overseas trade began is difficult to date because it was a slow evolutionary process.[2] But it has been pointed out that as late as the middle of the sixteenth century England was an underdeveloped country by continental standards.[3] English merchants were relatively less sophisticated in terms of financial techniques and general commercial expertise. Consequently, most of the country's overseas trade was in the hands of foreigners, particularly the Hanseatic and Italian merchants.[4] The principal exception was the cloth trade where the English Company of Merchant Adventurers played a key role. However, this company limited its activities largely to the continent.[5]

In the second half of the sixteenth century, the pace of commercial activity quickened and the level of English involvement increased, beginning with the opening of the Russian trade in the early 1550s. As the English merchants became more active participants in overseas trade, the presence of foreign merchants on English soil, particularly the Hanseatic traders, was considered to be detrimental to English interests. Accordingly, in 1597, Queen Elizabeth I ordered them to leave her realm.[6] By the early seventeenth century, control of the export trade was largely in English hands and the grounds had been laid for rapid commercial, industrial, and overseas expansion.[7]

As English commerce expanded, the character of British trading institutions changed. Initially, foreign trade was carried on by the so-called 'regulated companies.' These companies grew out of trading guilds, and many elements of their constitutions reflected this origin. For instance, the principle of apprenticeship was enforced, and membership was aquired ipso facto when a trader had served his time with a member. Membership could also be obtained by payment of a fee, provided everyone in the company agreed. Individual members traded solely on their own account, but were subject to the regulations of the association. When these regulations were broken, fines were levied by the company and the income thus obtained was used to help defray its costs of operation. Of importance, no subject of the crown could trade independently in any foreign district where a regulated company was established. Besides sheltering merchants against home rivalries, royal charters were designed to protect them from foreign aggression.[8]

Although most English trading companies of the sixteenth and seventeenth centuries were of the regulated type, the joint-stock company developed in the seventeenth century and eventually replaced the earlier type of organization. In contrast to the regulated company, in a joint-stock company members could transfer their interest to new associates without requiring consent of all members of the company. Also, new members did not have to serve time as apprentices. Furthermore, unlike the later regulated companies, in which members were liable to the whole extent of their means for the company's debts, in the joint-stock concerns shareholders were liable only to the value of their shares. Thus, this new corporate form, which was free of the old guild constraints and limited the liability of its partners, was capable of greater expansion and could finance extensive trade. At the end of the seventeenth century, there were only three English joint-stock trading companies, but it is generally believed that they were more important than all of the regulated trading companies combined.[9] These three companies were the East India Company, chartered in 1599, the Royal African Company, chartered in 1660, and the Hudson's Bay Company, chartered in 1670. Thus, the English trade of Hudson Bay was conducted under the aegis of a relatively new form of business organization.

Although the primary objective of the Hudson's Bay Company was an economic one, to make a sustained profit or gain through trade, the company was also charged with looking after other interests of the crown, notably exploration and territorial expansion. Hence, to foster commerce and to encourage the company to look after these other interests, the original charter granted the Hudson's Bay Company:

the sole Trade and Commerce of all those Seas Streightes Bayes Rivers Lakes Creekes and Soundes in whatsoever Latitutde they shall bee that lye within the entrance of the Streightes commonly called Hudsons Streightes together with all Landes and Territoryes upon the Countryes Coastes and confynes of the Seas Bayes Lakes Rivers Creekes and Soundes aforesaid that are not already actually possessed by or granted to any of our Subjectes or possessed by the Subjectes of any other Christian Prince or State ...

And further wee doe by these presentes for us our heires and successors make create and constitute the said Governor and Company for the tyme being and theire successors the true and absolute Lordes and Proprietors of the same Territory lymittes and places aforesaid And of all other the premisses Saving Always the Faith Allegiance and Soveraigne Dominion due to us our heires and successors for the same to HAVE HOLD possesse and enjoy the said Territory lymittes and places and all singular other the premisses hereby granted as aforesaid with theire and every of theire Rightes Members Jurisdiccions Prerogatives Royaltyes and appurtenances whatsoever to them the said Governor and Company and theire Successors for for ever To BEE HOLDEN of us our heires and successors as of our Mannor of East Greenwich in our County of Kent in free and common Soccage ... YIELDING AND PAYING yearely to us our heires and Successors for the same two Elkes and two Black Beavers whensoever and as often as wee our heires successors shall happen to enter into the said Countryes Territoryes and Regions hereby granted.

And that the said Governor and Company soe often as they shall make ordeyne or establish any such Lawes Constitucions Orders and Ordinances in such form as aforesaid shall and may lawfully impose ordeyne limitt and provides such paines penaltyes and punishments upon all Offenders contrary to such Lawes Constitucions Orders and Ordinances ...

And moreover ... WEE DOE GIVE and Grant unto the said Governor and Company and theire Successors free Liberty and lycence in case they conceive it necessary to send either Shippes of Warre Men or Amunicion unto any theire Plantations ffortes ffactoryes or Places of Trade aforesaid for the security and defence of the same and to choose Comanders and Officers over them and to give them power and authority by Commission under theire Common Seale or otherwise to continue or make peace or Warre with any Prince or people whatsoever that are not Christians in any places where the said Company shall have any Plantacions ffortes or ffactoryes ...

And further Our will and pleasure is And by these presentes for us our heires and Successors WEE DOE grant unto the said Governor and Company and to theire Successors full power and lawful authority to seize upon the Persons of all such English or any other our Subiectes which shall sayle into Hudsons Bay or Inhabit in any of the Countryes Islandes or Territoryes hereby Granted to the said Governor and Company without theire leave and lycence ...[10]

As constituted by royal charter, the company was thus virtually a sovereign state subject only to the supreme authority of the Crown of England. Although the prerogative of the Crown to grant such exclusive charters was questioned on constitutional grounds, and was later specifically limited by the Declaration of Rights in 1689 (which specified that an act of parliament was necessary to confirm any exclusive rights), the Hudson's Bay Company nonetheless managed to maintain its monopoly of trade in the bay vis-à-vis other English interests.[11] Also, it governed its territory, known as Rupert's Land; it attempted to arrange treaties and alliances with the Indians for trade purposes and to oppose the French; and it carried most of the expenses associated with the defence of its territory against incursions by the French on the bay in the late seventeenth and early eighteenth centuries, and in the interior after 1714. Significantly, these expenses were often a considerable addition to the company's operating costs.

By the seventeenth century, European society, as represented by the Hudson's Bay Company traders, had developed complex institutions for the purposes of trade and empire. The primary objective of the merchants was to trade for a sustained profit, but they were also required to invest some of their profits in the service of national interests.

INDIAN CULTURES

As late as 1670, British merchants had been largely accustomed to carrying on commercial intercourse with traders from other politically sophisticated state societies. Judging from the Hudson's Bay Company charter which granted the traders the right to make peace or war with any prince 'that are not Christian,' it appears that they anticipated having similar relationships with at least some societies of this type of North America. However, none of the Indian groups who occupied the drainage area of Hudson Bay had achieved such levels of socio-political organization by the time of contact. Indeed, even petty chiefdoms were lacking. The most advanced form of social and political organization was found among groups living on the periphery of the Hudson's Bay Company's territory, including such groups as the Huron (destroyed in 1649), the Ojibwa, and the northern Plains Indians. However, even these groups exhibited what anthropologist Marshal Sahlins has termed a segmentary form of tribal organization.[12] Such societies lacked any strong centralized authority and the constituent bands or villages all had essentially equal social status and authority. Collective action by the entire group was thus difficult even when its very existence was threatened. This proved to be a fatal flaw in political organization among the Huron, probably the most advanced of all of the Indian groups in eastern Canada, in that it enabled their rivals, the New York Iroquois, to divide and destroy them.[13]

The sizes of the social groupings varied spatially and seasonally, reflecting changing resource conditions. The largest settlements were formed during the warmer summer months. In the forest region, camps were generally established at good fishing sites where as many as two to three hundred people might gather.[14] In the grasslands, settlements of over a thousand people would form in the summer to hunt bison and engage in various ceremonial activities. During the winter, food supplies were more limited, forcing the Indians to scatter into smaller bands and micro-bands.

In the forests, these bands pursued the migratory moose and woodland caribou. The groups usually comprised at least two adult male hunters and their families. In better game-hunting areas, several hunters and their families might join together. Thus, winter bands in the woodlands commonly ranged from ten to thirty persons. In the parkland fringes of the grasslands where bison, wapiti, and moose were present, larger winter camps could be supported and settlements of as many as 700 to 1000 were reported by the early traders.[15]

The socio-political organization of these groups was based on kinship, and the predominant social unit was the nuclear family. The bands consisted of a number of related families, predominantly through the male side, and were exogamous. The Ojibwa appear to have been the principal exception to this pattern among the hunting and fishing groups of the woodland region. There is evidence that the Ojibwa fishing villages were organized on a patrilineal clan basis at the time of initial contact. These clans controlled the fisheries, which in turn supported a settled village life that enabled the clan system to operate.[16]

Band leadership was fluid, and a chief, or 'captain' as the Europeans called them, had little real authority by virtue of his position. Rather, he depended upon the consent of his followers. Consent was given as long as a chief was a successful hunter, warrior, or trader and continued to exhibit the kind of behaviour valued by Indian society, most notably generosity. Commenting on this facet of Cree society, Andrew Graham, chief trader at York Factory, wrote:

They have no manner of government or subordination amongst them. The father or head of a family owns no superior, obeys no command. He gives his advice and opinion of things, but has no authority to enforce obedience. The youth of his family obey his directions; but it is rather filial affection and reverence than in consequence of a duty exacted by a superior. When several tents or families meet to go to war, or to the Factories to trade, they choose a leader; but it is only a voluntary obedience. Everyone is at liberty to leave him when he pleases; and the notion of a commander is quite obliterated when the journey or voyage is over. Merit alone gives the title to distinction; and the possession of qualities that are held in esteem, is the only method of obtaining affection and respect out of his own house. Thus a person who is an expert hunter, one who knows the communications between lakes and rivers, can make long harangues, is a conjurer and has a family of his own; such a man will not fail of being followed by several Indians when they assemble in large parties at the building of their canoes. They follow him down to trade at the settlements, and style him Uckimow, that is a great man,

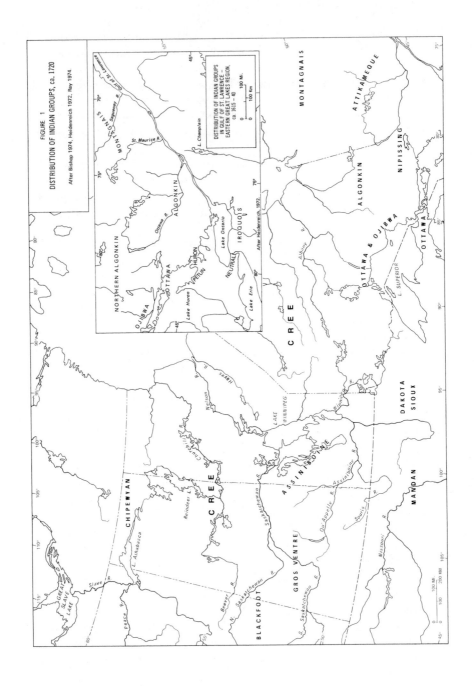

FIGURE 1

DISTRIBUTION OF INDIAN GROUPS, ca. 1720

After Bishop 1974, Heidenreich 1972, Ray 1974.

DISTRIBUTION OF INDIAN GROUPS
IN GULF OF ST. LAWRENCE –
EASTERN GREAT LAKES REGION,
ca. 1615 – 40

After Heidenreich, 1972.

chief or leader; but he is obliged to secure their attendance by promises and rewards, as the regard paid to his abilities is of too weak a nature to purchase subjection. In war a mutual resentment against their enemies forms their union for perpetrating their revenge. Personal courage, patience under hardships, and the knowledge of the manners and country of their adversaries, are the qualifications sought for in the choice of a leader. They follow him with fidelity and execute his projects with alacrity; but their obedience does not follow from any right in the leader to command, but what is founded on his merit, the affections of his followers, and the desire of subduing their antagonists. These actuate every breast, and cement the union which in civilized nations is effected by subordination to the laws of government.[17]

Significantly, Graham's comment suggests that, besides choosing leaders strictly on the basis of merit, Indian bands did not necessarily rally behind the same leader for hunting, war, and trade. Instead, they apparently followed the man best suited to lead the group in each activity.

Regarding territorial and resource control, recent historical research has suggested that band territories were not sharply delimited at the time of initial contact throughout most of the subarctic and northern plains regions, and the notion of trespass was not well developed.[18] Bands tended to hunt the same general areas each year (see Figure 1), but if they did not exploit a portion of their lands in a given year, neighbouring groups could do so if the resources in their own territory were inadequate.[19] Similarly, if a band did not hunt or trap a particular animal species in their home region, nearby bands were often allowed to hunt them. Such a system probably evolved out of the necessity to provide mutual assistance in times of need. Under such an arrangement, the Indians would have minimized the effects of short-term spatial variations in the availability of vital food resources, such as deer, which were often mobile. A more rigid, spatially fixed system of tenure, such as that of the Europeans, would have caused undue hardships and would have been a poor adaptive response to the environmental and technological conditions of pre-contact times. Indeed, the Europeans recognized this fact in the nineteenth century when proposals were being put forward to alter the Indian system in order to conserve diminishing resources.[20]

The pre-contact land tenure system, which has been called the 'hunting range system' by anthropologists, apparently did not give rights of passage across band ranges to groups for purposes of trade.[21] The historical record suggests that such rights had to be negotiated and that concessions, such as toll payments, were often exacted before permission was granted.[22] The right to restrict trading access had important implications for the evolution of the early fur trade because it was one of the factors that favoured the development of trading specialists, or middlemen groups.

3

The fur trade before 1670

THE BEGINNINGS OF REGULAR TRADE

Regular trading contacts began to develop between Europeans and Indians during the early sixteenth century. Until Jacques Cartier's voyage of 1534, trade was sporadic and largely limited to the Beothuk, Micmac, and Montagnais. These groups exchanged furs and other commodities with fishermen, particularly those who erected fish flakes along the maritime coast to dry their catches of cod.[1]

By 1534, the Micmac, and probably the Montagnais, had developed a strong demand for the wide variety of European goods which they had discovered through such contacts. When Cartier met a party of Micmac in Chaleur Bay in 1534, they were eager to trade with him, and in the course of two days they bartered away everything they possessed including the clothes on their backs. The Micmac were said to be particularly fond of European iron goods.[2]

Although the Indians thus exhibited a strong interest in trade, there was relatively little traffic in furs during the remainder of the century. The principal reason for the sluggish growth of trade was that the beaver felt hat did not become fashionable in Europe until the last quarter of the sixteenth century.[3] In Cartier's time, beaver pelts were of relatively little value. Since the Indians had no other commodities to offer which could be transported to Europe and sold at a large profit, barter continued to be carried on largely as an adjunct to the fishing industry.[4]

The growing popularity of the beaver felt hat in the late sixteenth century and the related development of a strong market for beaver pelts in Europe greatly altered the economic situation. Beaver pelts, especially the 'castor gras' or coat beaver worn as clothing by certain Indian groups, became very valuable. These coat beaver pelts, as well as the less-favoured 'castor-sec' or parchment beaver, could be obtained in large quantities from the Indians who had a techno-economic system that was well suited to harvesting the resource.[5] However, as Innis pointed out, one of the problems with the maritime region was that the drainage basins of the various coastal rivers were all relatively small and local Indian groups quickly hunted out beaver populations.[6] Since the traders depended upon a continuously high volume to cover their heavy transportation costs, rapid territorial expansion of the fur trade area became one of the primary concerns of the Europeans.[7]

By the late sixteenth century, the Gulf of St Lawrence became the focus of attention, and Tadoussac at the mouth of the Saguenay River was one of the most important trading centres.[8] The Saguenay River tapped a much larger hinterland than most of the other rivers in the region. The Montagnais, who controlled the mouth of the river and most of the north shore of the gulf, were eager traders, having already had considerable contact with Europeans since about 1544 when the Basques began whaling in the area.[9]

By 1588 the fur trade had become sufficiently lucrative for European merchants to begin to specialize in it, and two of Cartier's nephews petitioned King Henry III for a monopoly on the gulf trade.[10] Similarly, the Montagnais became trading specialists who monopolized the trade in the interior. They obtained a substantial proportion of the furs they bartered to the Europeans from other Indian groups, particularly the Algonkins. The latter groups in turn appear to have had contact with the Huron and passed European trade goods on to them.[11]

Significantly, as the Montagnais and Algonkins emerged as middlemen in the fur trade, they became skilled traders who learned to exploit European rivalries for their own ends. For example, at Tadoussac in the summer of 1611, the Montagnais refused to deal with any of the various European traders until all of the expected ships arrived. In the bidding for the Indians' furs that followed, prices were pushed so high that many traders could not make a satisfactory profit and ceased trading. A similar situation developed that summer at the Lachine Rapids where Champlain and a number of rival traders had gone to deal with the Algonkins and Huron.[12] The former groups participated in the bidding but the latter refused for reasons that will be discussed below.

Thus, the Algonquian groups (Montagnais and Algonkin) who lived to the north of the Gulf of St Lawrence and the St Lawrence River were heavily involved in the fur trade by the early seventeenth century, and had learned to make the most of European commercial rivalries. Indeed, while exploiting them, the Indians also apparently ridiculed the French, English, and Basques for their 'senseless' cut-throat competition. For example, when speaking of the Montagnais, Father La Jeune reported: 'The savages say that it [the beaver] is the animal well-beloved by the French, English, and Basques – in a word, by the Europeans. I heard my host [a Montagnais chief] say one day jokingly, ... "The beaver does everything perfectly well, it makes kettles, hatchets, swords, knives, bread; and in short, it makes everything." He was making sport of us Europeans, who have such a fondness for the skin of this animal and who fight to see who will give the most to these Barbarians to get it; they carry this to such an extent my host said to me one day, showing me a beautiful knife, "The English have no sense; they gave us twenty knives like this for one Beaver skin." '13

EXPANSION OF THE TRADE INTO THE ST LAWRENCE VALLEY AND GREAT LAKES

Until the beginning of the seventeenth century, Tadoussac had marked the western limit of the primary fur-trading area, and relatively few vessels sailed further up the gulf.14 However, trading expeditions were occasionally sent to the vicinity of present-day Quebec City in order to deal with the Algonkin allies of the Montagnais.

In 1608, Champlain set off from Tadoussac for the narrows in the St Lawrence River called Quebec, where he built a small wooden outpost. Champlain hoped to develop trade at this post and use it as a base to push exploration westward beyond the Lachine Rapids in pursuit of the elusive western sea.15 This expansion into the St Lawrence–Ottawa River area brought the French into a region whose socio-political climate was much different from that to which they had been accustomed in the maritime and gulf areas.

The St Lawrence Valley was a warfare zone contested by the powerful New York Iroquois and the Iroquoian-speaking Huron and their allies, the Algonkins and Montagnais. When Cartier first visited the St Lawrence River in 1535, the river marked the divide between these two power blocs. The Iroquois were found to the south, while to the north, the Montagnais held the lands east of the Quebec City area, the Algonkins occupied the lands between Quebec City and the head of the Ottawa River, and the Huron controlled the territory to the west of Lake Simcoe.16

By the time of Champlain's advance in the early seventeenth century, the situation had changed considerably. The Iroquois had taken control of the valley and had forced the Algonkins to retire to the Ottawa River region, in the vicinity of the Rouge River confluence and westward. The Montagnais, on the other hand, rarely visited the lands west of Quebec City and the Huron continued to withdraw into the area between Georgian Bay and Lake Huron.[17]

The war-like atmosphere of the region at the time of initial French contact and penetration had important consequences for fur trade activities. The trade took on a distinctly different character from that of the north shore region of the Gulf of St Lawrence, or the subarctic area in later years.

As has been pointed out, exchange between North American Indian groups was a political as well as an economic activity. Indians would not trade with groups with whom they were not formally at peace. Therefore, prior to the commencement of trade, ceremonies were held to conclude or renew alliances. Because open hostilities had led to a polarization of Indian groups in the upper St Lawrence Valley into two hostile alliance blocs, the New York Iroquois and the Algonquian-Huron, the political aspect of trade assumed prominence over the economic dimension in the region.

Thus, when the French pushed their trading establishments to the Lachine area in the early seventeenth century they found that the Algonkins and the Huron, particularly the latter, were as eager for military allies as they were for trading partners. In this important respect trade in the Lachine area differed sharply from that of the Tadoussac region. For instance, whereas the Montagnais welcomed and exploited European trade rivalries at Tadoussac in the summer of 1611, the Huron who met the French at Lachine the same summer were displeased and alarmed by the haggling that resulted from such unbridled competition. In particular, the Huron did not trust Frenchmen who were interested only in barter for gain and who were unwilling to aid the Huron in their wars with the Iroquois. Consequently, the Huron withdrew a short distance up river and sent a message for Champlain to come to them secretly. He was regarded as a trusted ally because he observed the political formalities of trade and he had accompanied the Huron on a war party against the Iroquois in 1610.[18]

Significantly, since the Indians of the St Lawrence Valley and adjacent territory were aligned into two hostile camps, the French, Dutch, and English who contacted them were obliged to ally themselves with one or another group. The French were allied with the Huron–Algonquian bloc because of the actions of Champlain. This precluded the French from dealing with the New York Iroquois. The Dutch and later the English were likewise unable to trade with the Huron since they were in league with the Iroquois. These over-riding political factors meant that competition for furs by Europeans did not take place through economic channels as it had earlier at Tadoussac, but rather was carried on by means of military activity. After a protracted struggle, the Iroquois destroyed the Algonkin groups controlling the lower Ottawa River and brought about the collapse of Huronia.[19]

NORTHWESTERN EXPANSION OF THE FUR TRADE, 1649–1670

The fall of Huronia was a serious blow to the French because the Huron had become important middlemen in the French trading network by the late 1640s. The Huron trafficked with the Ottawa, Northern Algonkins, Ojibwa, and Nipissing. These latter groups were all middlemen as well. The Ottawa and Northern Algonkins had trading connections in the west. They met the Huron on the shores of Georgian Bay each summer and passed on the furs they had collected in exchange for European goods brought from the St Lawrence by the Huron. The Ojibwa trading network reached to the northwest into Lake Superior country, while that of the Nipissing tapped the lands to the north. The Nipissing brought their furs to Lake Nipissing and Huronia.[20]

The destruction of Huronia in 1649 thus meant that the French faced the task of establishing direct contact with these former trading partners of the Huron. This was not easily accomplished, however, because the Iroquois wars led these other groups to retreat to the west and northwest. Also, the Iroquois continued to menace the Ottawa–St Lawrence route. Thus, contact with the Ottawa, Ojibwa, and Northern Algonkin was infrequent and had to be carried out via the more difficult and round-about routes of the Saguenay and St Maurice Rivers.[21]

In an effort to establish trade with the Great Lakes Indians on a more regular basis, Médard Chouart, Sieur des Groseilliers, was sent west in 1654 to persuade these Indians to come down to the St Lawrence settlements despite the Iroquois. He travelled as far as Green Bay, where he spent the winter. There he learned of the Cree of the far north and of the 'North Sea' or Hudson Bay.[22] In 1656 Grosseilliers returned to the St Lawrence with a flotilla of about thirty canoes and a large quantity of furs.

In 1659, Grosseilliers headed west again in company with Pierre Esprit Radisson. The primary objective of this voyage was to make contact with the Cree and explore the possibility of establishing a fur trade oriented to Hudson Bay.[23] The winter of 1659–60 was spent in the northern Wisconsin and Lake Superior area. In the spring the two Frenchmen met the Cree on the north shore of Lake Superior. Later Radisson claimed that he and Groseilliers had accompanied the Cree on an expedition to Hudson Bay. Although this is unlikely, Radisson and Groseilliers were nonetheless convinced that contact between the Lake Superior area and Hudson Bay was feasible, and that a profitable trade could be conducted from posts established on the bay.[24] A Hudson Bay oriented network would offer the advantage of shorter overland access to the primary fur source area, would make it possible to bypass Ottawa and Ojibwa middlemen, and would be safe from the threats of the Iroquois.

THE AWAKENING OF ENGLISH INTEREST IN THE FUR TRADE OF HUDSON BAY

Late in the summer of 1660, Radisson and Groseilliers returned to Montreal bringing a large quantity of furs with them. Because they had broken a colonial regulation that prohibited trade with Indians 'in their habitations,' the two Frenchmen were fined and forced to pay a heavy duty on the furs they had brought back.[25] Considering the reception that they had received on their arrival, Radisson and Groseilliers were convinced that the colonial authorities would not support their plan of opening trade to Hudson Bay, and they therefore set sail to France in the hope of obtaining the backing of the French government. Failing in this effort, they turned first to merchants in New England and eventually to the English Crown. In England, Radisson and Groseilliers received the support of Prince Rupert, cousin of King Charles II, and the statesman Sir George Carteret. These men believed that the scheme of Radisson and Groseilliers could fit into a plan for an imperial economy in which northern lands would counterbalance tropical territories, and control of trade routes would be all-important.[26]

The first voyage to the bay was planned for 1667 but had to be abandoned. In June of 1668 two ships set sail, but only one reached the bay. The ship was the Nonsuch with Groseilliers on board. Once in the bay the expedition proceeded to the 'bottom of the bay,' or James Bay, where they passed the winter near the mouth of the Rupert River. When the ship returned to England in 1669, it carried a large cargo of furs and the expedition proved to be a considerable financial success. During the winter that Groseilliers spent in the bay, the subscribers of the expedition had formed themselves into a legal corporation whose members were required to buy a share valued at £300. In June of 1669 a monopoly was secured for trade in northern North America. This grant was renewed on 23 October 1669, two days after the cargo of the Nonsuch was cleared through customs.[27] The renewed grant was more comprehensive and specific than that of June, incorporating information brought back by Groseilliers. These were preliminary steps towards the formation of the Hudson's Bay Company. The following summer, on 2 May 1670, that company was formally constituted when a charter was granted to the 'Governor and Company of Adventurers of England trading into Hudson's Bay.'

In this way, the English trading empire based on Hudson Bay began. Significantly, the original impetus came from Radisson and Groseilliers. They played an important role in establishing initial English contacts with the Indians in the bay and helped establish the conventions under which exchange took place. Thus, French trading experience and practices were carried over directly into the Hudson's Bay Company system.

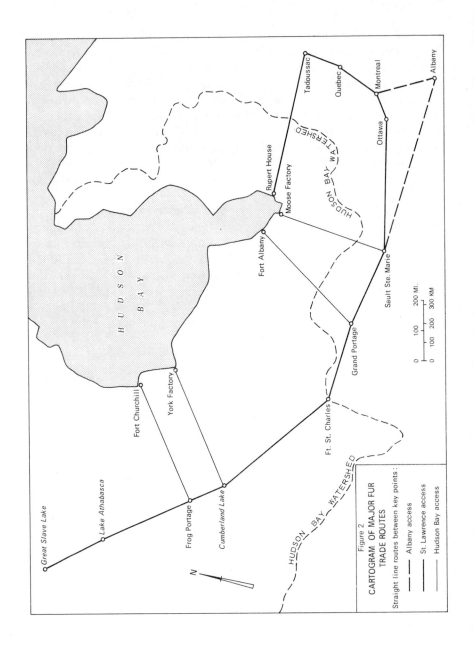

Figure 2

CARTOGRAM OF MAJOR FUR TRADE ROUTES

Straight line routes between key points:

— — — Albany access

– – – St. Lawrence access

——— Hudson Bay access

4

The struggle between
the English and the French for
the Hudson Bay fur trade

Prior to the founding of the Hudson's Bay Company, the French trading empire was exposed only along its southern flanks. After the establishment of this English company in 1670, it was menaced from the north also. Reference to Figures 1 and 2 will make the significance of geographic factors in this trade rivalry more apparent. As these maps show, several alternate routes provided access to the main fur-supply areas and territories of Indian groups engaged in trapping and trading.

The St Lawrence–Great Lakes route was the main corridor through which the French trade had been carried on. This route skirted to the south of the rugged and inhospitable terrain of the Laurentian Shield, following the more fertile lowlands to Lake Superior and beyond. However, the route suffered from a number of disadvantages which became apparent when rival British traders gained control of the alternative routes to the south (the Hudson River–Lake Champlain and Mohawk River route) and the north (via Hudson and James bays). First, the St Lawrence–Great Lakes route proved to be particularly vulnerable to interruption from the Iroquois-controlled Hudson River system. An alternative route via the Ottawa River and Georgian Bay was opened up by French traders in response to this threat, but this move did not successfully avert the danger to the fur trade. Also, the Great Lakes route involved numerous portages, which necessarily limited the size of craft and the payloads that each could carry. This meant that the French route was a high-cost one that covered a vast territory.

On the other hand, the Hudson Bay route to the north enabled large ocean-going vessels to penetrate more deeply the interior of the continent than was the case with the St Lawrence route, making canoe travel by European traders unnecessary. This substantially reduced the cost to

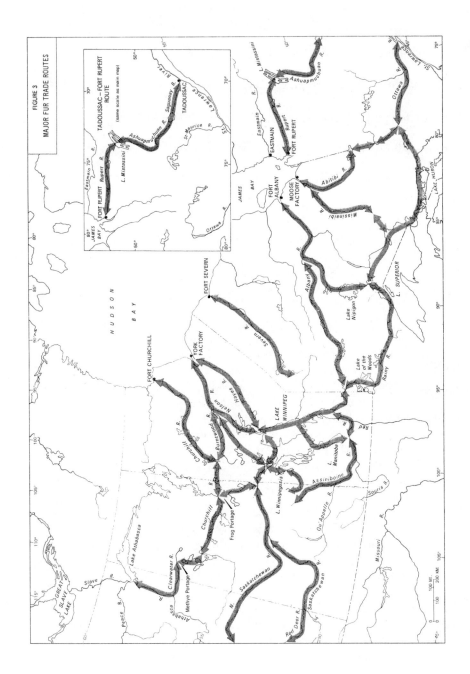

FIGURE 3

MAJOR FUR TRADE ROUTES

European merchants of transporting goods and furs, giving economic as well as military advantages to the British.

As early as 1657–8, the French had known that there were five major canoe routes that led overland from the Great Lakes region and the St Lawrence River Valley to Hudson Bay (see Figures 2 and 3). Not surprisingly, therefore, as soon as the English established themselves on the shores of the bay, the French moved to counteract the new threat. Initially, trade rivalries were centred on the James Bay area. In 1669 and 1670, the English carried on a profitable trade with the Indians at Fort Charles (in the vicinity of Fort Rupert), which was located on the lower Rupert River (Figure 3).[1] The Indians who visited this post came from the interior to the southeast of James Bay. The latter territory had traditionally been included in the hinterland of the Saguenay River system, and thus the English trade at Fort Charles had the immediate effect of drawing off some of the furs that normally would have reached the old French trading centre of Tadoussac (Figure 3).

The French reacted quickly to this new development. In 1671, the intendant Jean Talon sent the Jesuit Father Albanel overland via the Saguenay River, Lake St John, Lake Mistassini, and Rupert River to James Bay (Figure 3). The objectives of the voyage were the acquisition of first-hand knowledge of the interior and of James Bay, the encouragement of trade, and the establishment of a French claim to the shores of the bay by setting up the arms of the King of France as tokens of French sovereignty. Albanel spent the winter at Lake St John and arrived at the mouth of Rupert River in June 1672.[2]

Little came of the priest's visit. By the time he arrived at Fort Charles, the post had been abandoned, the English having returned home for the winter. However, Father Albanel learned from the Indians that the English had passed the previous winter in the bay. Clearly the French could do likewise. Having obtained this information, Albanel set up the French coat of arms and made a claim to the loyalty of the 'northern Indians' and to the territory lying between the bay and the St Lawrence River. It was in this manner that the English–French rivalry for control of the Hudson Bay fur trade began.

ENGLISH–FRENCH RIVALRY ON THE BAY

Shortly after Albanel left to return to the St Lawrence, three English ships arrived in James Bay. This rather large expedition had been sent out because the governor and committee of the Hudson's Bay Company had decided to make a settlement in the bay. By a settlement, the company meant a permanent 'fort' or 'factory' where a 'factor' could maintain continuous contact with the Indians and prepare cargoes for shipment. The decision to adopt a 'factory system' meant that the company had opted for the trading methods used by other English merchants in Africa and Asia.[3] Under this system the bulk of trade would be carried on at coastal establishments rather than from aboard ships as had previously been the case. By 1679, the Hudson's Bay Company had constructed factories on the lower Moose, Rupert, and Albany rivers.

Initially the French made no attempt to seize these posts because England and France were ostensibly allies at this time.[4] Rather, opposition was limited to the activities of independent *coureurs de bois* who operated in the interior on their own account, particularly in the vicinity of Fort Charles on the Rupert River.[5] The activities of the *coureurs de bois* were not sanctioned by the French Crown or colonial government, however, since these French traders were violating royal edicts that forbade unlicensed trade with the Indians outside of the colony of New France on the St Lawrence.[6]

Although the two European groups were thus not officially at war with each other, preparations were being made by both sides for the possible outbreak of open conflict. Besides using the three ships it despatched to the bay in 1679 for exploration and trade, the Hudson's Bay Company intended that they should play an important role in the defence of its establishments on the bay. Accordingly, the ships were armed with great guns such as could not be hauled overland from New France. Furthermore, when John Nixon was placed in charge of company operations in the bay in 1679, he was ordered to establish factories on the Nelson and Severn rivers to guard against any French incursions on the west side of Hudson Bay.[7]

Meanwhile, Radisson had rejoined the French and he began to press his view that the best way France could oppose England was by a maritime challenge – not by overland routes from the south. When first proposed, however, Radisson's scheme was not readily accepted in France, nor did it interest Louis de Buade, Comte de Frontenac, governor general of New France. Initially, Jean Baptiste Colbert, who assumed control of French colonial affairs in 1663, opposed any rapid expansion of the French fur trade, fearing that it would be detrimental to the establishment of a diversified economy in Canada. Colbert believed that such an economy was necessary to place the colony on a sound footing.[8] Also, at the outset, Colbert did not want to openly challenge the English in the bay because of the amicable relationship that existed between the two Crowns.[9]

Frontenac did not endorse Radisson's scheme because he was committed to an expansion of the fur trade to the south and west. Frontenac had managed to exert sufficient influence in the French court to obtain permission to establish trading posts in the Mississippi Valley and to pursue explorations to the mouth of that river. Frontenac had won the approval of Colbert and Louis xiv for this scheme by arguing that the fur trade would support exploration. Therefore, new lands could be claimed for France at no expense to the Crown. Once the approval of the Crown was obtained, explorations were pushed ahead rapidly to the southwest with Réné-Robert Cavelier, Sieur de La Salle, playing a key role. By 1682 La Salle reached the Gulf of Mexico via the Mississippi River. The network of posts that were established in the process of this expansion served to support an expanding fur trade that Frontenac and La Salle monopolized.[10] Thus, Governor General Frontenac had a strong vested interest in the fur trade of central North America. Although he believed that the English should be challenged in the bay, he opposed the idea of using naval forces and did not support the notion that the French fur trade should be extended in that quarter.[11]

In addition to the considerations mentioned above, the French were reluctant to push for a rapid expansion of the fur trade into the Hudson Bay area because in the 1670s the French fur market was glutted with parchment beaver. Parchment beaver were skins that were sun-dried immediately after the animal was skinned. These pelts contained the fine underfur, or beaver wool, which the felters used, and the longer glossy guard hairs. The parchment skins had to be sent to Russia for combing to extract the wool. Coat beaver, on the other hand, were pelts that had been worn by the Indians during the winter before they were traded. By wearing the pelts, the Indians greased the skin, producing a supple leather and wearing off the guard hairs, so that the wool could be easily removed from the skins and a useful leather could be obtained in the process. In the late 1670s, only about 4000 coat beaver were being obtained in Canada each year by the French, compared to almost 90,000 parchment beaver; whereas the French market could absorb 40,000 coat and only 20,000 parchment beaver a year.[12]

Once the Hudson's Bay Company's trade was firmly established, it became clear that the northern fur trade offered a number of advantages over the southern trade. A large proportion of all of the pelts that the northern Indians brought down to trade consisted of coat beaver. Furthermore, the beaver of the subarctic produced a fur that contained a heavier load of wool, especially if the pelts were obtained in winter. Thus, northern coat beaver fetched premium prices on the European markets.

The returns from the Hudson's Bay Company's 1680 shipment of furs exceeded the total capital invested in the company.[13]

As the advantages of the northern trade became clear, the French showed greater interest in the bay. However, opinion was still divided as to the best way of opposing the English. Frontenac wanted to avoid a direct confrontation and he favoured an overland approach. On the other hand, Charles Aubert de La Chesnaye, an influential local French merchant, supported Radisson's plan. La Chesnaye was unable to obtain sufficient backing for this more aggressive scheme when it was first put forward in 1679–80. Two years later, however, La Chesnaye obtained a permit from colonial authorities granting him the right to fish off Anticosti. He used this permit to organize an expedition of two ships. These ships set sail with Radisson and Groseilliers aboard. Once underway, the expedition headed for the bay and arrived at the mouth of the Hayes River on the west side of Hudson Bay in August of 1682.[14]

It was in this way that direct French–English naval confrontations began in the bay area. During the next thirty-two years, control of the posts commanding the outlets of the rivers flowing into Hudson Bay changed hands many times as French–English rivalries continued.[15] This period of instability in the bay came to an end with the Treaty of Utrecht of 1713 which gave England exclusive rights to the shores of Hudson Bay and halted confrontations between the two powers in the area for almost seventy years.

FRENCH ENCIRCLEMENT OF THE BAY

While the French and English struggled for control of the maritime approaches to Hudson Bay, the French continued to expand their inland trading empire. Their primary objective was to intercept the flow of furs to the bay and divert them southeastward towards the St Lawrence.

As noted above, Frontenac originally placed a higher priority on a southern and western expansion of trade and exploration than he did on a French push to the north. Accordingly, in 1678, Frontenac licensed Daniel Greysolon Dulhut (Duluth) to travel to the western Lake Superior area in search of the western sea. Once initiated, the western trade developed slowly. In 1684, Dulhut built a post on the northeast side of Lake Nipigon to intercept Assiniboine and Cree groups travelling down the Ogoki–Albany River route to Fort Albany on James Bay. Four years later, Jacques de Noyon travelled as far west as Rainy Lake where he traded with the Assiniboine (Figure 1). In addition, French *coureurs de bois* pushed westward to the interior to trade with the Indians in their home-lands, and by 1716 they had reached as far as Lake Winnipeg.[16]

After the Treaty of Utrecht excluded them from the bay, the French made a more concerted effort to expand and organize their overland trade in order to cut off the English posts from their hinterlands. The greatest impact of the French *coureurs* on the English trade before 1730 had been felt at the Hudson's Bay Company posts located on James Bay (Figure 4). The hinterlands of these posts were easily reached by traders travelling northward from Tadoussac up the Saguenay River, and they lay closest to the major French routes leading to the West (Figure 3). In contrast, on the west side of the bay, the hinterlands of York Factory and fort churchill were beyond the reach of most of the *coureurs*, and these two posts did not feel the effects of French opposition until the 1730s (Figure 4).

This situation changed rapidly beginning with the appointment of Pierre Gaultier de Varennes, sieur de la Vérendrye, as Commandant of the '*postes du nord.*' Initially, the post of Kaministikwia was La Vérendrye's base of operations, and he maintained two northeastern outposts at Lake Nipigon and on the lower Michipicoten River. These latter posts were intended to draw off the trade of Indian groups who travelled down to Fort Albany.[17]

Since La Vérendrye was responsible for exploration for the elusive western sea and needed the revenue of the fur trade to finance it, he quickly turned his efforts to the West. Between 1733 and the early 1740s, he built a string of posts at strategic points between Lake of the Woods and the lower Saskatchewan River (Figure 4). In the early 1750s, additional posts were constructed on the latter river downstream from the forks. As a result of this encirclement of the bay, by the late 1740s the French were in a position to intercept many of the Indians who travelled to the English trading posts. Yet, because of the great overland distances that they had to travel, and the limited cargo capacities of their canoes, the French were not able to provide the Indians with all of the trade goods that they demanded, nor were the French able to take all of the Indians' furs.

For these reasons, after 1714 the Hudson's Bay Company managed to hold on to the major share of the trade of the subarctic Indians. The company was the primary supplier of bulky, or heavy items such as kettles and guns that were difficult to transport overland in canoes in large quantities. Similarly, the English took most of the bulky, low value furs. Economic competition between the French and the English was thus focused on the acquisition of prime quality furs, such as winter parchment

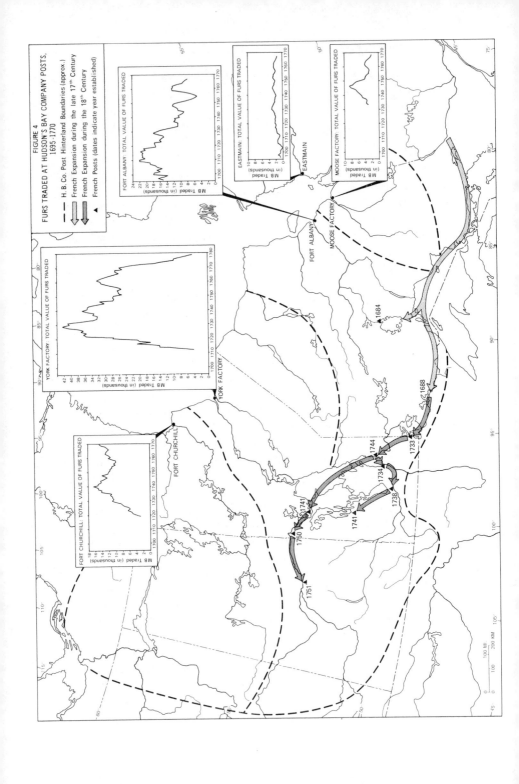

FIGURE 4
FURS TRADED AT HUDSON'S BAY COMPANY POSTS,
1695-1770

- - - H. B. Co. Post Hinterland Boundaries (approx.)
⇩ French Expansion during the late 17th Century
⇩ French Expansion during the 18th Century
▲ French Posts (dates indicate year established)

YORK FACTORY: TOTAL VALUE OF FURS TRADED

FORT CHURCHILL: TOTAL VALUE OF FURS TRADED

FORT ALBANY: TOTAL VALUE OF FURS TRADED

EASTMAIN: TOTAL VALUE OF FURS TRADED

MOOSE FACTORY: TOTAL VALUE OF FURS TRADED

FORT CHURCHILL

YORK FACTORY

FORT ALBANY

EASTMAIN

MOOSE FACTORY

1684
1688
1733
1744
1734
1738
1741
1741
1750
1751

and coat beaver or marten, which fetched premium prices on the European markets. These high value furs could be traded profitably by the French.

The French–English struggle for these prime Indian furs reached a peak in the late 1740s and early 1750s.[18] Although the French had built posts in the interior in Indian trapping territories and along the routes taken by Indian traders on their way to the bay, the Hudson's Bay Company did not attempt to counter these French moves with its own string of inland forts.

The company directors and traders believed that the boreal forest was an inhospitable environment in which it would be difficult to supply provisions for the posts and transport brigades that would be needed. Also, they doubted that the Indian population of the region was sufficiently large to support a profitable local trade.[19] For these reasons, Andrew Graham argued that 'Settlements within five hundred miles of the forts [on the west side of Hudson Bay] would avail nothing.'[20] Furthermore, he contended that the shallowness of the rivers would hinder boat travel to the interior, and therefore, canoes would have to be used.[21] The difficulty with employing this mode of transport, however, was that birch trees do not grow on the shores of Hudson Bay and the company would have to depend on the Indians for canoes and birch rind. Faced with these problems, the Hudson's Bay Company chose an alternative plan of action to counter the French in the interior. The governor and committee decided to send men inland to visit the Indians.

This approach had been championed by James Isham, one of Graham's predecessors at York Factory. In their letter of 24 May 1753, the governor and committee gave Isham permission to proceed with his plan when they wrote: 'As you are of opinion that if a proper Person were sent a great way up into the Country with presents to the Indians it may be a means of drawing down Many of the Natives to Trade We approve thereof and if you have any Person at your Factory whom you think Proper for that purpose and will undertake it you May assure him we will sufficiently reward him for any Services he may do the Company by such a Journey.'[22] A year later, Anthony Henday was sent inland from York Factory, and during the winter of 1754–5 he visited the Blackfoot in the southeastern area of Alberta. The governor and committee were pleased with the results of Henday's expedition and those of other men who followed him. In their letter of 26 May 1761 to Isham and the council at York Factory they observed: 'The Expediency of sending some of our Servants Annually up among the Natives a great Distance of York Fort inland is very evident from its effects. We therefore Direct that the same be Encouraged and continued.'[23]

While the practice of sending men inland did have a positive effect on the company's trade, the French nonetheless continued to siphon off a considerable number of the Indians' prime furs. Graham estimated that the two French posts built on the Saskatchewan River in the early 1750s (Figure 4) yielded six to eight large canoes of the 'richest furs' to the opposition.[24] It was not until the late 1750s that the situation changed, and the French were forced to abandon most of their western outposts after hostilities broke out between England and France. This meant that for a brief period during the late 1750s and early 1760s the Hudson's Bay Company monopolized most of the subarctic fur trade, excluding the southern James Bay region.

PART TWO

THE SPATIAL AND INSTITUTIONAL
STRUCTURE OF THE HUDSON'S BAY COMPANY
TRADING NETWORK

5

The inland trading network of the Hudson's Bay Company

The nature of French–English trade rivalries in the subarctic had important implications for the evolution of the fur trade in that region and for the Indians who participated in it. Since the Hudson's Bay Company did not move inland in force before 1763 to oppose the French, the Indians were obliged to travel to the bay if they wished to trade with the English. Concomitantly, a highly structured Indian trading network evolved. The character of this network was strongly influenced by the physical geography of the region, the locations of various Indian groups at the time of contact, and their cultural diversity.

THE LOWLANDS

The lowlands bordering on Hudson and James bays are most extensive along the western margins of the two bays. This physiographic area is low-lying and swampy, covered by northern boreal forest, muskeg, and tundra (Figure 5). Game and fur-bearing animals were never numerous in the region. Food was in short supply, except in the spring and autumn when great flocks of geese were present; thus the lowlands were not a favourable environment for permanent habitation. It is unlikely that many Indians lived in the region throughout the year prior to European contact. Rather, it is more probable that they only visited the region to hunt geese and in certain areas deer.

The decision of Europeans to establish fixed posts on the shores of the bay thus represented a radical departure from traditional aboriginal ecological adaptation to the regional environment, an adaptive strategy that stressed mobility. Rather than having the local food-consuming population move to the resources whenever and wherever they were

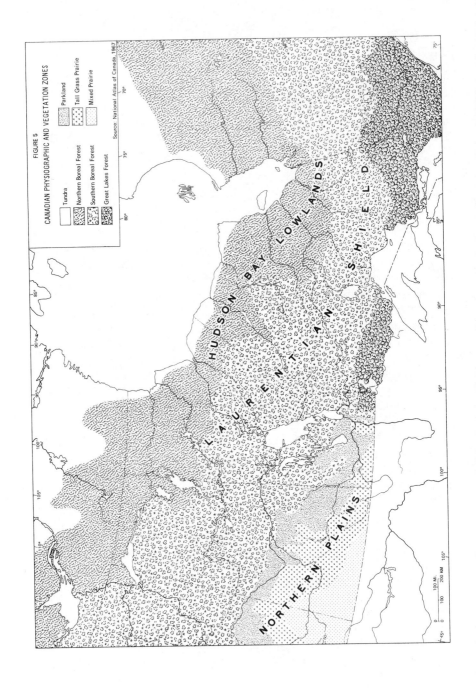

FIGURE 5
CANADIAN PHYSIOGRAPHIC AND VEGETATION ZONES

Tundra
Northern Boreal Forest
Southern Boreal Forest
Great Lakes Forest

Parkland
Tall Grass Prairie
Mixed Prairie

Source: National Atlas of Canada 1967

HUDSON BAY LOWLANDS

LAURENTIAN SHIELD

NORTHERN PLAINS

available, the Europeans chose to bring food and other supplies to their permanent forts.

Some of the food supplies that were consumed came from Europe, but such provisions were relatively expensive. To cut costs, every effort was made to obtain as much food as possible in the bay area. The company men did some hunting near the posts. But, since labour was in short supply and many of the men were not skilled hunters and trappers, the Hudson's Bay Company turned to the Indians for the major portion of the food supplies that were used. They encouraged the Indians to bring in moose and deer meat and geese when they came to the posts to trade. Indeed, some Indians were hired to serve as post hunters, particularly as goose hunters in the spring and autumn.

The end result of the dependence of the trading posts on the Indians for food supplies was that significant numbers of Cree Indians began living in the Hudson Bay lowlands year round. They became very dependent on the posts for the arms and munitions they used in hunting, as well as for a variety of other practical items such as firesteels, knives, hatchets, ice chisels, and clothing.[1] These Indians, who came to be known as the Home Guard Cree, were able to visit the company posts frequently during the year since they lived relatively close to these establishments. Thus, each post was surounded by what may be termed a *local trade* area inhabited by Home Guard Cree. They were the primary suppliers of what was called 'country produce.' Because the region the Home Guard Cree occupied was never rich in fur-bearers, these Cree did not figure prominently in the Hudson's Bay Company's trade in fur pelts.

THE LAURENTIAN SHIELD

Inland beyond the Hudson Bay lowlands lies the vast Laurentian shield, a rugged expanse of ancient crystalline rock with a broken cover of coniferous forest (Figure 5). In the late seventeenth and early eighteenth centuries this region was fairly well endowed with large game, particularly woodland caribou. Although fur-bearing animals were found throughout the boreal forest, the hard-rock shield area bordering on the Hudson Bay lowlands was not prime fur country. Rather, the richest fur lands lay along the southwestern and western margins of the Laurentian shield. Extensive marshlands are found in this sedimentary rock region. Here, also, birch (in the southern areas) and aspen (in the southwestern and western areas) grew abundantly and reached larger sizes than they did in more northerly sections of the boreal forest. Because of this relatively abundant food supply, beaver and muskrat were more plentiful in the zone arching northwestward from the Rainy River country through the lands bordering on the middle and lower Saskatchewan River to the Mackenzie River (Figure 5).[2]

As in the case of the Hudson Bay lowlands, the modest fur resources of the shield uplands were relatively quickly trapped out and the primary focus of Indian fur collecting shifted to the southern boreal and mixed forest areas. The spatial expansion of the fur trade system that resulted led to further economic specialization of the Indian groups who participated in it. In the boreal forest lands and the transitional southwestern woodlands of Manitoba, Saskatchewan, and Alberta, many Indian groups almost ceased trapping furs themselves. Instead, they obtained most of the pelts that they brought to the English or French through trade with other Indian groups. Thus, a new series of middlemen groups emerged, playing the same roles as the Montagnais, Algonkin, Huron, Ottawa, and Ojibwa had in the older French fur trade along the St Lawrence.

Of these former middlemen, only the Ojibwa participated in the Hudson's Bay Company trade. As noted earlier, the Iroquois wars led the Ojibwa to expand to the northwest from their aboriginal homelands adjacent to the northern shores of Lake Huron and the eastern shores of Lake Superior. By 1710 the Ojibwa occupied lands as far to the northwest as Lake Nipigon (Figure 1). Thirty-five years later they were found throughout the area south of the English River and east of Lake of the Woods. When the Treaty of Paris was signed in 1763, the Ojibwa had pushed as far north as Trout Lake in northern Ontario and as far to the west as Lake Winnipeg.[3]

As the Ojibwa took control over this territory, they came into contact with the Cree who occupied most of the shield uplands of northern Ontario, and with the Assiniboine who lived in the boundary waters area of Minnesota and Ontario in the late seventeenth century.

Generally, although there were occasional clashes between the Ojibwa, Cree, and Assiniboine, the three groups lived in comparative peace most of the time and were often formally allied against their common enemy the Dakota Sioux.[4] In part, this peaceful coexistence may be explained by the fact that between 1650 and 1670 the Ojibwa operated as middlemen in the French fur trade, supplying the Assiniboine and Cree with trade goods in return for furs.[5] These exchanges took place along the northwestern shores of Lake Superior and in the Lake Nipigon region.[6]

The establishment of trading posts on the shores of Hudson Bay led to a reorientation of trading networks in the forests to the southwest of Hudson and James bays. Once a post was established at the mouth of the

Albany river, a sizeable portion of the furs that previously flowed south-east through the Great Lakes to the St Lawrence River was diverted northeast from the Lake Nipigon region via the Ogoki River and Albany River to James Bay (Figures 3 and 4).[7]

Although the Ojibwa were involved in the transportation of furs to Fort Albany, they no longer handled the bulk of the trade of the Assiniboine and Cree. The latter two groups became directly involved in the fur trade themselves shortly after the establishment of the Hudson's Bay Company, and Assiniboine and Cree trading parties began visiting Fort Albany regularly. Knowledgeable French traders viewed this development with alarm since they knew that the Ojibwa and Ottawa had been obtaining most of their furs from the Assiniboine and Cree.[8] In an effort to counteract this threat to the French trading network, Dulhut built a post on the northeastern shores of Lake Nipigon in 1684. He hoped that this post would enable the French to intercept the Assiniboine and Cree on their way to James Bay. Dulhut's strategy achieved some success and a profitable trade was carried on with the Assiniboine and Cree, but many of them continued to trade with the English also.[9]

LOCATIONAL ADVANTAGES OF THE ASSINIBOINE AND CREE

Besides affording the Cree and Assiniboine an opportunity to trade their own furs directly with Europeans, the establishment of English posts on the bay also offered them an opportunity to play the role of middlemen, particularly when York Factory was built on the lower Hayes River.

In the late seventeenth century, the Cree occupied the boreal forest region of what is now northern Ontario and northern Manitoba between the Saskatchewan and Churchill rivers. The Assiniboine lived to the southwest of the Cree in a broad stretch of territory reaching from Rainy Lake to at least central Saskatchewan (Figure 1). Occupying these territories, the Assiniboine and Cree were in the strategically advantageous position of controlling the major trading routes that led to Hudson Bay.[10]

Using the steady supply of arms that were available at English posts, the Assiniboine and Cree were able to exploit their locational advantage preventing other more distant groups from having direct access to Hudson Bay. Although their languages were not mutually intelligible, the Siouan-speaking Assiniboine and Algonkian-speaking Cree became close military allies. In the Rainy River area to the south, these two groups were engaged in incessant warfare with the Dakota Sioux. The initial causes of this warfare are unknown.

However, by the end of the first decade of Hudson's Bay Company operations on the bay, these skirmishes appear to have become economically motivated. Evidence for this idea is contained in a report that Governor John Nixon wrote for the governor and committee of the company in 1682. Nixon observed: 'I am informed, there is a nation of Indians called the poyets [Dakota] who have had no trade with any cristian nation as yet, one [sic] whome (most parte of those Indians who trade with us) doeth make warr, and steall their beaver [.] It would be greatly to the advance of our trade if we could gaine a correspondence with them ... For they would faine have a trade with us but are affrayed to break through our neighbouring Indians for want of armes, we have had trade with their nixt [sic] nighbours the sinnypoyets [Assiniboine] lately ... our Indians [Assiniboine and Cree] are affrayed that they [the Dakota] will breake doune to trade with us, for by their good-will, they would be the only brokers between all strange Indians and us, and by all means kep both them and us in ignorance, the one of the others deallings ...'[11] It is clear from this commentary that within twelve years of establishment of the Hudson's Bay Company the Assiniboine and Cree were using English guns to establish themselves as middlemen.

When the French expanded into the western Lake Superior area in the late seventeenth century, they attempted to arrange a peace between the two warring groups, but failed.[12] Subsequently, in the early eighteenth century the French *coureurs de bois* attempted to use these hostilities to their own advantage. In an effort to discourage the Assiniboine and Cree from trading with the English, the *coureurs de bois* threatened to lead Siouan war parties against the former groups if they did not cease trading with the Hudson's Bay Company. These threats did not deter the Assiniboine and Cree. Consequently, in the 1720s, French *coureurs* led Siouan war parties into what is now northern Ontario and central Manitoba.[13]

The French thus attempted to use the Sioux to attack the flanks of the expanding Hudson's Bay Company trading network in much the same fashion as the Iroquois served English interests in the east by menacing the southern flanks of the French fur trade. However, the Siouan raids did not destroy the company's inland network.

When La Vérendrye took control of the French western fur trade in the late 1720s, it was clear that the Rainy River would have to serve as a major east–west thoroughfare for French canoes. However, the river had become essentially a no-man's land where battles were frequently fought between the Assiniboine–Cree–Ojibwa and the Sioux. In an effort to bring stability to the area, La Vérendrye attempted to call a truce among the combatant groups. Although he was unsuccessful, La Vérendrye did manage to neutralize the French in the conflict and, thereafter, they were able to trade with both factions.[14] The trade of the northern Ontario area remained under Assiniboine, Cree, and Ojibwa control, with the latter two groups dominating most of it. They visited Fort Albany, and after the 1720s the French posts located along the Rainy River route were frequented by these two groups also.

While Fort Albany served as the principal trading post for Indians living in the boreal forest uplands of northern Ontario, York Factory was the major entrepôt for Indians inhabiting the Nelson drainage basin.

In the early years of its operation, York Factory attracted the trade of many Indian groups from differing environmental zones and economic orientations. For example, prior to 1720, the horticultural Mandan from the Missouri Valley, the Blackfoot and Blood from the northern plains, and the Athabascan groups from the northern edges of the forests all visited the post. However, after 1720 most of these groups ceased travelling to York Factory, and the Assiniboine and Cree emerged as middlemen who controlled the inland trade of the post.[15] A number of factors enabled these two groups to assume a monopolistic hold on the York Factory trade.

Locational advantages and a secure access to a large supply of English arms were the primary factors which placed the Assiniboine and Cree in a favourable position. Since they occupied the lower Nelson drainage basin, all trading routes leading to York Factory passed through their territory (Figure 3). They were thus in a position to deny other Indian groups access to the fort.

However, unlike the situation at Fort Albany, the factors of distance, climate, and cultural geography were probably as important as were strategic and arms advantages in enabling the Assiniboine and Cree to take control of the inland trade of York Factory.

HAZARDS OF LONG DISTANCE TRADE

Tribes such as the Mandan, Blood, Blackfoot, and some Athabascan groups had a round trip of well over a thousand miles to York Factory (Figure 1). The records indicate that these expeditions took over three months to complete for many of the northern plains groups, and as much as two years in the case of some of the Athabascan groups who made the trek on foot.[16] Such trading expeditions were arduous and dangerous. For instance, the remote trading groups who used canoes to traverse part

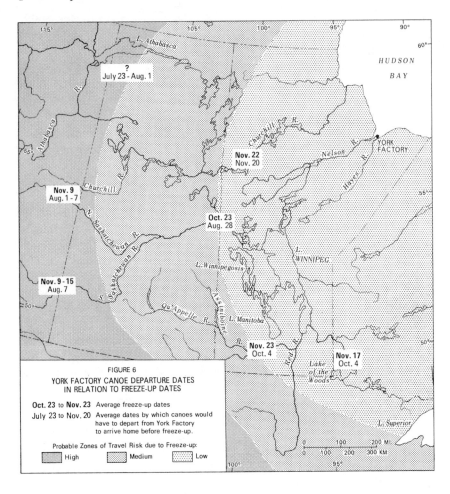

FIGURE 6
YORK FACTORY CANOE DEPARTURE DATES
IN RELATION TO FREEZE-UP DATES

Oct. 23 to Nov. 23 Average freeze-up dates
July 23 to Nov. 20 Average dates by which canoes would
have to depart from York Factory
to arrive home before freeze-up.

Probable Zones of Travel Risk due to Freeze-up:
High   Medium   Low

of the distance, such as the Mandan, Blood, and Blackfoot, had to contend with the problem of the short open water season that characterizes the lower reaches of rivers flowing into western Hudson Bay. Unless they reached the bay, traded, and departed before the second or third week in August at the latest, Indians from the Missouri, upper Saskatchewan, and Churchill rivers faced the danger of freeze-up before they reached their homeland (Figure 6). Starvation and death were usually the consequences if this occurred.

This hazard was further compounded by the fact that the English (prior to about 1717) and the French (1694–1714) traders who operated the Hayes' River post carried only a one year's supply of trade goods. Thus replenishment of trade good stocks depended upon the timely arrival of supply ships from Europe – usually in mid-August. Occasionally, however, a ship was lost or arrived late. Such occurrences delayed the departure of Indian trading parties, and increased the likelihood that they would be caught by freeze-up before arriving home.[17]

The Cree and Assiniboine, living between these more distant tribes and Hudson Bay, were able to make the trip to York Factory and return with a somewhat safer time margin. This enabled them to delay their departure from the bay until as late as the end of August and not run a serious risk of getting caught by freeze-up en route. Thus, there was an advantage to the Mandan, Blood, Blackfoot, Athabascans, and others in having the Assiniboine and Cree carry their furs down to the bay.

Also, in the case of Indians inhabiting the grassland region, many were in the process of adopting horses into their cultures in the early eighteenth century. As they did so, the use of canoes (which had never been extensive in this area) declined even further. Therefore, over time, fewer grassland Indians were able to undertake the canoe trip to the bay.[18] Furthermore, many of the plains Indian groups, such as the Blackfoot, disliked fish as a food or lacked the skills of catching fish, which necessarily constituted a major portion of the Indians' diet while their canoe flotillas travelled through the forests between the lower Saskatchewan River and Hudson Bay.[19] In this way, the cultural differences between grassland and parkland–woodland Indians worked to the advantage of the latter groups, making it easier for them to assume middlemen positions in the fur trade.

By about 1720, the Cree and Assiniboine had exploited these various advantages and had begun to dominate the inland trade of York Factory as they did earlier at Fort Albany. After 1720, other than the plains Assiniboine, relatively few plains Indians visited the post. Similarly, military pressures being exerted by the Cree were preventing many Athabascan-speaking Indians, or 'northern Indians' as they were called, from visiting York Factory.[20]

In an effort to deal with the latter problem and in order to establish direct contact with the northern Indians, the Hudson's Bay Company built Fort Churchill (then known as Fort Prince of Wales) near the mouth of the Churchill River (Figure 4). This effort was only partly successful. A number of Chipewyan did trade at the post, but the Cree dominated much of the trade of the middle and upper Churchill River region.[21]

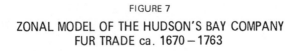

FIGURE 7

ZONAL MODEL OF THE HUDSON'S BAY COMPANY
FUR TRADE ca. 1670 – 1763

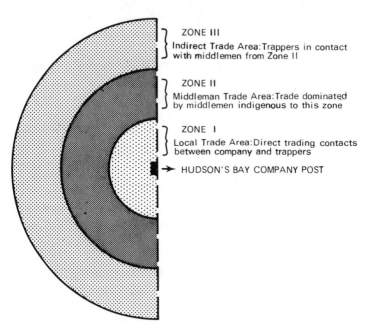

ZONE III
Indirect Trade Area: Trappers in contact
with middlemen from Zone II

ZONE II
Middleman Trade Area: Trade dominated
by middlemen indigenous to this zone

ZONE I
Local Trade Area: Direct trading contacts
between company and trappers

→ HUDSON'S BAY COMPANY POST

Thus, to a large extent, the Cree continued to maintain their middleman position in the fur trade of the Churchill drainage basin.

Similarly, when the French extended their network of trading posts to the middle Saskatchewan River area by the 1750s (Figure 4), they did not eliminate the Assiniboine and Cree middlemen operating in the Manitoba–Saskatchewan region. Rather, after the Assiniboine and Cree met their Mandan, Gros Ventre, Blood, or Blackfoot trading partners, the French intercepted them on their way to the bay and attempted to obtain the prime furs that the Assiniboine and Cree carried, in exchange for alcohol and other commodities. In this way the French attempted to work within the trading system the Indians had developed.

Lying beyond the area dominated by Assiniboine and Cree traders lay a third trade zone – the indirect trade area. This was a region inhabited by Indians who rarely, if ever, visited the English or the French, but rather obtained almost all of their trade goods from the above-mentioned middlemen groups. These Indians usually met the middlemen at predetermined locations each spring. For example, in the 1750s, the equestrian Blackfoot met the Assiniboine and Cree canoe brigades along the South Saskatchewan River and its tributaries.[22] Although there were occasional clashes between the various tribes living in the indirect trade region and their middlemen trading partners, these skirmishes were relatively minor by comparison with the wars between the Assiniboine–Cree–Ojibwa and the Dakota Sioux. The latter conflict had more of the character of a blood feud. No symbiotic economic relationship existed between these warring groups that could serve to hold hostilities in check. In the case of relationships existing between the Blackfoot and the Assiniboine–Cree, open warfare would have upset the stable trading system that had evolved to the benefit of both groups.

ZONAL PATTERN OF THE FUR TRADE

In summary, once the Hudson's Bay Company was established on the shores of Hudson Bay, an essentially zonal pattern of trade emerged in the interior. The essential elements of this pattern are illustrated in a simplified model (Figure 7). In the lowlands surrounding the posts a local trade zone emerged. Living in close proximity to the posts, Indians from this region, the Home Guard and Swampy Cree, visited the trading houses several times during the year, bringing in most of the 'country produce' that was consumed at the forts. Because of their close ties to the trading establishments of the various Indian groups, the Swampy Cree were the most acculturated to the Europeans.

The middleman trade zone was located further inland. Here distance generally prevented the Indians from making more than one trading visit to the bay a year. This zone was dominated by Assiniboine and Cree. In the case of the Fort Albany hinterland, the Ojibwa were important also. In the areas closest to the bay, the middleman trade was of an intratribal nature, that is Cree with Cree, etc., whereas near the outer limits of the middleman zone, intertribal exchange assumed major significance.

Beyond the middleman zone lay the indirect trade area. Distance and cultural differences often precluded any extensive contact between Indians living in this region with the bay-side posts. Thus, Indians from this zone, the Mandan, Gros Ventre, Blood, Blackfoot, Peigans, and many Athabascan groups, depended on the Cree and Assiniboine for their trade goods. As Figure 8 shows, the middleman and indirect trade zones

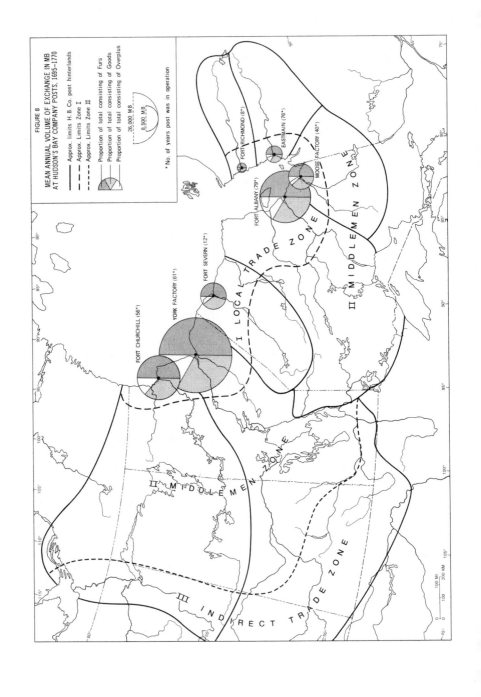

FIGURE 8

MEAN ANNUAL VOLUME OF EXCHANGE IN MB
AT HUDSON'S BAY COMPANY POSTS: 1695–1770

——————— Approx. limits H. B. Co. post hinterlands

— — — — Approx. Limits Zone I

–·–·–·– Approx. Limits Zone II

Proportion of total consisting of Furs
Proportion of total consisting of Goods
Proportion of total consisting of Overplus

26,000 MB

8,500 MB

* No. of years post was in operation

FORT RICHMOND (8*)

EASTMAIN (76*)

MOOSE FACTORY (40*)

FORT ALBANY (79*)

FORT SEVERN (12*)

YORK FACTORY (61*)

FORT CHURCHILL (56*)

I LOCAL TRADE ZONE

II MIDDLEMEN ZONE

II MIDDLEMEN ZONE

III INDIRECT TRADE ZONE

100 MI

0   100   200 KM

were most extensive and better articulated to the west of Hudson Bay (the York Factory and Fort Churchill hinterlands) than they were around James Bay (Fort Albany and Moose Factory). In the latter region, the Great Lakes to the southward and the main line of the French fur trade prevented the development of any significant indirect trade region. Similarly, on the east side of James Bay, the outer hinterland of Eastmain could be easily reached by French *coureurs* travelling north from Tadoussac via the Saguenay River.

The mean annual volume of exchange for the various Hudson's Bay Company posts, that is, the total turnover measured in *made beaver*[23] value of goods and furs traded, is shown in Figure 8. It is clear from this figure that the primary fur-producing areas lay to the west of Hudson and James bays. Furthermore, Forts Albany and Churchill and York Factory dominated the trade of this region. It was in the hinterlands of these three posts, especially Fort Churchill and York Factory, that the Indian middlemen played the greatest role.

FIGURE 9

FLOWS OF FURS AND GOODS IN THE HUDSON'S BAY COMPANY TRADING SYSTEM

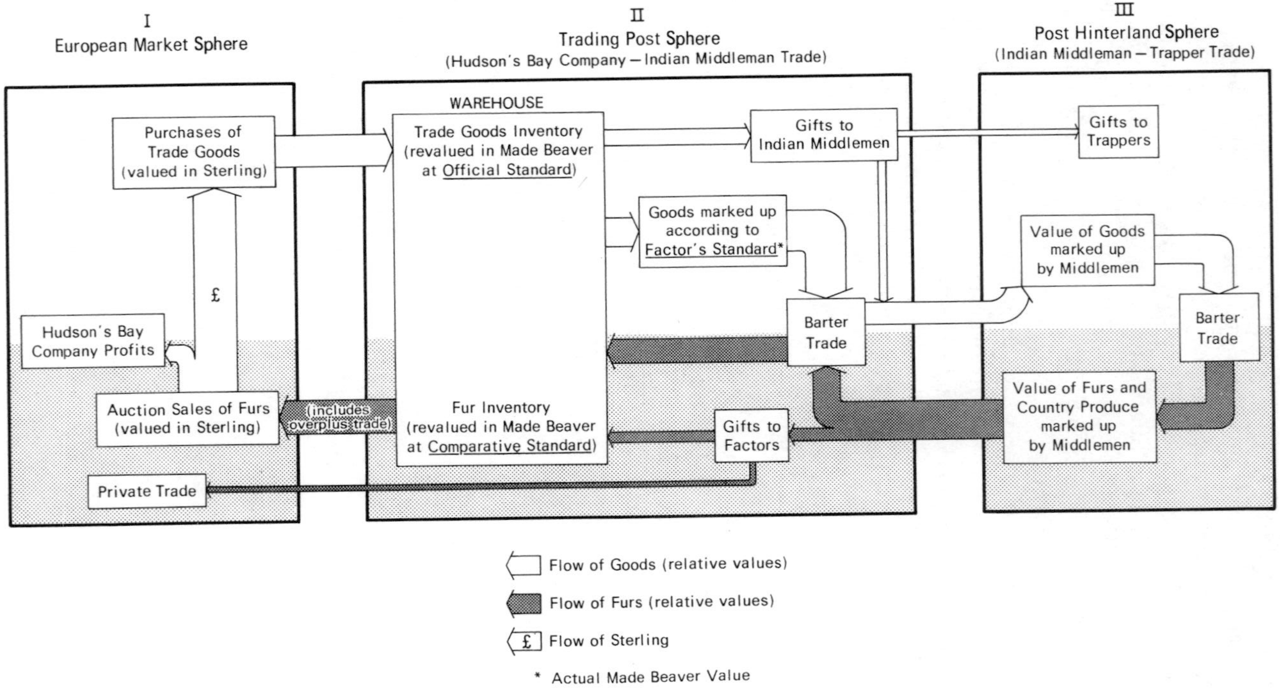

I
European Market Sphere

II
Trading Post Sphere
(Hudson's Bay Company – Indian Middleman Trade)

III
Post Hinterland Sphere
(Indian Middleman – Trapper Trade)

WAREHOUSE

Purchases of Trade Goods (valued in Sterling)

Hudson's Bay Company Profits

Auction Sales of Furs (valued in Sterling)

Private Trade

Trade Goods Inventory (revalued in Made Beaver at Official Standard)

Fur Inventory (revalued in Made Beaver at Comparative Standard)

(includes overplus trade)

Goods marked up according to Factor's Standard*

Gifts to Indian Middlemen

Barter Trade

Gifts to Factors

Gifts to Trappers

Value of Goods marked up by Middlemen

Barter Trade

Value of Furs and Country Produce marked up by Middlemen

Flow of Goods (relative values)

Flow of Furs (relative values)

Flow of Sterling

* Actual Made Beaver Value

6

Fur trading institutions

The spatially extensive Hudson's Bay Company fur trade was a very complex exchange system. For it to operate smoothly, a series of adjustments to customary practices had to be made by the company and the Indians. As Figure 9 shows, there were three distinct spheres of the trade. These were separated by time and place, but linked together by commodity, credit, and information flows. A series of institutions were adopted or developed to handle exchanges in the three spheres of operation.

EUROPEAN SPHERE

Beginning with transactions in the European market, the sustained demand in Europe for furs, particularly beaver, provided the primary driving force for the trade. Supplies of furs to meet this demand were offered at auction in a series of markets, most notably London, Paris, Leipzig, and Moscow. These furs came from a variety of sources, especially Rupert's Land (the Hudson Bay drainage basin), New France, and the Atlantic colonies.[1] The mechanism of supply and demand largely regulated prices in these fur markets, and, consequently, considerable price variation was a common feature. Since furs were essentially luxury items, the demand for them in Europe fluctuated markedly. Price fluctuations were therefore largely the result of the failure of European traders to adjust fur supplies in proportion to abrupt fluctuations in demand. According to E.E. Rich, this was one of the chronic problems that plagued the fur companies.[2]

On the other hand, the trade goods required for barter with the

Indians were purchased with the proceeds of the previous season's sales, or were obtained on credit (Figure 9). As with furs, the prices of these goods were determined by supply–demand conditions and again exhibited considerable variations. Most prominent amongst the inventories of the Hudson's Bay Company traders were firearms, ammunition, metal goods such as kettles, knives, hatchets, and firesteels, blankets, yard goods, and various items which might be termed luxury goods such as beads, liquor, and tobacco.

TRADING POST SPHERE

Goods and furs were purchased and sold in the European sphere of the fur trade under a market system based on monetary exchange in which the common principles of formal economics are applicable. The goods obtained for trade by the Hudson's Bay Company were valued in British sterling. However, these currency values could not be extended to cover transactions in the North American sphere of its operation because the pre-contact Indians of the subarctic had no conception of the use of money for the three purposes normally ascribed to it (as a unit of account, as a medium of exchange, and as a store of value).[3] Therefore, the Hudson's Bay Company was faced with the task of setting up an institutional framework that permitted it to carry on a barter trade on an accountable basis. To accomplish this end, the company invented a system of value measurement which could be applied to both the furs and goods bartered with the Indians. This accounting system was based on a unit called the *made beaver* (MB). The MB established an equivalence between volumes of goods traded and furs taken in return in terms of the number of prime, whole beaver pelts which they represented.[4]

Under the MB system, the company fixed the equivalents of trade goods in terms of MB units according to what was called the *Official Standard of Trade.* Furs, skins, and other 'country produce' (food mostly) were also assigned MB values. To distinguish the system for the valuation of commodities brought in by the Indians from that used to evaluate European goods, the term *Comparative Standard* was applied to the former. Both of these standards were set annually by the company directors in London, but, as will be shown subsequently, they remained remarkably fixed.

So that the system may be understood, it is important to stress that an adjustment was necessary on the part of both the English traders and the Indians in setting the MB standards. Initially, the Hudson's Bay Company traders were forced to operate without the use of currency for the purposes of indirect exchange, while the Indians were obliged to accept the alien concept of equivalence expressed in a single abstract unit, i.e., a system of accounting. In time, the traders extended credit to the Indians. Indian 'debts' were expressed in terms of MB, and therefore, the Indians learned to accept the notion of the MB as a store of value also.

Besides the above mutual adjustments that were necessary for the purpose of enabling the Hudson's Bay Company traders and Indians to carry on exchange on a regular basis, the company also had to accommodate itself to other Indian trade practices. As noted earlier, trade and politics had been closely linked in aboriginal Indian society. Before trade could take place between groups, the proper political climate had to be established. In particular, Indians would not trade with groups with whom they were at war. Consequently, gift-exchange ceremonies always preceded barter exchange. The purpose of these ceremonies was to formally establish, or renew, alliances of friendship between the participants. As the French had before them, the Hudson's Bay company traders were obliged to take part in these pre-trade gift-exchanges. Failure to do so would have meant that the Indians probably would have refused to trade. In time these ceremonies became very elaborate; they often took several days to complete and involved the exchange of considerable quantities of goods and furs.

One of the best descriptions of these pre-trade activities comes from Andrew Graham, who spent twenty-four years at York Factory in the late eighteenth century. According to Graham, when the Indian trading parties approached to within two miles of York Factory, they went ashore out of sight of the post so that the Indian leaders, or trading captains, as they were called, could organize the approach of their group to the Factory. Graham reported:

This being settled they re-embark and soon after appear in sight of the Fort, to the number of between ten and twenty in a line abreast of each other. If there is but one captain his station is in the centre, but if more they are in the wings also; and their canoes are distinguished from the rest by a small St. George or Union Jack, hoisted on a stick placed in the stern of the vessel. At the distance of four or five hundred yards is another fleet marshalled in the same manner; others behind them and so on until they are all come. Several fowling-pieces are discharged from the canoes to salute the Fort, and the compliment is returned by a round of twelve pounders, less or more for each division, and the Great Flag flying from the Fort, as it continues to do every day they stay.[5]

Once these canoe flotillas arrived at the Fort, the women set about making camp while the Indian captains and their 'lieutenants' proceeded into the Factory. Graham continued: 'The Governor being informed what Leaders are arrived, sends the Trader to introduce them singly, or two or three together with their lieutenants ... Chairs are placed in the room, and pipes with smoking materials produced on the table. The captains place themselves on each side [of] the Governor, but not a word proceeds from either party, until everyone has recruited his spirits with a full pipe.'[6]

The governor or factor and the Indian leaders then exchanged speeches. The latter indicated how many canoes they had brought with them, which Indians had stayed at home that year, and other news, and they also enquired as to the well-being of the English. In his turn, the factor welcomed the Indians, he assured them he had plenty of trade goods, and he promised them fair treatment. Also, he provided the Indian captains with the following items of dress:

A coarse cloth coat, either red or blue, lined with baize with regimental cuffs and collar. The waistcoat and breeches are of baize; the suit ornamented with broad and narrow orris lace of different colours; a white or checked shirt; a pair of yarn stockings tied below the knee with worsted garters; a pair of English shoes. The hat is laced and ornamented with feathers of different colours. A worsted sash tied round the crown, an end hanging out on each side down to the shoulders. A silk handkerchief is tucked by the corner into the loops behind; with these decorations it is put on the captain's head and completes his dress. The lieutenant is also presented with an inferior suit.[7]

After this outfitting was completed, the trading captains were given bread, prunes, tobacco, pipes, and brandy to take to their followers. The captains and the company servants then formed a procession that proceeded out of the Factory gates to the Indian encampment. Graham described the proceedings as follows:

Everything being prepared he is conducted to his tent with a procession. In the front are the spontoons [halberd or battle-axe and pike mounted on a six-foot pole] and ensigns, next the drummer beating a march, then several of the Factory servants bearing the bread, prunes, etc. Then comes the captain, walking quite erect and stately, smoking his pipe and conversing with the Governor and his officers; then follow the Second, and perhaps a friend or two who is permitted to come in with the Chief. The tent is all ready for their reception, and a clean birch-rind or beaver coats are spread on the ground for the chief to sit on; and before him are deposited the prunes etc. The Chief then makes a speech to his followers, and then orders his lieutenant, or some respectable person, to distribute the presents, never performing this himself.[8]

After this activity was finished, the Indians spent the next one to three days purchasing brandy. According to Graham, during this period: 'they get drunk and sing, dance, cry and quarrel for two or three days.' Once this release of tension and general celebration was completed, the Indians composed themselves and were ready to 'proceed to business.'[9]

However, before the trade of any other articles could begin, yet another ceremony had to be performed with all of the Indians in attendance. The Indians re-entered the fort to smoke the grand calumet (or pipe of peace and friendship) and make a present of furs to the factor. The object of this ceremony was to renew the 'league of friendship,' inspect the trade goods, and view the measures. Graham noted:

As the ceremony of smoking the calumet is necessary to establish confidence, it is conducted with the greatest solemnity, and every person belonging to that gang is admitted on the occasion. The Captain walks in with his calumet in his hand covered with a case, then comes the lieutenant and the wives of the captains with the present, and afterwards all the other men with the women and their little ones. The Governor is genteely dressed after the English fashion, and receives them with cordiality and good humour. The captain covers the table with a new beaver coat, and on it lays the calumet or pipe; he will also sometimes present the Governor with a clean beaver toggy or banian to keep him warm in the winter. The Puc' ca' tin' ash' a' win [gift of furs] is also presented. Then the Governor sits down in an arm-chair, the captain and the chief men on either hand on chairs; the others sit round on the floor; the women and children are placed behind, and a profound silence ensues.[10]

The governor then lighted the calumet and the smoking ceremony began. Once the smoking of the calumet was completed, the Indian captains and the governor exchanged lengthy speeches. When the speeches were concluded, the governor distributed baskets of bread and prunes to the Indians who then retired to their tents.

Trade could now begin. A roll of the drum at five AM announced that the company traders were ready to do business. Similarly, at eight PM, drums announced that the warehouse was being closed for the day.[11]

Business was conducted in a trading room that was attached to the warehouse. The company servants dealt with the Indians at a window or 'hole-in-the-wall,' as it came to be known, which was located in the trading room situated at the side of the warehouse. According to Graham, at York Factory, 'this window is in the trading room in the south curtain, and accessible only by boarded passage railed in from the outer works, so that all other communication with the factory is excluded.'[12] Thus, with the exception of the Indian captains, no Indians were permitted to enter the warehouse or factory while trade was being carried on. This company practice represented an adjustment by the English traders to Indian attitudes towards private property rights.

The Indians came from a society that stressed the need for mutual aid and generosity. Edward Umfreville offered an insightful account of this aspect of Indian life: 'When we view the fair Side of their characters We find them Kind, courteous, and benevolent to each other, relieving the wants and necessities of their distressed bretheren with the greatest good-nature, either by counsel, food or cloathing. The good effects of this excellent disposition are frequently experienced by themselves; for, as in their mode of life no one knows how soon it may be his own fate to be reduced to the verge of extremity, he secures for himself a return of kindness, should he experience that vicissitude.'[13] Since generosity was highly esteemed and general reciprocity the dominant form of exchange between close kin, the Indians did not place much value on the private ownership and control of material goods. The hoarding of such wealth was considered to be antisocial behaviour. Therefore, whenever an individual had more knives or hatchets than he could use, it was quite acceptable for close relatives to help themselves to whatever they needed. The Indians carried this practice over to their affairs at the trading houses. Clearly, the traders did not need all of the goods stored in the warehouse, so the Indians saw nothing wrong with helping themselves to the items that they wanted. The English regarded such actions as stealing, since they had a different perception of individual and corporate ownership rights. By keeping all of the goods in the warehouse, and forcing the Indians to deal through the 'hole-in-the-wall,' the company could keep a tight control over its inventories of merchandise.[14]

Only the trading captains, who were admitted into the warehouse, had the opportunity to take goods, and therefore had to be watched. If the traders observed them picking up any items, they were dealt with very discreetly. In describing the actions of the captains in the warehouse and the company factor's reactions to them, Graham wrote:

What a pity it is, that pride which makes him [the Indian Captain] aspire to be thought great cannot deter him from actions which must degrade him even in the sight of those Europeans by whom he wishes to be respected; for while he walks about in the trading room under the sanction of good faith and confidence he does not scruple to purloin a hatchet, knife or other article. And if observed it is taken from him with a smile, and without the least expostulation at the time, or recrimination afterwards. Should the Governor come into the trading room he will cut off a foot or two of tobacco [it was twisted into a rope], and put it into the captain's pocket, at the same time shaking hands, and talking familiarly with him as if he was as honest a man as ever breathed.[15]

Thus, although Graham's comments suggest that the English and the Indians did not fully understand each other's attitudes and motivations with respect to property rights, the two groups had worked out a trading procedure and pattern of interpersonal behaviour that accommodated their differences.

While the band was conducting its trade, the traders at York Factory gave presents to the Indian medicine men, some of whom were also trading captains. Graham reported: 'The Captains and several others are doctors, and are taken singly with their wives into a room where they are given a red leather trunk with a few simple medicines such as powders of sulphur, bark, liquorice, camphorated spirit, white ointment, and basilicon [an ointment], with a bit of diachylon plaster [a vegetable juice ointment]. The use of everything is explained, and the women are bid to remember, and indeed their memories are very tenacious. A picture is generally put up with the things, for it is held in great reverence and thought to add to the efficacy of the remedies.'[16]

A final presentation of gifts was made to the Indians as they concluded their business and prepared to return to the interior. Once again, the presents were given to the captains. The procedure was as follows: 'Each leader at his departure is presented by the Chief [Factor] with a new gun, a two gallon rundlet of brandy, a small trunk, a yard and a half of cloth, two beaver [2MB] in beads, half a pound of powder and shot conform, six lb. brazile tobacco, a beaver [1MB] in vermilion, one fish-hook, ice-chisel, gun-worm, hatchet, burning-glass, two pairs hawks bells, two knives, a looking-glass, a needle, net-line, powder-horn, a ring, scraper, one pound coarse twine, a pair scissors, two thimbles, and one tobacco box ... and the leader gets a small bag of oatmeal and prunes at his going away ...'[17] Thus, the departing gift to the Indian leaders was a substantial one. The Indians were now ready to leave. As a final gesture of respect, the cannon of the fort was fired as the Indians headed away to their homelands.

INLAND SPHERE

In the interior, exchange between the middlemen groups and their trading partners was no doubt conducted, in large measure, along the lines outlined above, considering that many Hudson's Bay Company practices were adopted from, or represented adjustments to, Indian cultures and modes of behaviour. For example, the ceremonial exchange of gifts prior to trade would have been an essential ingredient in interband transactions for the reasons that have already been outlined. Unfortunately, the general lack of European observations of trade among Indian groups in the interior means that the details regarding various aspects of these exchanges are not well known. For example, it is unclear whether or not the middlemen gave presents to the medicine men of the groups with whom they were in contact. Also, the extent to which gifts were exchanged between Indian leaders is not known. Presumably, such exchanges took place, but probably on a smaller scale.

INTERPRETATION OF THE TRADING CEREMONY

The foregoing discussion has highlighted the more important aspects of the various trading institutions that were developed to facilitate exchange between the disparate European and native economies. The manner in which the trade was conducted raises some important issues.

There is no doubt that the pre-trade gift-giving ceremony was an Indian institution that was adopted by the company. It clearly had certain political overtones. Rich and Rotstein have suggested that the company was forced to adopt such an institution because trade and politics were inseparable in the native mind.[18] Rotstein argued that by adopting the ceremony the company was drawn into the existing native political alliance networks and these networks served to channel trade.[19] Thus, he contended that native trading preferences (i.e., with English or French) were more a reflection of their concern for political and strategic situations than they were a function of price competition between the two European groups.[20]

There are a number of problems associated with this interpretation. It suggests that the native concern with the political dimension of trade was one of the behavioural characteristics that set them apart from their European partners.[21] The early records of the Hudson's Bay Company do not support that viewpoint. From the outset, the governor and committee in London were concerned with security and acquisition of territorial rights, and hoped to establish alliances that would serve to exclude their French rivals from trade with native groups who visited the bay. For example, on 29 May 1680, the governor and committee sent a letter to Chief Factor Nixon instructing him:

There is another thing, if it may be done, that wee judge could be much for the interest & safety of the Company, That is, In the severall places where you are or shall settle, you contrive to make compact wth. the Captns. or chiefs of the respective Rivers & places, whereby it might be understood by them that you had purchased both the lands & rivers of them, and that they had transferred the absolute propriety to you, or at least the only freedome of trade. And that you should cause them to do some act wch by the Religion or Custome of their Country should be thought most sacred & obliging to them for the confirmation of such Agreements.[22]

In a postscript to the above letter, Nixon was further informed:

As wee have above directed you to endeavour to make such Contracts wth. the Indians in all places where you settle as may in future times ascertain to us all liberty of trade & commerce and a league of friendship & peaceable cohabitation, So wee have caused Iron marks to be made of the figure of the Union Flagg, wth wch wee would have you to burn Tallys of wood wth such ceremony as they shall understand to be obligatory & sacred, The manner whereof wee must leave to your prudence as you shall find the modes & humours of the people you deal with, But when the Impression is made you are to write upon the Tally the name of the Nation or person wth. whom the Contract is made and the date thereof, and then deliver one part of the Stock to them, and reserve the other. This wee suppose may be suitable to the capacities of those barbarous people, and may much conduce to our quiet & commerce, and secure us from foreign or domestick pretenders.[23]

Clearly the company directors had their own political motivations and they were prepared to accept any native institution that would serve their ends. The Indian custom best suited for that purpose was the reciprocal gift exchange ceremony.

Indeed, once this institution was adopted, the governor and committee hoped that giving gifts to the Indians would instill in the minds of the recipients a sense of obligation towards the company. In a letter sent to Radisson on 20 May 1686, the governor and committee wrote: 'Wee will also that you be permitted by the Governor & every one else to *dispose such presents as you shall thinke fitting to the Captaines of the Nations to further our trade & oblige them to bring their Families Downe.'*[24]

In short, the directors of the company willingly adopted an Indian institution in the hopes that it would serve their own political objectives and work to their commercial advantage as well. However, the political climate of the central subarctic was different from that of the St Lawrence valley in the early seventeenth century. There were no well-defined native power blocs, such as those of the New York Iroquois and the Huron and their trading allies, with whom the French and English could establish strong bonds, thereby channeling competition through the military sphere. Instead, the uplands surrounding the bay were occupied by sophisticated Cree and Assiniboine middlemen who were in a position to take advantage of the commercial rivalry that existed between the English and French. And, as early as 1682, they were using English arms to tighten their middleman cordon around the bay, blocking the efforts of groups like the Dakota Sioux to trade directly with the Hudson's Bay Company.[25]

Reflecting these political–economic conditions in the subarctic, the trading ceremony – while retaining many of the trappings of the political institution it had once been – increasingly served purely economic ends, as the subsequent discussion will show. The subject of trading speeches centred on the rates of exchange and the quality of goods. Also, bands of Assiniboine and Cree readily traded with both the English and the French. Often bands would arrive at the Hudson's Bay posts wearing French clothing or carrying French goods. The company traders often referred to such groups as the 'Frenchified Indians.' Clearly, in the central subarctic political alliances or pacts concluded between the two European groups and the Assiniboine and Cree middlemen did not channel the flow of goods and furs.

7

The factor and the trading captain

Following the examination of the institutional and social aspects of trade, the roles which the factor and trading captain played as well as the economic aspects of exchange will now be considered in greater detail.

THE TRADING CAPTAIN

The foregoing discussion has shown that the trading captains and the company factors played key roles in the complicated exchanges that took place between the Indians and the Europeans. Yet, in representing the interests of their respective backers, each was faced with fairly stringent operating constraints. As was pointed out in chapter 2, the egalitarian society of the Indian meant that the trading captains had little real authority. Trade leaders or captains were men who were good hunters, knew the trading routes, had a family, could make 'long harangues,' and could deliver the rewards they promised to their followers.[1]

Regarding oratorical abilities, an examination of the kinds of speeches that were exchanged during the ceremony of the calumet prior to the commencement of trade suggests that the captain's success as a bargainer would have been one of the criteria that his followers would have used to assess his performance. Although the pre-trade gift exchanges initially had been primarily political in character, in time the captains and the factors appear to have used the event to come to general terms regarding the rates of exchange that would be used in a given year. As noted earlier, the official Hudson's Bay Company rates were set forth in the *Standard of Trade* and *The Comparative Standard*, and, for the most part, these price schedules remained fixed over time (Table 1). However, the actual rates of exchanges did vary more often and more widely. The factors at-

TABLE 1

A comparison of the official standards of trade at Fort Albany and York Factory, 1710-60 (value shown in MB)

Item	1700 Albany		1700 York		1720 Albany		1720 York		1740 Albany		1740 York		1760 Albany		1760 York	
	Amt.	Value	Amt.	Value	Amt.	Value	Amt.	Value	Amt.	Value	Amt.	Value	Amt.	Value	Amt.	Value
Powder, lbs.	1½	1	—	—	1½	1	1	1	1½	1	1	1	1½	1	1	1
Shot, lbs.	5	1	—	—	5	1	4	1	5	1	4	1	5	1	4	1
Guns:																
4½ ft.	1	10	—	—	1	10	1	14	—	—	1	14	—	—	1	14
4 ft.	1	8	—	—	1	10	1	14	1	12	1	14	1	12	1	14
3½ ft.	1	6	—	—	1	9	1	14	1	11	1	14	1	11	1	14
Flints, no.	20	1	—	—	20	1	16	1	20	1	16	1	20	1	16	1
Ice Chissels	2	1	—	—	2	1	1	1	2	1	1	1	2	1	1	1
Hatchets	2	1	—	—	2	1	1	1	2	1	1	1	2	1	1	1
Broad Cloth, yds.	1	2	—	—	1	2	1	3	1	2	1	3	1	2	1	3
Tobacco, lbs.*	1	1	—	—	1	1	1	2	1	1	3/4	1	1	1	3/4	1
Brandy, gals.	1	4	—	—	1	4	1	4	1	4	1	4	1	4	1	4
Knives	8	1	—	—	8	1	4	1	8	1	4	1	8	1	4	1
Twine, Skein	1	1	—	—	1	1	1	1¼	1	1	1	1	1	1	1	1
Kettles	1	1	—	—	1	1	1	1½	1	1	1	1½	1	1	1	1½

TABLE 1 cont'd.

Item	1700 Albany Amt.	1700 Albany Value	1700 York Amt.	1700 York Value	1720 Albany Amt.	1720 Albany Value	1720 York Amt.	1720 York Value	1740 Albany Amt.	1740 Albany Value	1740 York Amt.	1740 York Value	1760 Albany Amt.	1760 Albany Value	1760 York Amt.	1760 York Value
Comparative Standard																
Wolverine	2	1	—	—	1	1½	1	2	1	1½	1	2	1	1½	1	2
Wolf	—	2	—	—	1	1	1	2	1	1	1	2	1	1	1	2
Bear	—	—	—	—	1†	2	1	2	1	2	1	2	1	2	1	2
Grey Fox	2	1	—	—	1	1	1	2	1	1	1	2	1	2	1	2
Red Fox	2	1	—	—	1	1	1	1	1	1	1	1	1	1	1	1
White Fox	2	1	—	—	1	1	2	1	1	1	2	1	2	1	2	1
Black Fox	2	1	—	—	1	1	1	3	1	1	1	3	2	1	1	3
Deer	2	1	—	—	2	1	2	2	1‡	1	1‡	1	2	1	1	1
Moose Skins	1	2	—	—	1	2	1‡‡	2	1	2	1	2	2	1	1	2
Lynx	1	1	—	—	1	2	1	1	1**	2	1	1	1**	1½	1	1
Marten	4	1	—	—	4	1	3	1	3	1	3	1	3	1	3	1
Fisher	—	—	—	—	1	1	—	—	1	1	2	1	1	1	2	1
Feathers, lbs.	10	1	—	—	10	1	—	—	500††	1	10	1	500††	1	10	1

*Brazil, †Black Adult, ‡Buck, **Adult, ††Number, ‡‡Parchment

SOURCE: Fort Albany Account Books, 1700-1760, PAC HBC B 3/d/5-59, and York Factory Account Books, B 239/d/12-51

tempted to exceed the official rates by as large a margin as local conditions permitted. The Indian captains countered this pressure as best they could.

The dialogue that took place regarding the standards is reflected in the substance of speeches that were exchanged during the smoking of the calumet prior to trade. According to Graham and one of his predecessors at York Factory, James Isham, an Indian captain's 'harangue' was roughly as follows:

You told me last year to bring many Indians, you see I have not lied, here are a great many young men come with me; use them kindly ... I say: Let them trade good goods ... I say: We lived hard last winter and hungry, the powder being expended ... Tell your servants to fill the measure up to the brim; take pity on us ... I say: We paddle a long way to see you. We love the English, let us trade good black tobacco [i.e., Brazil tobacco] ... let us see it before opened; take pity on us ... Let the young men have more than measure [i.e., than specified in the official standard]: roll tobacco cheap, kettles thick ... give us good measure in cloth, let us see the old measure: do you mind me, the young men love you by coming to see you ...[2]

Significantly, the trading captain did not ask that the official rates be changed. Rather, he asked that he and his followers receive full measure, i.e., that the official rates of exchange be used as the guideline for trade. He tried to obtain the factor's acceptance of this proposal by stressing the hardships that his people had suffered over the winter and the long journey they had to make to reach the posts. Threats that he and his followers would go to the French the next year were sometimes employed also.[3]

The factor typically responded telling the Indian Captain and his assembled followers: 'that the great men in England loves the Indians so well, that with great trouble and danger, sends the great ship yearly full of goods to supply their wants, and strongly talks to them not to be lazy but get furs in the winter, and all the young men to come down with their canoes full of beaver etc., ... and harangues upon the largeness of the measures, and the smallness of the Canadians [opposing traders], strongly advising them not to deal with them etc.'[4] In this manner, a general understanding was eventually reached. An examination of the account books reveals that the factors always managed to advance the terms of exchange above the official standards. As later discussions will show, the over-all markup averaged between ten and fifty percent depending primarily upon the intensity of French competition, which influenced the bargaining position of the Indians. The excess of furs obtained by advancing the terms of trade above the standard was termed the 'Overplus.' The manner in which the factors calculated the amount of 'Overplus' they gained each year will be outlined in the subsequent examination of the post account books (chapter 9).

After an understanding had been reached regarding the general terms of trade, and barter through the 'hole-in-the-wall' was ready to begin, the captain was admitted into the trading room of the warehouse to make sure that the company servants operated within the limits of the agreement. Regarding this procedure Graham wrote: 'Whilst any tribe is trading their captain is admitted into the trading room to satisfy them that everything is measured fair, and that they have their due. He frequently talks to them out of the window, receives their furs, and carries the goods in exchange now and then to show his familiarity and consequence with the English.'[5]

Although the captain remained in the trading room to see that the general terms of trade were adhered to by the company, the traders still had some latitude in bargaining with individual Indians as they approached the trading wicket. James Isham left an account of how this aspect of the trade was conducted. According to Isham, a typical interchange between a band and a company trader would have proceeded roughly as follows:

A [1st Indian] ... friend come I want to trade ...

E [Trader]   ... come and trade

B [2nd Indian] ... take pity of me give good measure with a little over

B [2nd Indian] ... this is very little [less than measure]

E [Trader]   ... your coate [beaver] is bad and half summer Beaver [a low grade of pelt]

D [4th Indian] ... a steel 2 combs & a worm a hatchett a narrow Ice chissel, and a shirt, their [sic] is 4 beaver

E   ... one is $\frac{1}{2}$ Beaver the other all $\frac{3}{4}$ beaver [i.e., $2\frac{3}{4}$ MB]

D   ... Let them go I have no more Beaver

E   ... No I can not their is two whole Beaver wanting

E   ... You forgett 2 half Beaver is equal to one whole Beaver.

D   ... their is one Beaver you are hard you will not pity me, I will not come any more

E   ... they will not take so much pity on you at another factory [French] ...[6]

Thus, while the captain looked on, his followers attempted to obtain the best terms they could, employing many of the same tactics which the captain used in his speech – i.e., mixing pleas for pity with threats that they would go elsewhere. As the interchange between the trader and the fourth Indian reveals, compromises were reached. In this hypothetical transaction the Indian offered $2\frac{3}{4}$ MB in furs for goods the trader said were worth $4\frac{3}{4}$ MB. After initially saying that he had no more skins, the Indian offered one more and the trader accepted. Thus, the two came half way.

Besides being a good bargainer, speechmaker, and an effective watchman, a successful trading captain had to fulfil the promises that he made to his followers and deliver the rewards that he said would be forthcoming to any who travelled with him.[7] There is little doubt that one of the promises he made was that he would obtain favourable treatment for his comrades.

Regarding rewards to his followers, it should be recalled that during the course of trade at the post, the captain received two or three sets of gifts from the factor: the captain's outfit before trade began, the medicine man's gifts if the captain also served in that capacity, and the parting gifts that were presented to the captains when their bands had finished trading. In total, therefore, the quantities of goods that a captain received as gratuities from the factor could be substantial. But the captain did not keep all of these goods for his own personal use. Rather, many of these presents were redistributed to his followers.

For example, the captain obtained the *Puc' ca' tin' ash' a' win*, or gift of furs, that he presented to the factor during the smoking of the calumet, by taxing his followers one or two beaver skins each. Since the captain's gift to the factor was therefore a present from the band as a whole, the captain was obliged to distribute the presents he received in return amongst all those who had made a contribution. Regarding the captain's and factor's obligations, Graham observed: 'there is a return to be made for the Puc' ca' tin' ash' a' win which though given as a present yet is only a mere form of kindness, because it is expected to be paid for; and as it belongs to the whole gang brandy and tobacco being the articles returned for it, the Governor always greatly exceeds its value as mark of his approbation of their conduct, and to encourage them to come down again the next year.'[8]

Although Graham thus indicated that the captain was obliged to return to his followers the alcohol, tobacco, and other commodities he received in exchange for the *Puc' ca' tin' ash' a' win*, there is evidence indicating that the Indian leaders gave away most of the articles which they received as personal presents at the post. Such action is not surprising given the fact that generosity was considered to be a prime virtue of a chief. Thus, even the captain's outfit was given away. As late as the 1860s trading chiefs still gave away their company uniforms excepting the hat which was regarded as a symbol of office.[9]

The captain's redistribution of gifts other than tobacco and alcohol took place shortly after the band left the trading post. Graham reported that:

it frequently happens that the young men are ready to go away before the Captain. On these occasions he gets upon the top of the tent or some elevated situation, and assuming an imperious air and voice he tells them to go away for the sake of provision, and hunt as they go to avoid quarrelling; to stay at such a place until he and the rest come up to them, when he will make a feast and settle everything for the next year. As for himself he has been used very well at this Factory, and seen that they had good measure and fine goods for their furs; and concludes them with acquainting them that he intends to come here again.[10]

Thus, the trading band assembled for a final feast before they separated and headed for their winter camps. The captain settled his accounts at this ceremony. If his followers were satisfied with the way he had treated them and had looked after their interests at the trading post, they agreed to follow him the next year, and selected a location where they all would assemble the following spring.

From the above, it follows that the more favourably a captain was treated at the post, the more presents he would have had to redistribute to his supporters. This would improve his chances of retaining or increasing the number of Indians who followed him. Consequently, he must have been in a somewhat difficult position since his continued success as a leader was partly dependent upon maintaining the continued goodwill of the local factor.

THE FACTOR

The factors also faced some difficult problems. They were in the position of having to understand the motivations and conventions of their Indian trading partners as well as of their London employers.

Regarding their relationships with the Indians, the factors had to possess a good understanding of the position of the trading captain in Indian society as well as an appreciation of the considerations that motivated an Indian to seek that role. On this subject, Samuel Hearne, a Hudson's Bay Company trader wrote:

The Leaders have a very disagreeable task to perform on those occasions [visits to the post]; for they are not only obliged to be the mouth-piece, but the beggars for all their friends and relations for whom they have a regard, as well as for those whom at other times they have reason to fear. Those unwelcome commissions, which are imposed on them by their followers, joined to their own desire of being thought of as men of great consequence and interest with the English, make them very troublesome. And if a Governor deny them any thing which they ask, though it be only to give away to the most worthless of their gang, they immediately turn sulky and impertinent to the highest degree.[11]

Although Hearne suggests that the captains sometimes had their office imposed on them, most traders indicate that individuals sought out the position and struggled to retain it. For example, Graham reported, 'during the voyage [to the factory] each Leader is canvassing with all imaginable art and earnestness for people to join his gang, and influences some by presents, others by promises; For the more canoes under his command the greater he appears at the Factory.'[12]

Thus, the factors realized that the captain's position was precarious and that he needed a good stock of gifts to maintain it. Furthermore, there was a general realization by the traders that status recognition, as manifest through preferential treatment at the post, was the primary incentive that motivated Indians to act as captains. This was one of the reasons that these leaders were given the 'captain's outfit' prior to trade. Also, it explains why the factors never reproached a captain for taking goods while he was in the trading room. The traders regarded such actions as degrading, but chose to overlook them, treating the captain '... as if he was as honest a man as ever breathed.'[13]

Many other courtesies were extended to the captains. Unlike their followers, who were forced to trade at the 'hole-in-the-wall,' the captains were, as we have seen, admitted into the factory to transact their business. Furthermore, at York Factory, if the captain led a party of fifteen or more canoes, he was invited to breakfast and dine every day with the factor and officers. Leaders of smaller parties had an oatmeal porridge prepared for them every day and they were given prunes.

Since they had become accustomed to such treatment, any curtailment of these hospitalities would be regarded as an affront by a captain and he would threaten not to return with his followers the next year. As Graham noted, deferential treatment of the captain by the factor 'is a sure means of keeping up the Company's trade, and ingratiating himself into the natives' favour, who are a good natured people and very susceptible of wrongs done them. Each leader leaves his grand calumet at the Fort he trades at unless he is affronted, and not designed to return next summer, which is sometimes the case ...'[14]

Besides having to deal delicately with the Indian captains, the factors had to attempt to implement policies of the London directors, or convince the latter that their plans needed to be modified in instances where they were unworkable. Some of the most difficult problems the factors confronted related to the rates of exchange and the costs of operating their posts. For example, during the late seventeenth century when England and France were at war, the company was plagued with inflated trade goods prices, rising transportation costs, and a declining fur market. The directors therefore wanted the factors to raise the standards. After their initial correspondence on the subject failed to produce the desired results, the London committee wrote to Chief Factor Geyer at York Factory in 1693 informing him:

... We take Notice that you have made noe Allteration in the Standard of Trade wch. we earnestly expected, for all considered, it ought be done, every thing standing us in double what it did in time of peace and that must be reason to all men of Understanding, to Consider the Arguments and reasons that have bin write you in this very affaire. Nay you know if we would force the Indians they must give double the price or starve. Therefore we doe againe recommend to you that you get two skins more p. Gun & soe proportionable in all other Comodityes that vend there, for inducemt. to the Indians to give you more for our goods, you may make a larger present then usuall to the Cheif Capt. of Rivers and leading men; and not expect more in returne from them then formerly soe that they may be induced to advance the standard wch. will make the rest to follow theire Example the more willingly Soe that by a littell more then ordinary given away you will bring a considerable advance in the hole with them this may be done privately the Comon Indians not knowing of it, Wch. yet notwithstanding we refer to your Discretion.[15]

In short, as was typical of most dispatches from London, the directors stated the policy changes they wanted made and suggested approaches to accomplish them, but they left it to the factors to determine whether a proposed scheme would work. If it were not feasible, then the latter were expected to arrive at an alternative solution.

In this instance, the factors were being told by London businessmen that all men of reason would accept increases in trade goods prices given the market conditions that the company faced in Europe. Yet the factors knew that such arguments would not convince the Indians, since the latter had no conception of the distant European market in which exchange rates were governed by supply-and-demand pressures. Also, the traders would have been aware that the plan of action that the London directors proposed to obtain Indian consent to the price changes was not workable, because it was based on a poor understanding of the relationship that existed between Indian captains and their followers. Since these captains redistributed most of the gifts they received, any increases in company generosity would have become common knowledge to all Indians. Furthermore, if the captains had been given preferential terms of trade as proposed, it would have served to undermine their support in the band. In an effort to solve the problem, it appears that the traders resorted to advancing the unofficial exchange rate thereby increasing their overplus trade.

Another persistent difficulty which confronted the factors was that of attempting to hold their 'out-of-pocket' costs to a minimum. These costs included expenditures of trade goods for services such as the transport of letters between the posts by Indians, the free distribution of alcohol and tobacco to the company men on holidays, the purchase of provisions from local Indians, and the presentation of gifts to trading captains and their followers. The latter two items accounted for a large proportion of the expenses that were incurred. Significantly, during periods of strong competition by the French, the factors attempted to retain their trading partnerships with the Indians by more generous gift-giving.[16] However, this added substantially to their out-of-pocket costs.

The factors attempted to cover these costs by obtaining as much overplus as conditions permitted. As has been noted, a large proportion of the overplus of most posts was derived by application of the factor's standard. In addition, at some posts, overplus was taken by giving gifts to the Indians that were of lesser value than those received. Indeed, Richard Norton, chief factor at Fort Churchill, wrote in 1739 that although most of the traders gained their overplus by use of the factor's standard, he managed to take his by: '... the respect and acquaintance I have with the natives. ... I have from the help of long acquaintance with the nature of the natives, and how to converse upon any subject with them, and good treatment, have often received a great part of this overplus from them by presents ...'[17] It therefore would appear that at Fort Churchill counter gift-giving was the major source of the overplus trade while Norton was in command. His method of obtaining it contrasted sharply with those of the traders at York Factory. At the latter post, counter gifts to the Indians were of greater value than those which the traders received from them.[18] Consequently, at York Factory most of the overplus must have been obtained by unofficially advancing the terms of trade.

Regardless of which method was used most extensively at a particular post, it is clear that, when the demand for the Indians' furs was strong, the Indian captains were in favourable bargaining positions. As subsequent detailed analysis of trade data shows, the captains took advantage of these situations and forced the factors to relax the actual rates of exchange and be more generous in their presentations of gifts before, during, and after trade. Thus, at the very times when the factors needed to increase their overplus trade to cover rising expenses, they were under pressure from the Indians to relax the terms of trade.

Clearly the factor's job was a difficult one even under the best of circumstances, and to be successful, he needed to have considerable experience prior to assuming the position. Richard Norton's record at Fort Churchill is a good example. In 1723 he was appointed as chief trader at the post to serve under Nathaniel Bishop, the factor. However, Bishop died in the summer of 1723 and Norton was placed in charge of the post at the age of twenty-two. He held that position until the summer of 1727 when he was relieved of command and sent to York Factory as an apprentice clerk.[19] In explaining their actions to him, the London directors wrote:

We observe in the Accounts you have sent us, that your over Trade [overplus], hath been every Year very small compared, with that of our other Factories, and former Accts. from the Fort you are at, likewise that your expence of Provissions, hath been very large ... we have therefore ordered that you shall be remov'd to York Fort, and their [sic], to be under the direction of Governr. Macklish, which we are certain, will be very much to your advantage and improvement, in the knowledge of our Trade and Accounts, for we do not think, that you have converted any of our Goods to your own use, with any design to defraud the Company, but believe that what we observed, relating to your over Trade, and expences, hath been for want of your knowing perfectly the method of Trade, used at our other Factories ...[20]

In evaluating the performance of a factor, the London committee was therefore keeping a close watch on expenses and overplus and comparing the trend of these two variables at a given post with those of the other forts and the past record of the establishment in question.

In summary, the Indian trading captain and the factor played key roles in the fur trade. They orchestrated the complex trading ceremony (Figure 10). Acting as spokesmen for their respective backers, they attempted to bridge the gap between their disparate cultures so that the trade

FIGURE 10

PHASES OF THE TRADING CEREMONY

Phase 1 : Pre—Trade Gift Exchange

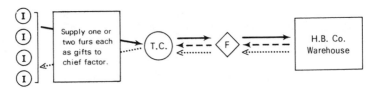

Phase 2 : Barter Trade

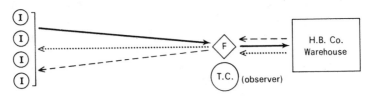

Phase 3 : Gift to Trading Captain after Trade

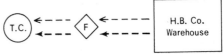

Phase 4 : Redistribution of Gifts after Departure from Post

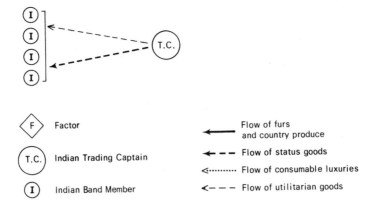

operated to the benefit of both groups. The interplay between the captains and the factors in the context of changing economic conditions is reflected in the trade data contained in the early account books of the Hudson's Bay Company. These records and the data contained in them will now be analysed in detail in an effort to obtain a fuller understanding of the economic behavior of the seventeenth- and eighteenth-century European merchants and their Indian trading partners.

PART THREE

THE ECONOMIC STRUCTURE OF THE FUR
TRADE SYSTEM: A QUANTITATIVE ANALYSIS

8

Analytical objectives and approach

The preceding chapters of this book have provided an overview of the antecedents and early development of the Hudson's Bay Company fur trade, giving the necessary background to a detailed analysis of the economics of the fur trading system. The third part of the book develops this economic analysis, using original Hudson's Bay Company data pertaining to the value, nature, and patterns of exchange of European goods for Indian-procured furs.

This inductive analysis provides an empirical basis for explaining the economic characteristics of the trading system as well as the behaviour and motivation of participants in the trade, especially the Indian trappers and middlemen. By using statistical data pertaining to the exchange of European goods for Indian furs, we hope to avoid the pitfalls inherent in viewing the trade through preconceived interpretations or theories and to provide a new viewpoint on clouded aspects and contentious issues.

More specifically, our objectives in this part of the study are: (1) to investigate temporal and spatial variations in the volume of trade, the rates of exchange between furs and trade goods, and the profits or losses incurred at the posts by the company factors before 1770; (2) to demonstrate and explain the regulatory mechanisms of the trade, particularly the operation of unofficial exchange rates (factors' standards), the significance of effective price variations, and the impact of competition within the trading system; (3) to use the above-mentioned characteristics as indicators of patterns in the behaviour of Indian traders and middlemen, so as to test various inferences concerning their basic motivations in trading furs for European goods. As a result of this part of our study, it is anticipated that a number of earlier statements or conclusions about the fur trade which hitherto have not been adequately supported by empirical evidence may be either solidly confirmed or finally laid to rest.

The inductive analysis of Part III will, in its turn, form the basis for a theoretical reappraisal in Part IV, focusing on the conceptual underpinnings of comparative economic analysis. In particular, we shall reconsider the applicability of various concepts explaining 'non-western' as opposed to 'western' modes of exchange. It is hoped that this will lead to the verification of a more satisfactory set of concepts applicable to economic interactions among widely differing cultures.

The approach adopted here builds on the quantitative data contained in the Hudson's Bay Company account books in the first century of the company's operations. A number of key indices are developed from these original data which form the basis of subsequent analysis and interpretation. It is therefore crucial that a clear understanding be obtained both of the original data provided by the account book sources, and of the derived indices, especially the measures involving overplus data, since these are vital to the later analytical arguments. Chapters 9 and 10 provide a detailed appraisal of the sources and nature of our data. Then in chapter 11 we explain the operation of the overplus trade and outline the usefulness of this variable in formulating indices of actual price, competition, and underlying behavioural traits. Chapter 12 deals with the competitive struggle of the English and the 'Canadians' for control of the Hudson Bay fur trade, probing causes and impacts of competitive manoeuvres with the aid of insights gained from the analysis of overplus trade. Since change through time is an important dimension of fur trade competition, various moves and counter moves are dealt with in a chronological sequence. Chapter 13 deals with an aspect of the fur trade which has not hitherto been given adequate attention – the relationship between the ebb and flow of European competition and the fluctuations in those costs and expenses of conducting the trade that were under the factors' control. Such considerations are a necessary prelude to the consideration of factors' profits and losses, which are also dealt with in chapter 13. The empirical analysis culminates in an appraisal of the Indians' role in the trade, which forms the subject matter of chapter 14. This examination involves a synthesis of evidence and interpretation from earlier chapters of this book and from previous works to give an empirically supported appraisal of the economic behaviour and motivation of Indian participants in the fur trade. Behaviour of European traders in face-to-face contact with Indians at the posts is also examined within this context. However, no systematic analysis of the attitudes and economic behaviour of the London directors has been undertaken in this study, except in so far as these were germaine to specific developments at the bayside posts.

9

The early Hudson's Bay Company account books

The Hudson's Bay Company trading post account books contain a wealth of statistical information about the exchange of furs for goods at bayside posts. They provide empirical data for this study which is remarkably accurate and complete (duplicate copies were kept in Canada and England, so there are a few gaps).[1] Available post accounts span a very long period of the company's operations.

Prior to the present analysis, little use had been made of these account books. There are a number of possible reasons for this. First, few scholars seem aware that this data source exists and contains such complete information.[2] Second, the books are organized in a complex fashion, using some outdated accounting conventions. Third, there is a lack of any guide or explanatory note dealing with these accounting conventions since the company accountants at the time learned 'on the job' as apprentices to experienced post accountants, rather than from written texts or notes.

This chapter deals with the format of the accounts and explains the conventions, since such knowledge is necessary for the reader to understand the nature of the data on which the ensuing quantitative analysis is based.

THE POST ACCOUNT BOOKS: BASIC STRUCTURE

One of the most important responsibilities of the chief factors who commanded the Hudson's Bay Company posts was to ensure that a complete set of accounts of the business operations of the posts was kept. These records were sent home at the end of each trading year, so that the company directors in London could scrutinize them, make sure that adequate, but not excessive stocks of goods were available at the posts, evaluate the performance of their trading representatives and guard

TABLE 2

Account book outline

I. TRADE GOOD ACCOUNTS
A. The Journal (with commonly used subtitles)
1 'Trading Goods Remaining as per Balance of the Last Years Acct. are as Follows Viz.' (beginning inventory)
2 'Trading Goods Received as per Invoice from on board [ship name and captain's name]'
  a. less goods invoiced but not received
  b. less goods damaged
  c. plus any goods shipped but not invoiced
  d. plus any goods made at the post
3 'General Charge' (inventory of goods available for trade, i.e., beginning inventory [1 above] plus goods received or made [2 above])
4 'Standards of Trade' (official rates of trade)
5 'Men's Debts' (goods sold to company employees)
6 'Expenses' (goods given or used at the post)
7 'Being ordered to make up ye Acct to ... [end of year] by an Exact acct taken of ye trading room itt appears their hath been traded ... the following goods, Viz.' (a list of all of the goods traded to the Indians)
8 'Furs and Other Commoditys' Receiv'd in trade for the aforesaid goods ...' (itemized fur receipts)
9 '... by an over hawl taken of ye warehouse I find there is trading goods remaining as follows' (closing inventory of goods)
B. The Ledger
1 Alphabetical index to the ledger
2 Reconciliation of accounts with the general charge
  a. Beaver account (fur receipts)
  b. Men's debts account (sales to men)
  c. Expense account (expenditures of trade goods)
  d. Profit and loss account (overplus and expenses)
  e. Balance remaining account (closing inventory)
3 Reconciliation of goods accounts (guns, kettles, etc.)
4 Reconciliation of beaver, men's debts, expenses, balance remaining and profit and loss accounts with the respective account totals
  a. Beaver account
  b. Men's debts account
  c. Expense account
  d. Profit and loss account
  e. Balance remaining account
II. STORES ACCOUNTS (commodities and goods for factory use)
A. 'State of Provisions' (European foods)
B. 'Armourer's Stores' (gunsmith)
C. 'Carpenter's Stores'
D. 'Cooper's Stores'
E. 'Factory Stores' (silverware, dishes, etc.)
F. 'Gunner's Stores' (defensive arms for post)
G. 'Harpooner's Stores' (if whaling was an activity)
H. 'Bricklayer's Stores'
I. 'Naval Stores'
J. 'Smith's Stores'

against embezzlement. For ease of analysis and comparison of the state of the fur trade at the various posts, the format of the account books was standardized to a high degree, as were the accounting procedures. Fortunately for present-day researchers, this means that the basic structures of all of the surviving seventeenth- and eighteenth-century account books are fundamentally alike. Variations in the records between posts and over time before 1763 are minor, being primarily matters of detail involving mostly the page layouts used in data presentation.

In their accounting procedures, the traders were required to keep separate sets of records for goods shipped to their posts to be used in trade and for stores intended to be used at the post. The latter would include such items as cannons, tools used by the carpenter, the blacksmith, and the 'armourer' (gunsmith), and food intended for consumption by the company employees. Accordingly, as Table 2 shows, the account books can be subdivided into two parts. The first half, beginning with a subsection usually entitled 'Trading goods Remaining as Per Balance of the Last Years Acct ...' deals with trade, while the second half of the books generally opens with a 'State of the Stores,' and provides a list of the goods that were used to maintain the post. The structure of these two basic divisions will now be examined in detail.

THE ACCOUNT OF TRADE GOODS

For discussion purposes, the trading portion of the account books can be divided into two separate units, the journal and the ledger, each of which includes several subsections (Table 2).

Journal accounts
As noted above, the journal opens with an itemized list of the goods remaining in the warehouse at the close of the previous year's trade (Illustration 1). This inventory gives the quantity of each type of good remaining, but the values of the items are not provided in this portion of the record. Significantly, the quantities noted in this inventory are the only sets of figures that are carried over from one year to the next in the journal portion of the account books.

It is unclear when the governor and committee first began to request that the factors include their closing inventories in the accounts that they sent back to London every year. One of the earliest references to these inventories is contained in a letter that the London directors sent to Governor John Nixon on 29 May 1680. In that letter, Nixon, who was in charge of the company's operations in the bay, was informed: 'Wee have

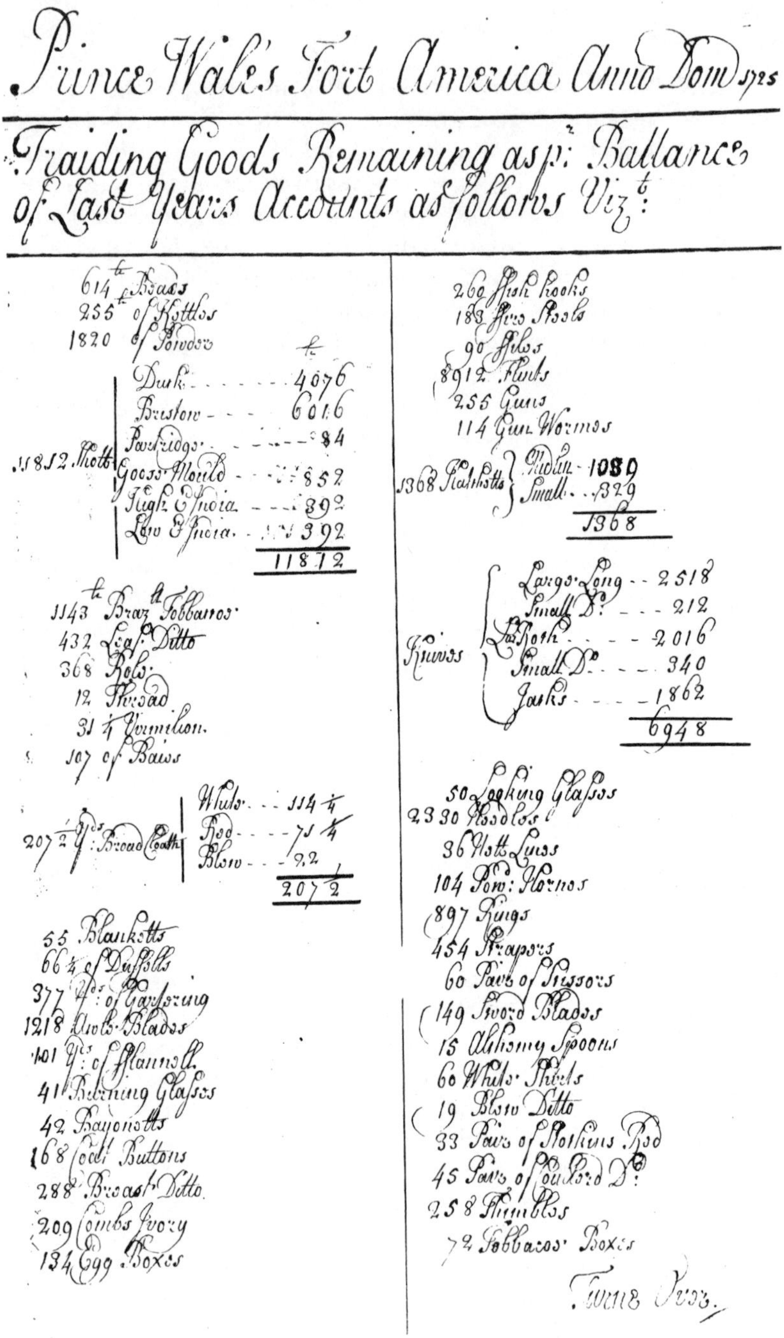

Prince Wale's Fort America Anno Dom 1725

Traiding Goods Remaining as pr: Ballance of Last Years Accounts as follows Viz:

614 lb Brass
255 lb of Kettles
1820 of Powder

11812 Shott
Duck - - - 4076
Bristow - - - 6016
Partridge - - - 84
Goose Mould - - - 852
High E India - - - 392
Low E India - - - 392
11872

1143 lb Braz: Tobbacco
432 Leaf Ditto
368 Roll
12 Thread
31 ¼ Vermilion
107 of Beads

207½ Yds: Broad Cloth
White - - - 114 ¼
Red - - - 71 ¼
Blew - - - 22
207½

55 Blanketts
66 ¼ of Duffells
377 Yds: of Garterring
1218 Awl Blades
101 Yds: of fflannell
41 Burning Glasses
42 Bayonetts
168 Coat Buttons
288 Breast Ditto
209 Combs Ivory
134 Egg Boxes

260 ffish hooks
188 ffire Steels
90 ffiles
8912 fflints
255 Guns
114 Gun Wormes

1368 Hatchetts
Medium - 1039
Small - - 329
1368

Knives
Large Long - - 2518
Small Do: - - - 212
Large Roth - - - 2016
Small Do - - - 340
Jacks - - - 1862
6948

50 Looking Glasses
2330 Needles
36 Nett Lines
104 Pow: Hornes
897 Rings
454 Scrapers
60 Pair of Scissors
149 Sword Blades
15 Alchimy Spoons
60 White Shirts
19 Blew Ditto
33 Pair of Stockins Red
45 Pair of Coulered Do:
258 Thimbles
72 Tobbacco Boxes

Turne Over.

1 Balance remaining inventory, Prince of Wales Fort (Fort Churchill), 1724–5 (courtesy Hudson's Bay Company Archives)

written to Mr. Phips our Warehouskeeper [at Moose Factory], requiring him to give us an Account by every return of our ships what goods of every sort are remaining in our several Factories, And wee desire you to see that he observes our commands therein, that wee may be the better instructed to know what provision is fit for us to make, and may not be in the dark in a thing of so great importance.'[3] Since no account books survive from this period (1670–80), it is uncertain whether this was the order that initiated the practice of enclosing the 'balance remaining inventories' in the post account books. In any event, it is clear that the governor and committee intended to use these inventories primarily to guide them when making decisions as to the quantities of trade goods that should be ordered and shipped to the bay.

In later letters, the London directors frequently stressed the importance of receiving closing inventories that were detailed and accurate. For example, in their 27 April 1683 letter to John Bridgar, they told him: 'We expect to receive a very exact account from you of all our concernes and perticulerly of what goods you have traded and what remaines wth you of all sortes of Provisions & stores as well as of goods & Merchantdizes which you must carefully observe to doe every yeare that we may the better know how to suppley you.'[4]

Similar orders were sent to other factors in subsequent years. A failure to comply with this order meant that the factor ran the risk of being reprimanded or dismissed by the governor and committee. For instance, the company directors were not satisfied with the performance of John Nixon for a number of reasons, one of which related to his failure to comply with their accounting instructions. In their 16 May 1684 correspondence with Chief Factor Henry Sergeant they wrote: 'When you meet with Mr. Knight & Mr. Vernor at Charleton Island the Generall Rendevouse. we doe expect not only a just account of what they & you have traded for & the Remaines of Merchantdizes but an account of all the stores & provissions which Governour Nixon did alwaies decline to our Detriment. all which accounts we require you to signe & not the Warehouse keepers.'[5] Thus, the importance of providing accurate inventories of goods and stores remaining in the warehouse at the end of the year was underscored. And, the factor, not the warehouse keeper, was to be held responsible for the report since the former was required to sign the accounts.

Having copies of the closing inventories enabled the governor and committee to determine whether or not the factors' orders for trade goods were reasonable. For example, in their 16 May 1684 letter to Sergeant

Prince Wales Fort America 1728.

Trading Goods as pr Invoyce Sent over from England on board the Hannah frig: Capt: Chris: Middleton Comr: Anno 1727 Are As follows Viz:	Trading Goods Sent to York Fort by Govr: Mack Lish's Order Are As follows Viz:
Kettles 327 ℔ N? 110	Beads 150 ℔
Powder 1000 ℔	Kettles 164 ℔ N? 30
Brazl Tobacco 332 ℔	Powder 400 ℔
Role Do: 500 ℔	Shott Bristow 952
Virmilion 30 ℔	Do Low Ed India 560 ℔
Broad Cloath Blew 225 ¾ yds	Tobacco Braz: 420 ℔
Do Red 180 ½ yds	Do Role 122 ℔
Brandy 406 ⅜ Galls	Broad Cloath Blew 113 yds
Baies 95 yds	Brandy 93 Galls
Blanketts 30	Ivory Combs 48
Flannell 60 yds	Guns 75
Gartering 144 yds	Hatchetts 400
Guns 100	Knives L Long 720
Gun Wormes 576	Do Jacks 648
Needles 1000	Looking Glases 24
Nett Lines 60	Nett Lines 24
Scrapers 250	Powder Hornes 50
Stockins Red 12 pair	Rings Plain 48
Do Blew 12 pair	Runcetts 20
Tobacco Boxes 84	Scrapers 100
Thread 12 ℔	Shirts White 24
Runcetts 40	Stockins Red 6 pair
	Stockins Blew 6 pair
	These Afore Mentioned Trading Goods you will find Deducted from the Generall Charge

2 Shipping invoice, Prince of Wales Fort (Fort Churchill), 1727–8 (courtesy Hudson's Bay Company Archives)

cited above, the governor and committee questioned the previous year's order for goods that they had received from the men in the bay. Attention was focused on the requisition for firearms. The London committee pointed out that 1150 guns had been ordered, while average annual trade to the Indians usually totaled 363. The governor and committee continued: 'And by your Accte. there are 962 remaineing in the Countrey (though our bookes mentions 991) yet take your Accte. thereof there are enough to last you above 2 yeares and a halfes Trade & now we are upon this subject we wold have you remove our Merchantdizes & likewise Provissions which does exceed two yeares supply from one Factorey to the other where is most need.'[6]

Normally the closing, or 'balance remaining inventory,' is followed in the journal by a section entitled, 'Trading Goods Received as per Invoice' (Illustration 2). As the illustration shows, a detailed breakdown is given of the goods shipped, but the value of the shipment is not provided. The factors were expected to carefully check the cargos they received against the invoices. The earliest known order to that effect was sent to Governor Nixon in June of 1681: 'Pray lett us heare from you how each parcell of goods proves whether they bee truely packed and whether they hold out accordinge to the Invoice in contents and condition as well provisions as merchandize.'[7] In compliance with this instruction, the clerks usually enclosed a reconciliation of the shipping invoice in the account books if it was required (such as when goods were damaged or the quantities received did not tally with those listed). Usually very little was missing or damaged in transit.

Occasionally, as occurred at Fort Albany in 1698, the supply ship did not arrive from England, and therefore the inventory of goods received was omitted. In its place was a section with the heading, 'Made here in the Factory by the Govr.s order the following particulars which hereafter you will find I have given the Company credit for.'[8] In years when significant quantities of goods were made at the post for trade, and shipments were received from England as well, the account of the former merchandise was inserted after the shipping invoice. Generally, in terms of the total trade good inventories, relatively few articles were made for trade, and in most years none were listed. After reconciling the shipping invoice, the inventory of trade goods remaining from the previous year was added to it, along with the quantities of goods made at the post, if any, and the resulting total was termed the *general charge*. It represented the total quantity of goods available for trade.

York Fort America. Anno 1724

Mens Debts   *Mens Debts*

Brought over	£12 : 10 : 9	
To Sugar 24 lb	£1 : 4 :	
To Tobacco Pipes ss 1 dz	£— : — : 6	
To Wäte Soap 4 lb 2 qrt	£— : 2 : 6	

John Wateridge

nicholas Rauffian	£14 : 3 : 9	
(Enh)		

John Wateridge

To Tobacco Lea: 44 lb .... 9 : 6 : —
To Brandy 6 Gall .... 1 : 16 : —
To Broad Cloth White 2 y ..... 3 : 3 :
To Duffels 2 y .... 1 : 6 :
To Flannel 33 y 2 qr ..... 1 : 6 : 6 :
To Shoose s Pr ..... 5 : 6 —
To Sugar 15 lb ..... 15 :
To Hard Soap 8 lb 3 qr ..... 4 : 6 —

£ 8 : 4 : 9 —

Tho. Riddell

To Tobacco Lea 46 lb £3 : 9 :
To Brandy 6 Gall £1 : 16 —
To Broad Cloth White £ : 73 : 9
To Bays s y £— : 2 : —
To Duffels s y £— : 2 : —
To Flannel 18 y £1 : 16 —
To Shoose 2 Pr £— : 11 : —
To Stockins 3 Pr £— : 9 : —
To Sugar 9 lb £— : 9 : —
To Tobacco Pipes 8 Doz £— : 4 : —
To Hard Soap 4 lb £— : 8 : —

Thomas Reddall — 9 : 9 : 3
Ent

David Allen

To Tobacco Lea 24 lb .... 1 : 16 —
To Brandy 6 Gall .... 1 : 16 —
To Broad Cloth White 3 y .... 4 : 9 —
To Duffels 2 y .... 1 : 6 —
To Flannel 8 y .... 16 —
To Shoose s Pr .... 5 : 6
To Sugar 9 lb .... 9 —
To Pipes 4 Doz .... David Allen

(Enh) £ 5 : 10 : 9 —

James Fettus

To Brandy 4 Galls .. £1 : 4 —
To Broad Cloth White £ : 8 : 3
To Sugar 8 lb £— : 3 : —
James Fettus his mark †
(Enh) £1 : 10 : 3

Willm Norgrave

To Brandy 6 Gall .... 1 : 16 —
To Flannel 2 y .... 4 —
To Sugar 10 lb .... 10 —
Ent Wm Norgrave £2 : 10 : —

3 Men's debts, York Factory, 1723–4 (courtesy Hudson's Bay Company Archives)

The general charge
The itemized breakdown of the general charge thus constitutes the next major section of the journal. As with the above inventories, the values of the stock items are not indicated. In terms of bookkeeping procedures, the quantities of goods listed in the general charge were extremely important in that the traders had to give an exact accounting of how these supplies of merchandise were used during the following year. As the subsequent discussion will show, most of the subsidiary accounts had to be reconciled with the totals listed in the general charge.

After the general charge is presented, there is a segment dealing with the standards of trade. All European goods and the commodities received from the Indians were assigned MB values. The current official company rates of exchange were listed in this part of the account books under two subheadings: the standard of trade, which, as we have previously noted, gives the MB prices demanded for European trade goods, and the comparative standard, which provides a schedule of prices offered for furs and provisions brought in by the Indians.

Men's debts
After listing the standards, the accounting clerks included a section variously entitled 'Men's Debts,' 'Men's Accounts,' or 'Sold to the Men,' where the purchases of each company employee were recorded (Illustration 3). As the subsequent discussion will illustrate, the debits to the men's accounts were entered as credits to the appropriate trade good account. The men's debts portion of the journal closes with a listing of the 'Men's Debts Collected' (i.e., summarized). Here, usually on a single page, it is possible to find the total quantities of cloth, thread, tobacco, etc., that the contingent of men at the post had bought.

Expenses
As noted earlier, the pre-trade gift exchange was an Indian institution that became a central feature of the trading ceremony. Accordingly, the governor and committee authorized the factors to use whatever quantities of trade goods or provisions that they thought were necessary to treat the Indians in a sufficiently generous manner.[9] But, the governor and committee wanted to know how much was being given away. For instance, in the 16 May 1684 letter to Governor Sergeant, they informed him that he could give the Indians provisions when the latter were in need, adding, 'when they are in want we must leave it to your Discretion to give what is fitting but then let us know what you yearly give away which hithertoo

4 Expenses, Prince of Wales Fort (Fort Churchill), 1724–5 (courtesy Hudson's Bay Company Archives)

your Predecessors kept us in the Darke.'[10] Concerning the matter of gifts of trade goods the governor and committee continued, 'we wold have you yearely acquainte us what presents are remaining in the Countrey & what yearely distribute.'[11] In compliance with these instructions, an expenses section was included in every account book that showed how many trade goods and what quantities of provisions were given to the Indians each year. In this same section, payments of goods to Indians for services rendered, such as carrying letters between posts, hunting for provisions and so forth, were also recorded. Similarly, the quantities of alcohol, tobacco, and food that were dispensed *gratis* to the company men on festive occasions were noted in this portion of the accounts.

As in the preceding 'Men's Debts' segment of the journal, the expense data are presented in two parts. The first provides an itemized accounting of the ways in which the goods were 'used and otherwise expended.' The second gives a summary statement of the total quantities of each type of trade good that was given or expended. Illustration 4 shows portions of both sections of the expenses segment of the account book for Fort Churchill in 1725. As in the case of the men's debts summary, no MB values are included.

Significantly, the men's debts and the expenses accounts appear to have been the only ones that were kept current during the year. Records of transactions with individual Indians were not kept during this early period. As one of the factors pointed out in a letter to London, this was not possible because of the shortness of the trading season, which often meant that the bulk of the business was conducted in a few days. Furthermore, Indian trading parties often numbered 60 to 200 men or more at the larger posts, such as York Factory. Under these time constraints, and the confusion at the post which was associated with these visits of large bands, detailed records could not be made. Rather, the volume of goods traded was determined by inventory of the warehouse at the end of the year.[12] The closing inventory, the men's debts, and the expenses were added together and subtracted from the general charge, and the result equalled the year's trade of goods to the Indians.[13] Apparently in the earliest years the factors did not provide the governor and committee with enough information about the goods traded. Concerning this matter, in their letter of 16 May 1684 to Governor Sergeant, they wrote:

In the account of sales you sent us we are sattisfied as it is an account Currant or a Collection of the whole which we wold have you constantly follow yet we must tell you we are not sattisfyed in that only because it is not perticular enough[.] for take

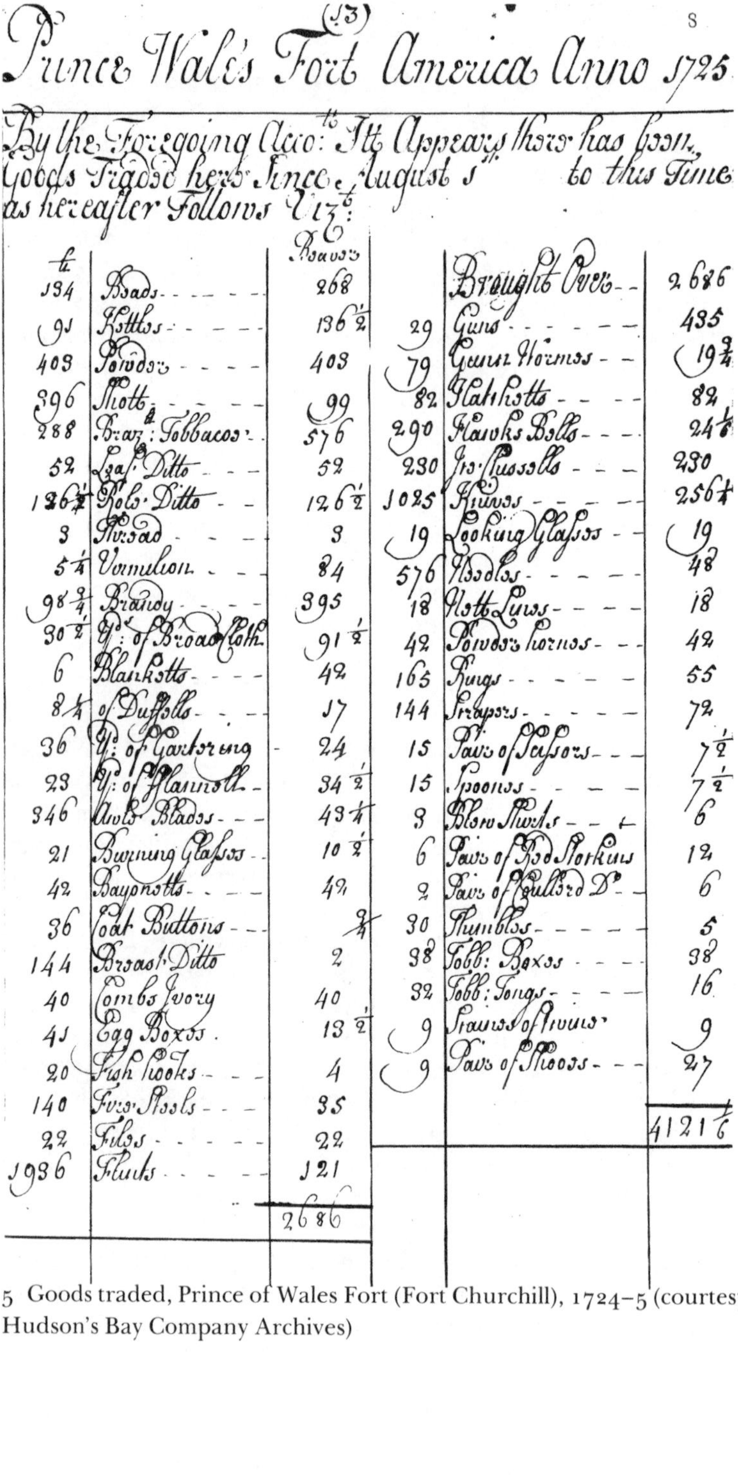

(13)

S

Prince Wale's Fort America Anno 1725

By the Foregoing Acco:ts Itt Appears there has been Goods Traded here Since August 1st to this Time as hereafter Follows Viz:t

		Beaver			
134	Beads	268		Brought Over	2686
91	Kettles	136 1/2	29	Guns	435
403	Powder	403	79	Gunn Wormes	19 3/4
396	Shott	99	82	Hatchetts	82
288	Braz: Tobbacco	576	290	Hawks Bells	24 1/6
52	Leaf Ditto	52	230	Ice Chissells	230
126 1/2	Role Ditto	126 1/2	1025	Knives	256 1/4
3	Thread	3	19	Looking Glasses	19
5 1/4	Vermilion	84	576	Needles	48
98 3/4	Brandy	395	18	Nett Lines	18
30 1/2	Yd: of Broad Cloth	91 1/2	42	Powder hornes	42
6	Blanketts	42	165	Rings	55
8 1/4	of Duffells	17	144	Scrapers	72
36	Yd: of Gartering	24	15	Pair of Scissors	7 1/2
23	Yd: of Flannell	34 1/2	15	Spoones	7 1/2
346	Awls Blades	43 1/4	3	Blew Shirts	6
21	Burning Glasses	10 1/2	6	Pair of Red Stockins	12
42	Bayonetts	42	2	Pair of Quilted Do	6
36	Coat Buttons	3/4	30	Thimbles	5
144	Breast Ditto	2	38	Tobb: Boxes	38
40	Combs Ivory	40	32	Tobb: Tongs	16
41	Egg Boxes	13 1/2	9	Skaines of Twine	9
20	Fish hooks	4	9	Pair of Shooes	27
140	Fire Steels	35			
22	Files	22			4121 1/6
1936	Flints	121			
		2686			

5 Goods traded, Prince of Wales Fort (Fort Churchill), 1724–5 (courtesy Hudson's Bay Company Archives)

that account of Albany River you mention 243 guns sold at 8 beavor 51 at 9 beavor & 30 at 10 beavor not expressing what kinde of guns they are whither 3½ foote guns, 4, 4½ or 5 foote guns Chissells 316 at 2 beavor & not mentioning what Chissells whither large, midle or small Chissells, Roles of Tobacco 165 at 8½ beavor & not mentioning how many pound in the role, 824 hatchets at 2 beavor not mentioning 2 lb. hatchets, 1½ lb. or 1lb. hatchets, & so shott 8250 lb. are 165 caskes at 10 beavor by Caske & not mentioning what sort of shot whither Bristoll, Calliver[,] goods, etc., by which hudling acct. we cannot discerne what sorte of Goods goes best which alwaies has beene a fault in your Predecessors which we expect other things from you because you are Intelligent in Trade and that we may the better provide with Judgment what is wanting.[14]

In compliance with these orders, the factors began to include reasonably detailed accounts of the goods that were traded (Illustration 5). As the illustration shows, the summary list provides an itemized breakdown of the total quantities of beads and other items that were sold to the Indians. The MB value of the goods traded is also given here (Illustration 5).

Calculation of the overplus
Next in the journal is an accounting of the 'Furs and other Commodities Receiv'd in trade of the aforesaid Goods are as follows Viz.' (see Illustration 6). The total quantity of each type of fur or country produce brought in by the Indians is then listed along with the aggregate MB value of these commodities as determined according to the comparative standard. The value of the goods traded (priced according to the standard of trade) is then subtracted and the remainder is termed the overplus. Illustrations 5 and 6 are taken from the 1725 account book for Fort Churchill and demonstrate the procedure. If all of the goods and furs had been exchanged according to the official standards listed in the account books, then the value of the furs received should have equalled that of the goods traded and there would be no overplus. However, as the subsequent analysis of account-book data shows, this was never the case. It appears that the official standards served only as accounting devices, and as a 'language of trade,' or terms of reference that the Indians and the factors used to negotiate the actual rates of exchange. This interpretation will be pursued more fully below.

At present, it should be pointed out that an examination of the early account books shows that the standard of trade and the comparative standard were relatively fixed at the various posts, but that the amount of overplus varied a great deal over time. Thus, as we indicated in Part II of

6   Furs received in trade, Prince of Wales Fort (Fort Churchill), 1724–5 (courtesy Hudson's Bay Company Archives)

this book, the traders were bartering fewer goods than the official rates called for, given the quantities and quality of furs and other commodities they were taking in, and in effect were forcing the Indians to trade at an unofficial rate of exchange, termed the *factor's standard*, that was applied each year.[15] Evidence presented in chapter 5 confirms that the Indians and the traders haggled over the setting of these unofficial rates. In the bargaining process, the Indians frequently asked to receive full measure (i.e., exchange at the official rates) while the traders always refused, as is evidenced by the fact that they always showed an overplus trade in their books. The dickering was therefore carried on in relation to official prices and in that sense the latter served as a business language that Indians and traders understood. The traders' gain, or the overplus, was determined by using the official standards when closing the accounts at the end of the year. It bore no relationship to the actual cost of goods purchased by the company in London nor to the revenue that was derived by fur sales in European markets. Yet, the practice of using the standards as an accounting device to arrive at an overplus figure did provide the traders and company directors with a means to measure the general trend of the trade at the various posts (i.e., to determine the quantity of furs being received, relative to volume of goods traded).

The closing inventory

The concluding portion of the journal consists of the inventory of the goods remaining in the warehouse at the end of the year. This is the inventory which was used to determine the quantity of goods traded in the manner outlined above, and it is the one which is carried over in the first section of the following year's account book where it forms a part of the subsequent general charge. The inventory of goods remaining was usually sizeable because, as the letter quoted on page 87 indicated, the company attempted to keep a two years' supply of goods in the warehouse. This practice ensured that there was a stock surplus that could be drawn upon in the event a ship failed to arrive.

THE LEDGER

The various accounts were balanced in the ledger, which follows the journal. The ledger section of the account books is divided into four parts (Table 2): (1) the index; (2) the reconciliation of accounts with the general charge, taking into consideration the men's debts, expenses, goods traded, and balance remaining (e.g., closing inventory) accounts; (3) the

Anno Domini

Company

	Number	Folio	Beaver
P:ᵈ Flints Value' att 16 p:ᵉ Beaver - - - -	8912	17	557
P:ᵉ Guns Value att 15 p:ᵉ Beaver - - -	255	17	3825
P:ᵉ Gunn Wormes Value at 4 p:ᵉ Beaver - - -	114	17	28½
P:ᵉ Gloves Yarn Value at 1 Paur p:ᵉ Beaver - -	9	17	9
P:ᵉ Hatchetts Value at 1 p:ᵉ Beaver - -	1368	18	1368
P:ᵉ Hawks Bells Value at 12 p:ᵉ Beaver - - -	910	18	75⅚
P:ᵉ Ice Chussells Value at 1 p:ᵉ Beaver - - -	1208	19	1208
P:ᵉ Knives Value at 4 p:ᵉ Beaver - - - -	6948	20	1737
P:ᵉ Looking Glasses Value att 1 p:ᵉ Beaver - -	50	20	50⅙
P:ᵉ Needles Value at 12 p:ᵉ Beaver - - -	2330	21	194⅙
P:ᵉ Nett Lines Value att 1 p:ᵉ Beaver - - -	36	21	36
P:ᵉ Powder Hornes Value att 1 p:ᵉ Beaver - - -	104	21	104
P:ᵉ Scrapers Value att 2 p:ᵉ Beaver - - - -	454	22	227
P:ᵉ Twigs Plains Value att 3 p:ᵉ Beaver - -	897	21	299
P:ᵉ Scissors Value att 2 p:ᵉ Beaver - - - -	60	22	30
P:ᵉ Sword Blades Value at 1 p:ᵉ Beaver - - -	149	22	149
P:ᵉ Spoons Alchomy Value att 2 p:ᵉ Beaver -	15	22	7½
P:ᵉ Shirts White Value att 3 Beaver Each -	60	23	180
P:ᵉ Shirts Blew Value att 2 Beaver Each -	19	23	38
P:ᵉ Shooes Value at 3 Beaver p:ᵉ Pair - -	59	23	177
P:ᵉ Stockins Red value att 2 Beaver p:ᵉ Pair - -	33	23	66
P:ᵉ Stockins Collerd Value at 3 Beaver p:ᵉ Pair -	45	23	135
P:ᵉ Thimbles Brass Value at 6 p:ᵉ Beaver -	258	24	43
P:ᵉ Tobacco Boxes Value at 1 p:ᵉ Beaver -	72	24	72
P:ᵉ Tobacco Tongs Value at 2 paur p:ᵉ Beaver -	32	24	16
P:ᵉ Twine Value at 1 Beaver p:ᵉ Plain -	324	24	324
	24021		10944⅞

7 Index to the ledger, Prince of Wales Fort (Fort Churchill), 1724–5 (courtesy Hudson's Bay Company Archives)

reconciliation of each trade good account (kettles, knives, etc.); and, finally, (4) the reconciliation of the men's debts, expenses, goods traded, and balance remaining accounts with the actual quantities of goods sold to the men, expended, traded, and remaining, respectively. This last section also includes a profit-and-loss account in the early years.

The index to the ledger
The first part of the ledger, the index, contains an alphabetical list of all of the goods available for trade, along with the page references indicating where accounts of particular items can be found. The page numbers refer to those numbers written in longhand in the upper left-hand margin of each folio and not to those printed in the upper right-hand corners. The latter were added later when the documents were indexed (Illustration 7).

Account balancing to the general charge
In the second portion of the ledger, the traders balanced their account totals to the general charge. A standardized procedure was generally followed. Pages were ruled into two columns to facilitate debit–credit entries. On the credit or right-hand side, the general charge inventory was recorded. Besides listing the total quantities of each item that were on hand at the beginning of the year, as was done earlier in the journal, the MB values which these stocks represented were also included. In addition, the value of the overplus trade was entered and the column was then tallied to arrive at a credit total. The example taken from the Fort Churchill account books of 1724–5 illustrates the operation (Table 3). On the debit side, the total MB value of the beaver account (the furs and other commodities received in trade and shipped home) was entered along with the totals for the men's debts, expenses, and balance remaining accounts. When summed, these debits equalled the credits, or general charge and overplus. The reason for adding the overplus to the general charge on the credit side (the profit and loss entry) was that the furs received were of greater value than the goods that had been traded for them due to the application of the factor's standard. Thus, the surplus furs, or the overplus, constituted a part of the beaver account total on the debit side. A failure to make an adjusting credit entry therefore would have meant that the debits would have exceeded the credits by the amount of the overplus. An example of this accounting practice is shown in Illustrations 8 and 9. Illustration 8 is the debit entry page and Illustration 9 the credit entry page. The two sets of page totals are equal.

In many of the account books, the inventory of the general charge is of

	Number	Folio	Beavers
Prince Wales Fort America Company. Dr:			
To Beaver Parkd up to be Sent home. This Effects of this Poss within Trade — — — —	4752	13	1540½
To Mens Debts for Goods of this Fort taken up	34	15	112
To Proffitt & Loss Presented and Otherways Expended — — — — — — —	450	14	141
Remaining in Factory Uss — — — —	25	25	109
To Ballance Remains — — — — —	19360	23	9042⅞
	24621		1094 4⁷⁄₇

8 Reconciliation of the general charge, debit entries, Prince of Wales Fort (Fort Churchill), 1724–5 (courtesy Hudson's Bay Company Archives)

Prince Wales's Fort America Anno 1725

Henery Bullin Dr

To 8 yd: of Flannell	12	
To 2½ yd: of Broad Cloth	3	3
To 1 yd: of Duffells	4	
To 1 Gallᵗ of Brandy	7	6
To 2 ℔ of hard Soaps	4	
To 4 of Shugar	4	
To 1 pairs of Shooss	5	6
To 2 ℔ of Leaf Tobbaros	2	

Henery Bullin £ 2 2 3

Wm Manning Dr

To 2 Gallᵗ ½ of Brandy	15	
To 6 ℔ of Shugar	5	
To 2 ℔ of hard Soaps	4	

£ 1 4

Wm Pratt Dr

To 1 pairs of Shooss	5	6

Land Mens Debts

Mr James Anderson Dr

To 17 Gallᵗ of Brandy	5	2	—
To 3 ½ of Whits Rolls Tobb	—	5	3
To 32 ℔ of Shugar	1	12	—
To 4 ℔ of Whits Rolls Ditto	—	6	—
To 1 Blankett	—	10	—

Sam: Anderson £ 7 15 3

Samᵗ Walker Dr

To 14 Gallᵗ of Brandy	4	4	—
To 25 ℔ of Shugar	1	5	—
To 1 Blankett	—	10	
To 1 yd ½ of Broad Cloth	—	9	9
To 2 yd: of Duffells	—	2	
To 8 yd: of Flannell	—	12	
To 13 ℔ of Leaf Tobbarros	—	13	—
To 3 pairs of Shooss	—	16	6

Sam Walker £ 8 12 3

James Worrall Dr

To 14 Gallᵗ ¼ of Brandy	4	5	6
To 4 yd: of Duffells	—	1	—
To 5 ℔ of Shugar	—	5	—

James Worrall £ 4 11 6

9 Reconciliation of the general charge, credit entries, Prince of Wales Fort (Fort Churchill), 1724–5 (courtesy Hudson's Bay Company Archives)

TABLE 3

Reconciliation of the general charge, Fort Churchill, 1724-5

	Dr		Cr			
	Beaver*		no.	wt.	meas.	Beaver*
[A] To Beaver Packt up effects of the overwritten trade with overplus	4,669⅝	[E] To beads valued at 2 beaver pr. lb.	614			1,228**
[B] To men's debts for goods of this sort taken up by the men	978½	[etc., down the listing for the general charges of each item, the last of which was twine]				
[C] To Profits and Losses Presented and Otherwise Expended	1,280½	Total general charge				16,613⅝
Remaining in Factory use†	201	[F] To Profit and loss gained on this whole trade				567††
[D] To Balance Remains	10,051					
Total	17,180⅝‡	Total				17,180⅝

I-B Ledger, Section 2 (see Figure 1)

* Made Beaver value

† An uncommon entry. Items in general use were usually charged to a stores account.

‡ Because of the length of the list of goods in the general charge, these totals are broken down into two subtotals, one balancing debits against the credits of beads through files and the other for flints through twine.

** This figure, the general charge for beads, can be found in section A-3 of the journal portion of the account book and in the debit section of part B-3 of the ledger under the entry for beads.

†† This was the overplus gained that year.

such a length that it could not be placed on a single page. Consequently, the balancing of the accounts is spread over several pages. The factors arbitrarily divided the general charge into two to four segments and balanced them to subtotals of the beaver, men's debts, and expenses accounts. Because the operation shown in Table 3 was broken down into two to four steps, the figures make little sense at first glance. An added source of confusion relates to the fact that the accountants often did not add their subtotals together to obtain a single debit and credit figure. For this reason, it is easier to understand the bookkeeping operation used here by looking at some of the earliest records. The more limited inventories meant that the account balancing could be done on one or two pages with one or two sets of figures.[16] In the case of Fort Churchill, the 1724–5 reconciliation was done using two sets of figures. Figures 8 and 9 are the second of these two sets.

Trade good accounts

Following the balancing of accounts to the general charge, there is a lengthy section in the ledger that provides a detailed picture of the ways in which the stock of every item was used during the course of the year. Table 4 serves as an example. As can be seen, the general charge for the various articles that are shown as credit entries on Table 3 and Illustrations 10 and 11, were entered as debits in the left-hand column and the quantities traded, sold to employees, expended, and remaining at the end of the year were entered as balancing credits in the right-hand column. Thus, by examining this part of the ledger one can quickly see what percentage of the stock of a commodity was being given or traded to the Indians or consumed by the company's own servants. The relation of the local supply to the demand is also readily apparent. Of significance to the accounting operations, the figures appearing in these accounts are the ones used to derive the various totals in the reconciliation procedure outlined previously and in those which will be discussed below.

Reconciliation of beaver, men's debts, expenses, profit and loss, and balance remaining accounts

The fourth and last section of the ledger provides a breakdown of the account totals that appear as debit entries in Table 3 (A, B, C, and D). For example, Table 5 shows the beaver-packing account for Fort Churchill for 1724–5. The credit entry in Table 5 (A) is the same as the debit entry (A) in Table 3. The debit entries in Table 5 (G) were taken from the credit entries (G, to beaver traded) of the various trade good accounts (see example for

TABLE 4

Reconciliation of the trading account for beads, Fort Churchill, 1724-5

Beads	Dr				Cr			
	wt.	no.	fol.*	MB	wt.	no.	fol.*	MB
[E] To Company at 2 beaver [per pound]	614			1,228†				
[G] To Beaver traded					134			268
[H] To Men's Debts‡					—			—
[I] To Expenses‡					—			—
[J] To Balance Remains					480			960
[E]†					614			1,228

(I-B ledger, Section 3)

* Folio or page number of ledger

† See entry (E) Table 3 and the first entry in Illustration 11.

‡ Normally when there are no charges, men's debts and expenses entries would simply be omitted. They were inserted here simply to show where they would be found in this portion of the ledger.

TABLE 5

Reconciliation of the beaver account, Fort Churchill 1724-5*

	Dr				Cr			
	wt.	no.	meas.	beaver		wt.	no.	meas.	beaver
[G] To beads value at 2 MB per pound	134			268†	[A] Pr. Company to Be Packed up to be Sent Home the Efforts of This Overwritten Trade With the Overplus				4,669 5/8*
[etc., giving the quantity and value of each type of trading good]									
Total value of all goods traded				4,102 5/8**					
[E] To Profit and Loss Gained in the whole Trade				567‡					
[A]				4,669 5/8††					

(I-B Ledger, Section 4a)

 * This appears as entry A on Table 3.
 ** This was the accounting of the goods traded for the furs being shipped back to England.
 † This appears as entry G on Table 4.
 †† A subtotal for total value of goods was not included, but rather, the overplus of 567 was simply entered after the list of trade goods was completed and then the column was summed.
 ‡ This was the overplus for the year; it appears as entry F on Table 3, and as last credit entry on Illustration 6.

Prince Wale's Fort America	Weight	Number	Folio	Beaver
Beads Dr.				
To Compy: valus: at 2 Beavers p:tt - - - - -	614		✓	1228
Kettles Dr.				
To Compy valus: al s 2 Beavers p:tt	499	79		748½
Powder Dr.				
To Compy Valus: al s Beavers p:tt - - - - -	3120		✓	3120

10 Reconciliation of bead, kettle, and gunpowder accounts, debit entries, Prince of Wales Fort (Fort Churchill), 1724–5 (courtesy Hudson's Bay Company Archives)

	Dr.	Weight	Number	Folio	Beaver
Anno Domini					
Beads					
P:. Beaver Traded		134		12	268
P: Ballance Remains		480		26	960
		614			1228
Kettles					
P: Beaver Traded		91	24	12	136½
Remaining in ffactory 9ho.		30	5	25	45
P: Ballance Remains		378	50	26	567
		499	79		748½
Powder					
P: Beaver Traded		103		12	103
P:. . . .		277		14	277
P: Ballance Remains		2740		20	2740
		3120			3120

11 Reconciliation of bead, kettle, and gunpowder accounts, credit entries, Prince of Wales Fort (Fort Churchill), 1724–5 (courtesy Hudson's Bay Company Archives)

TABLE 6

Reconciliation of the men's debts account, Fort Churchill, 1724-5

	Dr				Cr		
	wt.	no.	meas.	beaver	wt.	no.	meas.	beaver
[H] To beads value at 2 MB per pound*								978½
					[B] To Company for the Overwritten			
[etc., giving quantity value of each type of goods purchased by men]								
[B] Total value of Men's Debts†				978½				

(1-B Ledger, Section 4b)

* As Table 4 shows, no beads were purchased by the men. Generally, in such cases no entry would have been made for beads. Rather, entries were made only for the items used. This entry equalled entry [H] in the appropriate trade good account. See Table 4.

† This total appears as entry [B] on Table 3.

beads, Table 4). These were then tallied along with the overplus (entry F in Table 5 and last credit entry Illustration 9) to arrive at a debit total. This total equalled that shown as entry A on Table 3. The men's debts account was balanced in a similar fashion (Table 6). The credit of 978½MB appears as debit entry (B) in Table 3. The debit entries shown in Table 6 were taken from the appropriate credit entries (H) of the various trade goods accounts (see Table 4 for an example). Likewise, the total for expenses which appears as a debit in Table 3 (entry C) is registered as a credit in Table 7. The debit total of Table 7 was obtained by tallying the appropriate credit entries from the trade good accounts (see Table 4, entry I).

In the early account books, the reconciliation of the expense account was followed by a balancing of what was labelled the 'profit and loss account.' As Table 8 shows, the total expenses (entry C, Table 7) were registered as a debit and a credit (entries C) as was the overplus, or gain on trade (entries F). It is unclear why expenses and the overplus were added together to balance the account. In any case, the traders and the company directors could readily see the relationship between the two. These were important figures, because the local factor's expenses such as gift-giving and the overplus were key aspects of the trade. Furthermore, they were among the few items which were under the direct control of the factors at the posts. A skilful factor held his local expenses as low as was possible, while at the same time he obtained as much overplus as trading conditions permitted. Not surprisingly, evidence contained in eighteenth-century letters from London to the posts on the bay indicate that the factors' performances were evaluated partly on the basis of these two variables. As will be discussed, Richard Norton was dismissed as chief trader at Fort Churchill in 1727 because of his high expenses and declining overplus trade.

The ledger was normally brought to a close with a reconciliation of the balance remaining account (Table 9). The credit figure for this account appears as a debit entry (D) in Table 3. The debit total was obtained by summing the appropriate credit entries in the various trade good accounts (see Tables 4 and 9, entries J).

In the case of the Fort Churchill Account Books of 1724–5, the ledger does not end with the balance remaining account, but rather with the 'factory use account' (Table 10). As noted earlier, goods that were earmarked for trade were not normally put to use at the factory. However, in this particular year, some trade goods were put into service in this manner. Since these goods were listed in the general charge, an accounting had to be made. This was provided in the 'factory use account.' An

TABLE 7

Reconciliation of the expenses account, Fort Churchill, 1724-5

Dr				Cr			
wt.	no.	meas.	beaver	wt.	no.	meas.	beaver
To beads value at 2 MB per pound*							
[etc., giving the quantity and value of each type of good expended or used]†				[C] Pr. company for the Overwritten			1,280½††
[C] Total value of Expenses			1,280½††				

(I-B Ledger, Section 4c)

* As Table 4 shows, none were expended.
† Taken from entry D of each Trade Good Account.
†† Entry C on Figure 3.

TABLE 8

Reconciliation of profit and loss, Fort Churchill, 1724-5

Profit and loss	Dr Beaver	Profit and loss	Cr Beaver
[C] To Expenses of this sort	1,280½*	[F] Pr. Beaver Assort	
[F] To Company for the hitherto Gain	[567]†	Gained in the whole Trade	[567]†
	1,847½‡	[C] To Company for the Overwritten used and Expended	1,280½*
			1,847½‡

* This amount appears as entry [C] in Table 3 and the debit and credit totals [C] in Table 7.
† Although the heading was made for this entry, the clerk did not insert the amount. However, an examination of other account books for the period, including those for Fort Churchill, indicates that the overplus value was added here. This amount appears as entry [F] in Table 3 and is included in the total value of beaver packed and shipped home (entry [A] in Table 3).
‡ The debit and credit entries were often left untotalled. However, in some instances they were added together as in the case of the Fort Churchill accounts for 1718. It is clear in this case that the chief trader, Richard Norton, would have shown a net loss of 713.5 MB in terms of the system of accounting used at the post.

examination of Tables 3, 4, and 10 shows that this account was treated in the same manner as the above-mentioned accounts.

Occasionally the accounting clerks used a different format for their records. Tables 11 to 15 were taken from the 1718 account books for Fort Churchill. In this set of books, the data normally included in sections 4 of the journal and 2 and 3 of the ledger (see Table 2) were presented in column form on two pages (Table 11). The balancing of the general charge (Table 12), the beaver account (Table 14), and the profit and loss account (Table 15) follows this statement. The entries in these account reconciliations refer to columns A through F in Table 11. This unusual layout is of particular interest in that it provides one of the clearest outlines of the accounting procedures that were being used.

THE STATE OF THE STORES

All of the preceding accounts were kept to provide a detailed record of the manner in which trade goods were expended, and of the services, furs,

TABLE 9

Reconciliation of balance remaining account, Fort Churchill, 1724-5

Goods	Dr					Cr
	no.	wt.	fol.	beaver		beaver
[J] To beads at 2 beaver per pound	480			960*		
[etc., giving the quantity and value of each of the trade goods remaining in stock]					[D] To Company Goods Remains of the Overwritten	10,051†
[D] Total				10,051†		

* This amount appears as Credit entry J in Table 4. This credit entry is taken from the appropriate section of each of the trading goods accounts (i.e., beads, cloth, kettles, etc.) and entered as a debit to the balance remaining account.
† This amount appears as debit entry D in Table 3.

and produce that were received for them. We have explained these accounts with a view to providing a better understanding of the data employed in our analysis of the trade. However, it should be noted that the factors were expected to keep an equally close tally of the goods destined for use at the post. These records were included in the latter half of the account book and usually begin with a 'state of provisions.' Here an accounting is provided of the quantities of European food that were being consumed at the post. As in the trade goods portion of the books, the balance of food remaining from the previous year is added to the reconciled cargo invoice for the current year to arrive at a general charge. The quantities of food that were consumed during the year are then listed. The inventory of food on hand at the close of the year appears next. Since the objective of these accounts was primarily one of stock control, no values are assigned to any of the commodities. This is the case with all of the records in this portion of the account books.

The state of the various 'stores' follows after the provision account. The number of stores varied from post to post and increased over time. At mid-century, York Factory, the largest post, had nine stores not including provisions. They were as follows: Armourers' Stores (gunsmith), Carpen-

TABLE 10

Reconciliation of factory use account, Fort Churchill, 1724-5*

	Dr						Cr
Goods	no.	wt.	meas.	fol.	beaver		beaver
The listing included kettles, cloth, fish hooks, guns, hatchets, and powder horns					201†	To Company for the overwritten	201†

* Normally trading goods were not put to use in the factory. Rather, items intended for factory use were sent under a separate invoice and included in the statements of the 'State of the Stores.' Thus, most account books do not have a factory use account in the ledger.
† Appears as a debit entry in Table 3.

ters' Stores, Coopers' Stores, Factory Stores, Gunners' Stores (post defensive arms), Harpooners' Stores, Bricklayers' Stores, Naval Stores, and Smiths' Stores. The statement of each of these stores provides the same kind of information as that found in the provision account, i.e., balance remaining from previous year, the invoice of goods received, the general charge, the quantities of goods used, and the closing inventory.

Significantly, although the trade good accounts and stores accounts were separate, occasionally an item intended for factory use was traded or given to the Indians. Such transactions meant that adjusting entries had to be made in the two sets of accounts. For example, in 1698, when Fort Albany failed to receive a shipment from England, the stock of trading goods was low and some items which were in use at the post were expended in trade. One of these was an old sword that was given to an Indian captain. It was deducted from the stores inventory as an item used. In the expenses section of the trade accounts more details of the transaction were recorded by the following entry: '1 Sword presented the upland Indian of the Christins [Cree] of which you will find further acctt. among the stores.'[17] Similarly, three old muskets were taken out of factory use and sold to the Indians for eight MB each. The appropriate deduction was made from the state of the stores account and a credit of 24 MB was made to the beaver account.[18] In this way transfers were made between the trade and stores accounts when the need arose. However, the value of such transfers was usually very low in comparison to the total trade.

TABLE 11

Fort Churchill schedule of accounts, 1718

Val. as Beaver	The Whole of Sev'll Sorts of Goods on This Year's Accounts	The Whole Qty. of Goods	Val to Beaver [A]	Goods Traded of them	Val to Beaver [B]	Fact. Exp. & Presented	Val to Beaver [C]	Goods Sold to Men	Val to Beaver [D]	Goods Aboard Houy Gone No.	Val to Beaver [E]	Remains of Goods to Balance of Them	Val to Beaver [F]
	[Name of each trade good entered here and the appropriate sums in the columns. As an example, *Shot*]												
lb. pr 1	21,974 lbs	5493*	156	39*	1,646	411½*	—	—	616	154*	19,652	4,890½*
Total Value in Beaver of all ye Goods†		32,174[A]*		540[B]*		1,537[C]*		244[D]*		816[E]*		29,035[F]*

* In the original, all the entries in the value columns were in red and the quantities columns were in black.
† The column totals shown include the values of all other commodities in addition to those shown here for shot.

TABLE 12

Reconciliation of the general charge, Fort Churchill, 1718

	Dr			Cr
Company	Beaver	Company		Beaver
To Company Value of all the trading Goods as pr Weight, Number & Measure with the Skins taken out of Stock all together added Amounts to in Beaver as Appears pr thee total of thee first Columns of Red figures added up wch is at thee bottom of it [e.g., the sum of column A in Table 11].	32,174*	Pr.† Goods Traded Valued as Beaver Amounts to the Wt., No. & Measure Appears at the bottom of the 2nd Column of Red Figres [e.g., sum of column B, Table 11].		540
		Pr. Factory Expenses & Presented Do. as appears at Bottom of the 3rd column of Red Figures [e.g., sum of column C, Table 11].		1,537
		Pr. Men's Debts taken up As Appears at the bottom of ye 4th Column of Red Figures [e.g., sum of column D, Table 11].		244
		Pr. Goods Put Aboard the Succss Houy Gone to the North upon Discovery as Valued appears at bottom of 5th Column of Red Figures [e.g., sum of column E, Table 11].		816
		Pr. Ball. Remains the Sev'll Goods as Appears at the bottom of the 6th column Red Figures [e.g., sum of column E, Table 11].		29,035
				32,174*

* In tallying this column the clerk appears to have made an error. It in fact amounts to 32,172.
† Per

THE RELIABILITY OF ACCOUNT-BOOK DATA

Since previous attempts to analyse the economics of the Hudson's Bay Company fur trade have failed to make extensive use of the statistical data provided in the account books, some interpretations of the trade are called into question by the data presented below. Consequently, as we

TABLE 13

'The Acct of the Several Skins & Furs Valued into Beaver as pr ye Comparative Trade wch is the Product of ys Years Trade Commencing from July ye 14th to July ye 16th 1718,' Fort Churchill, 1718

No. Skins	The Sev'll Following Skins Purchased in ye time of ye acct.	Valued as Beaver	Amts. to in Beaver
320	Whole Parch Beaver Skins	1 pr 1	320
150	Half Parch Beaver Skins	2 pr 1	75
175	Coat Beaver	1 pr 1	175
2	Catts [Lynx]	1 pr 1	2
	[etc., giving number and value of all items received in trade]		
Packt up to be sent home ye Years Trade valued to Beaver			674½

have stressed earlier, a through understanding of the accounting sources and the nature of the statistical information contained therein are prerequisites to the following economic analysis.

An accurate and balanced assessment of the importance of the account books as a source for analyses of the present kind must include consideration of the limitations of this data source. Our efforts to assess the accuracy of these records are greatly assisted by an examination of the outward correspondence books of the governor and committee in London. In order to properly manage their affairs, the London committee needed to have a reliable set of accounts. Therefore, the account books were scrutinized closely every year. Any deficiencies that the governor and committee detected they called to the attention of the appropriate factor and council in their next general letter. For this reason, the official outward correspondence of the company provides us with a yearly commentary on the account books.

As might be expected, these letters reveal that inaccuracies in the accounts were attributable to three causes: the deliberate attempts of clerks to defraud the company; efforts to 'cook' the books to present a more favourable picture of trade; and carelessness. Of these problems, embezzlement appears to have been the least significant. An examination of all of the London correspondence before 1763 reveals that only one serious case of fraud was ever suspected. On 26 May 1721 the governor and committee sent a private letter to Henry Kelsey at York Factory informing him: 'Wee having Several Informations on Oath of Some of Mr. Halls transactions which are contrary to ye Comps Interest & ye

TABLE 14

Reconciliation of the beaver account, Fort Churchill, 1718

	Dr		Cr
Beaver	Beaver		Beaver
To ye Sev'll Goods as is Valued to Beaver as Appears at the Bottom of 2nd Column of Red Figures [e.g., sum of column B, Table 11] Amts to	$540^{30}/_{48}$	Pr. The Sev'll Sorts of Skins as is Purchased by Trade and is Pack'd up to be sent home valued as Beaver pr Comparative Trade Above Written amounts to	$674\frac{1}{2}$†
Overgained pr. Trade as P Value of Stock is	$145^{18}/_{48}$*	Pr. 9 moose skins & 2 Deer Skins which was taken out of stock & sold to men and being purchased by goods	
Neat Proceed Purchased by Goods Traded is	686	traded valued as beaver I here add	$11\frac{1}{2}$
		Neat Purchased by Goods Traded	686

* The overplus for the year
† The total value taken from Table 13; it includes the overplus.

Express direction given our officers, not only ye Embezzlement of Brandy & Other ye Comps goods, in Selling & bartering them on his own Acct but in Exchanging ye Martin he used to Catch by traping or procured to himself by Others from some of ye Comps best Martins taking ye best of ye Comps out of ye Bundles & puting his worst Martins Instead thereof which as Warehouse keeper he had oppertunity of doing ...'[19] Kelsey was ordered to seize Hall's books and papers and relieve him of his duties. If Hall could clear himself of the charges, Kelsey was instructed to send him to Fort Churchill. Nothing more is said of this case in subsequent letters so it is uncertain whether Hall was guilty.

In the case of one factor, Richard Norton, there is evidence that indicates that certain accounts were 'adjusted' to present the affairs of his post as favourably as possible. As noted earlier, and as will be discussed in detail subsequently, Norton was relieved of his command at Fort Churchill in 1727 because of his high expenses and low overplus trade. He was not reinstated until 1731. Judging from later correspondence between the governor and committee and Norton, it appears that Norton altered these two accounts if he believed they did not cast his operations in a

TABLE 15

Profit and loss, Fort Churchill, 1718

	Dr		Cr
Profitt and Loss	Beaver	Profitt and Loss	Beaver
To Factory Expenses and wch is Presented of Trading goods Valued as Appears at the bottom of ye 3rd Column of Red Figures [e.g., sum of column C, Table 11].		Pr. Beavor on Acct Gained Ye Whole Trade	$145^{18}/_{48}$
		Pr. Company for the Overwritten Expenses	$1,537^{13}/_{48}$
			$1,682^{31}/_{48}$
	$1,537^{13}/_{48}$		
To the Company for thee hithertoo gains	$145^{18}/_{48}$		
	$1,682^{31}/_{48}$		

favourable light. For example, on 17 May 1739 the governor and committee made the following extensive criticism of Norton's accounts.

On examination We find your Invoice agree in ye Balance of every Article of Furrs & Beaver with the account of Trade kept in the Book Whereby it evidently appears to us that the quantity's of each Sort of Goods put down in the book as the produce of the Trade is not an exact Just and True account which it ought to have been for how Can it Ballance when what is given away is not Entered, as to our Looking into the overplus, it can in no ways be Satisfactory to us, it being made up as the Chief directs, and the overplus set down more or less as he thinks Fit to inform us, On the whole we think is a very pernicious Practice for a Chief to give and take away what he pleases out of the Company's Goods and no account thereof given or Entered in the Books, and yet the Books made to Ballance wherefore we do Direct that you retrench the Gifts as much and as soon as Possibly you can in prudence, and what ever is given or taken out of the Company's Goods be it little or much must be particularly Entered in the account book you send home by the Ship.[20]

Responding to this letter Norton wrote:

I must acquaint you that I have from the help of long acquaintance with the nature of the natives, and how to converse upon any subject with them, and good treatment, have often received a great part of this overplus from them by presents but some years it will run short of what have been customary and other years somewhat more. But one year with another we make it balance and this is as punctual as we can be, but we presume it would have been much better liked by your honours and we think a fairer account would appear to send home every year what is received either in trade or otherways without regard to the balance, be the overplus more or less.[21]

Thus, when challenged, Norton admitted that he was not providing the governor and committee with a true set of accounts, but was adjusting them to reflect average conditions. He was not trying to defraud the company of its trade, but rather was attempting to make sure that his position was not threatened by fluctuations in the overplus trade as it had been in 1727.

Careless mistakes were the most widespread sources of error in the account books. The most serious case of sloppy bookkeeping occurred at Fort Albany in 1734. Commenting on this set of Albany accounts, the governor and committee wrote: 'Samll Walker who kept the books last Year hath made so many mistakes in the Accots that it was impossible for us to find out the Exact remains of several Particulars, therefore hope You will be very carefull to compare the remains of all manner of trading Goods Provisions & Stores at the Factory with the Accott Enter'd in ye Books before the Ship comes away ...'[22] Usually accounting errors were not this serious. Rather, they were limited to specific trade good accounts, such as beads, or kettles, etc., and resulted from inaccurate entries of the number, volume, or weight of items contained in boxes or barrels. The governor and committee readily detected these mistakes by comparing their shipping invoices against the goods received inventories of the various posts (part two of the journal section of the account books).

In short, the correspondence of the governor and committee indicates that the account books do provide a reasonably accurate picture of the business affairs of the company. This committee needed a good set of accounts to properly manage the business and, by monitoring the activities of the bookkeepers closely, the governor and committee checked abuses.

Although the account books are a generally reliable source of information, it should be pointed out that they do not provide us with a complete picture of all of the trading activity that took place at the company's posts. Some of the company's servants and officers engaged in trade for their own personal benefit even though such activity was forbidden. The servants and officers obtained the goods they traded to the Indians by smuggling them on board ship in London, by purchasing them from ship captains and crew members, or by buying them from other employees of the company who were not engaged in this illegal exchange.

The governor and committee made a concerted effort to stop this activity by cutting off these supplies of goods. In the sailing orders for 1727, the ship captains were instructed: 'to prevent our Servants having more Liquors and other Goods sent them out of England than we allow of, herewith given you the particulars allowed by us to each Servant and hereby order you to be very careful not to permit any thing to be sent on shour [*sic*] at the Factory to any Person whatsoever but what you find mentioned in the said List of particulars.'[23] This measure apparently did not achieve the desired results. In their general letter of 12 August 1738, the London committee tightened their controls further by ordering the chief factors:

not to Suffer or permit any English or French Brandy or any sort of goods whatever to be brought on shore from on Board our Ships by any Person or Persons whatsoever, Except allowed by the Gover and Committee, and are mentioned in the list Signed by the Gover and Committee which wee send you here inclosed Mark'd C with the Package and Mark of Each parcel licenced by us which will be viewed and packed by our officers, and a peice of red Tape put on the outside Case or Cask and Sealed with our Seal, and if you find any Goods or Brandy brought to the Factory or found in the Custody of any of our Servants, or attempted to be brought on shore without our licence as aforesaid you are to Seize and take away the Same and acquaint us thereof at the return of the Ship mentioning the Persons name the quantity and sorts of Goods so Seized and the Value thereof that the persons may be prosecuted by the Company for doing contrary to his contract.[24]

Despite these directives, illegal private trade continued. In 1739 Robert Pilgrim, a servant at Moose Factory, attempted to smuggle some furs into London on his return home. He was caught and his actions prompted the governor and committee to write the following to Richard Staunton and the council at Moose Factory:

You Could not be Ignorant but that Pilgrim was Possessed of some furrs and not being Packt up among ye Other Servants furrs he must of Course have put them Clandestinly on board to hinder their coming to the Companys Knowledge to prevent which for the Future you must Examine the Chests of all Servants before sent on board the Ship and take out all the Skins and furrs you find, and put them in a Case giving us an account thereof and what belongs to each Person for Goods run from on board Ship and sold Privately here does the Company a great deal of damage in their Publick Sales.[25]

Nonetheless, the smuggling continued. In a further effort to stop it, the 5 May 1743 sailing instructions to the ship captains included the order that they were: 'not to suffer any Officers Sailors Passengers, or others in their behalf, in your Ship to carry on Shore, after their arrival in the River Thames, any Chest, Trunks, Packs, Fardels[?] or Beds untill such time as the Same be viewed by such person as the Committee shall entrust and Employ for that purpose and whoever shall be found to transgress in this particular shall be deemed and adjudged guilty of Private Trade and consequently incur the Forfeiture of his or their goods and Wages.'[26]

In the end, the company directors never did manage to halt this clandestine trade of its servants. Thus, some of the interchange between the Indians and the English was not reported. However, the volume of this trade was very small in comparison to that recorded in the company's account books since it had to be carried on out of sight of the watchful eye of the governor and committee. And even if the servants managed to sneak furs passed the committee and sell them in London, the committee frequently learned who was responsible because of its business connections with auction houses and furiers.[27] As the above series of instructions from directors have shown, if detected, the servants ran the risk of losing their jobs and accumulated wages. For these reasons, we can assume that illegal private trade accounted for a small percentage of the total English trade with the Indians.

10

Variables and methods of analysis

In order to achieve the analytical objectives outlined in chapter 8, it was necessary to extract data from the Hudson's Bay Company account books which would permit a comprehensive, comparable, and accurate overview to be obtained of activities at all major posts. The magnitude of this task dictated that a systematic procedure be set up to handle the selection, preparation, and analysis of these data. This procedure is described below.

SELECTION OF BASIC VARIABLES FROM THE ACCOUNT BOOKS

To provide a basis for analysis of the salient economic characteristics of the trade, four variables were assembled from the account books: (1) total furs traded; (2) total goods traded; (3) total overplus gained; and (4) total factor's expenses. All of these variables are expressed in common units of value (made beaver). In the case of furs and goods, these variables can also be regarded as a crude measure of volume, given that the official standards that were being used by the bookkeepers did not vary significantly during the period under consideration. Also, there is considerable evidence that suggests that there were no major changes in the mix of goods that was being traded. In the case of fur receipts, the subsequent discussion will show that the French siphoned off some of the most valuable fur, particularly marten and prime coat beaver, when competition was strong. Hence, the aggregate fur returns expressed in made beaver exaggerate, to some extent, the volumetric fluctuations that occurred as a result of French opposition.[1] Since the analysis of the overplus and expenses variables forms the focus of several later chapters, they will not be described in detail here. However, a number of preliminary comments are in order at this point regarding the reasons for their selection. Total furs traded and total goods traded, of course, provide us with a view of the size and relative importance of each trading post in the system, and show the over-all scale of trade fluctuations and secular changes through time. Although in aggregate the patterns of exchange of goods and furs are similar, they do not coincide because the factor's standard, rather than the official standards, were used at the time of trade. Therefore, the value of goods traded was always less than that of furs, but the amount of the difference varied reflecting changes in the unofficial rates of exchange (the factor's standard).

The general pattern of fur returns at each of the posts, excepting Fort Severn, is shown in Figure 4. This figure was derived from the annual values of trade contained in the account books of the posts indicated. However, closer comparative analysis of economic performance at various posts requires that differences which are strongly linked to volume be 'screened out.' Thus, the furs and goods variables are used as the denominators of various ratio measures which permit such comparisons, as will be explained subsequently. The variable total overplus gained, as we have seen, represents in accounting terms the discrepancy between the MB value of total traded furs and total goods traded. As such, it is a potentially important economic measure of the actual performance of the chief factors as well as a very useful component of indices measuring the economic 'climate' of the fur trade. Indeed, this variable can, as we have suggested, be considered a measure of the factors' gains relative to the standards and thus occupies a central position in subsequent analysis of aspects of the trade.

Total factors' expenses comprises all expenditures under the control of the chief factor at each post that were not part of actual barter. These do not include cost of stores of trade goods, which were controlled by the company's London headquarters and were beyond the jurisdiction of the factors on the bay. Factors' expenses are again an important complementary measure of economic performance of Hudson's Bay Company posts and are used to derive other economic indicators.

DATA COMPARABILITY

Since the data are all expressed in common units and have been collated and recorded in the same original source (the account books of the

Hudson's Bay Company, described in chapter 9), it is assumed that they are of equal accuracy and reliability for the period during which all the posts operated. That is, it is assumed the data may confidently be employed for comparative analysis of operations of the various trading establishments keeping in mind the limitations discussed in chapter 9.

TIME PERIOD

The time frame of this study is the first century of operation of the Hudson's Bay Company. However, it should be noted that quantitative data are not available for the whole of this period at the majority of the bayside posts. As indicated in Part II of this study, the history of trading operations by the company was interrupted for several decades prior to 1713 by French military activity. Moreover, a number of the company's posts did not begin operation until later in the period. Consequently, recorded data measuring simultaneous operation at major posts are available for only a relatively short period (1720–70). The specific lengths of operation for which there are usable accounts of each post are shown in Figure 4.

CALCULATION OF ECONOMIC INDICES

Three main economic indices have been formulated using combinations of the original variables outlined above. These comprise the following percentages and ratios: (1) ratio of goods traded per unit of overplus gained; (2) percentage gross factors' gain over standard (percentage of overplus over total furs traded); (3) percentage net factors' gain over standard (overplus less expenses as a percentage of total furs traded). The term factors' gain used above refers to the difference between gains and expenses under the control of each factor and is not equated with company profit which involves dealings in the European markets also. Of the three indices, the most useful is the ratio of goods traded per unit of overplus gained. As will be demonstrated in the following chapters, this measure permits comparative analysis of effective exchange rates of goods for furs, acting as an index of actual fur prices. It also gives some idea of demand competition on the fur market (since this index correlates fairly well with fluctuations in French trading activity).

The percentage gross and net factors' gain over standard indices are used in conjunction with the variable total factors' expenses to flesh out the picture of variations in the fortunes of trade and the response of both factors and Indians to such variations. These topics are taken up in chapter 13.

PREPARATION OF DATA FOR ANALYSIS: SMOOTHING TECHNIQUES AND COMPUTER CODING

In any time-series data, and the present case is no exception, there are a number of trends which normally are combined: secular or long-term trends, periodicities which may be cyclical or seasonal, and random variations (short-term, erratic fluctuations). The latter may at times be severe enough to distort or obscure underlying regularities in the data. However, random fluctuations may be eliminated or 'dampened' by using data-smoothing techniques such as moving averages (running means).

In the present case, use has been made of a five-year moving average for preliminary data smoothing. Thus, where use of this technique is indicated the annual values of a variable actually represent means of successive overlapping five-year periods for which each particular year is the midpoint. In this way the occasional anomalous or erratic value is rendered less disruptive of meaningful underlying trends. In instances where trade values for specific years require discussion, the general trend data are supplemented by original (non-smoothed) quantities.

The sheer volume of data involved in this study dictated that all calculations be handled by an electronic computer. York University's IBM 370 computer was used. Computation made use of library programs from the *Statistical Package for the Social Sciences*[2] as well as specially written programs.

ANALYTICAL PROCEDURES

For the purposes of the following analysis, relatively simple univariate and bivariate statistical techniques were considered adequate. The standard techniques used are Pearson's Product-Moment Correlation, linear regression, and lagged regression. These have been supplemented with graphic displays of the relationships being analysed. Since the techniques of correlation and regression are in common use in the social sciences, they will not be discussed in detail here. It should be noted, however, that lagged regression (the dependent variable being lagged one or more observations in the data set) has been used where it is expected that a relationship involves a time-lapse between application of a stimulus and the generation of a response in the dependent variable. Such situations were considered to be highly likely in the fur trade, where such large distances are involved in the movement of furs and goods, and where some Indian bands made contact with European traders only once in several years.

11

The terms of trade

The statistical data from Hudson's Bay Company account books provide an excellent basis for the examination of a key element in the trading system: the rate at which goods and furs were actually exchanged. The variable which permits us to unravel the complexities of the terms of trade is *total overplus gained*.

THE ORIGIN AND MEANING OF *Overplus*

Given the importance of overplus in any effort to understand how local rates of exchange varied in response to changing economic situations, it is necessary to have a clear picture of what the term represented and it is important to know if it had different meanings over time.

As originally drafted, the Hudson's Bay Company's system of standards was too rigid to be followed closely. For instance, the comparative standard assigned MB values to the furs Indians brought in on the assumption that all of these pelts were of prime quality. This of course was not the case, and allowance had to be made for the fact that the Indians brought in summer furs, damaged peltry, and pelts that were not full size. John Lawson, who kept the account books at York Factory in 1688, gives us some insight into how the traders dealt with this problem. In his account book for that year he included a note to the governor and committee explaining what the overplus represented and asked them if they objected to the system of accounting that was used to derive this value. Lawson wrote:

The Reason how this overplus Beavr ariseth is many times an Indian Bringing Summer Skins to Trade for wch I give but half as much as I doo for Winter Beav'r wch is considerable, likewise their doth arise many times amongst Indians Beavr Coates some of them very much worn & have little furr upon them & is not reasonable that Wee should take them for Merchantable Beavr. Should Wee, the Inds would laugh at us & would not take care of their Beav'r but would bring us much more then they doe of such Tattered Torn Stuff and Summer Beav'r which I apprehend not to have above halfe as much furr upon it as ye Winter Beaver hath. therefore I thinke it not convenient to give soe much for yt as I doe for Winter Beav'r & good Beav'r nither doe ye Indians Expect it. But when Wee pack this Beav'r for England Wee accott all Beav'r Skins that will hold ye Size of a Beav.r & those that will not for halfe Beav'r Skins. Now if there be any Damage in this I would desire to know it. I can see none from hence ariseth this overplus as it is called, but it really belongs to ye Number.[1]

Lawson's commentary provides much important information. He makes it clear that the traders recognized variations in the quality of peltry and valued it accordingly when dealing with the Indians. However, when tallying their books at the end of the year, the company traders adhered closely to the comparative standard. As Lawson points out, all pelts that were full size were valued at the rate specified in the official tariff whereas any that were less than that size were valued at one-half that rate. Hence, in the early years the total annual returns of a post expressed in MB was, in essence, really a skin count, and the overplus was therefore a statement of the difference between that count and the value that had been assigned to those furs by the traders when they dealt with the Indians.

It is uncertain how long the traders had been in the practice of keeping an account of their trade in this manner. Lawson's commentary is contained in the earliest surviving Hudson's Bay Company post account book. Since he apparently believed that an explanation was in order, this system of accounting may not have been in use much before 1688.

Significantly, the fact that allowance had to be made for variations in the quality of peltry that the Indians brought to the posts meant that there was a way that the traders could depart from the rigid standards of trade when the need arose. Rather than altering the official tariffs directly, the traders accomplished the same objective by haggling with the Indians over assessments of the quality of their furs. The manner in which this was done was outlined in the previous discussion regarding the factor and the trading captain.[2]

In later years, the traders departed more widely from the standards of trade, and therefore the overplus increasingly represented the net effect of unofficial changes in the terms of trade. For instance, in the late seventeenth century, when England and France were at war, the Hudson's Bay Company was plagued with rising prices of trade goods in Europe, escalating seamen's wages, and a decline in fur prices. To combat this problem, the company's governor and committee urged the factors to advance the standards of Trade.[3] The latter were unable to obtain Indian approval for direct alterations of these tariffs for reasons cited earlier. Nonetheless, the effective terms of exchange were apparently changed and the gains thereby achieved reported as overplus. Evidence to this effect is contained in the York Factory Account Book of 1691. After recording that 27,577 MB of goods had been traded, a notation was added stating:

But having for sundry reasons this War time advanced upon the standard and traded dearer then Usuall I have Outgone this Sum & delivered into the Warhousekeeper (as will be found more at large in his Accotts) Beaver and other furrs and skins made beaver to ye Sum and Value of 34,905
From wch deducting the Value of ye Goods 27,577
There appears Overplus in this year trade 7,327[4]

From this account it is clear that the overplus had come to have a somewhat different meaning than that indicated by Lawson. It increasingly represented the measure of success that traders had achieved in their efforts to alter the actual terms of trade in favour of the company. Had the traders been able to overtly change the standards of trade, fewer goods would have been traded per fur received, but this would not have influenced the difference between the MB value of goods traded and the MB value of furs received for them. Hence, there would be no change in the amount of overplus reported. For instance, if the traders wanted to raise the price of a pound of powder from 1 MB to 2 MB, and did so by changing the standard of trade, they would receive 2 MB in furs from the Indians for each pound traded. No gain in overplus would occur because the traders would have been obtaining the quantity and value of furs that were specified in the accounts. On the other hand, if, in this example, the change was made unofficially, then the traders would have obtained 1 MB of furs per pound more than the tariff specified. This surplus would then be recorded as an additional unit of overplus per pound of powder traded.

As the factors increasingly departed from the company's standards of trade, they derived their overplus in a variety of ways. Initially it appears that the primary way the factors advanced the standards was by haggling with the Indians over assessments of the quality of their peltry. By the early eighteenth century, the factors had expanded the scope of their operations and were taking most of their overplus by unofficially advancing the price of trade goods. This was done in several ways, depending on the nature of the goods being traded. In the case of discrete items such as guns, hatchets, or knives, the factors simply insisted that the Indians pay more than the standard of trade specified. Table 16 illustrates how this was done, drawing on an example provided by Andrew Graham who was stationed at York Factory in the late eighteenth century.

Although Graham's price list suggests that a considerable quantity of overplus could be obtained this way, in practice it is likely that only a small percentage of the total was derived by this means. The trader Richard Staunton provided a good explanation of why this was the case. In a letter from Moose Factory in 1738 he discussed the subject of the overplus trade in some detail in a response to the governor and committee's call for more information regarding the manner in which the traders obtained it. Staunton wrote: 'As for your overplus it is an easy matter to know from whence it proceeds, for if you have 100 skeins of twine or 100 guns of any sizes, and as many files and blankets, your honours will not have one skin of overplus, all the Indians knowing what they must give for everything they trade, and Brazil tobacco when the roll proves thick, will yield no overplus for an Indian must have his length small or thick, also broad cloth which they trade in small quantities will yield no overplus.'[5] It is clear from Staunton's commentary that it was not an easy matter to blatantly advance the prices on items like kettles, guns, and blankets.

Rather, most of the overplus was obtained by using shortened measures and biased scales when bartering items that had to be measured out at the time of trade. Analysis of trade data for Fort Albany in 1715 reveals that broadcloth, gun powder, shot, Brazil tobacco, brandy, vermilion, duffles, beads, and English tobacco, in order of importance, accounted for over 80 per cent of the post's overplus trade. According to James Isham, it was these kinds of commodities, particularly brandy, beads, and paint (vermilion) that provided the York Factory traders with most of their overplus in the early eighteenth century.[6] Indeed, an examination of Graham's price list (Table 16) reveals that 71 per cent of the 53 5/24 MB of overplus gained on the sale of trade goods was derived from articles that were bartered by the yard, pound, or gallon.

There is little doubt that of all the items the company traded, brandy was the one that yielded the greatest quantity of overplus. Brandy had become an important article in the fur trade by the late seventeenth century. The French *coureurs de bois* carried considerable quantities of spirits to the interior in spite of the efforts of colonial officials in New France to curtail this traffic.[7] In order to counter the influence of the *coureurs de bois* among the Indians, it was necessary for the Hudson's Bay Company to make sure that its factors had adequate stocks of brandy in their warehouses. As early as 1716, Thomas McCleish noted its importance for the trade of Fort Albany. In his annual letter to London in that year he commented: 'Brandy is a rare commodity, for I can have more done towards the promoting the trade in small furs for two gallon of brandy than for forty beaver in any other sort of goods in the factory, it is become so bewitching a liquor amongst all the Indians especially amongst those that trades with the French.'[8]

As is generally known, as competition intensified, the importance of brandy also increased. It became a key item in the gift exchange ceremonies and was a commodity that the Indians purchased in ever greater quantities. These trends are graphically portrayed in Figures 11 to 18 and are documented in Table 17. The graphs show the amount of brandy that was traded and given (used) to the Indians at each of the posts.

Several important facts emerge from the data. The quantities of brandy that were traded annually at Moose Factory and Fort Albany appear to have been more strongly influenced by the changing intensities of French opposition than was the case at York Factory and Fort Churchill. French competition was strongest during the period from the late 1730s to the mid 1750s, as subsequent chapters will document, and these were the peak years in the brandy trade at Moose Factory and Fort Albany. At Fort Churchill and York Factory, on the other hand, a general upward trend in the trade is evident.

Regarding the quantities of brandy that were 'used,' all of the graphs show a general increase over time. Significantly, Table 16 reveals, however, that more brandy was traded every year at the various posts than was given away.

Much has been written about the negative effects of the alcohol trade on Indian societies, but to the traders the brandy traffic had a positive side if viewed in cold economic terms. It was a commodity that could be consumed on the spot and did not have to be transported. This was an important consideration given that the Indian's purchasing power increased substantially during competitive periods but his per-capita transport capacity remained fixed at a relatively low level. Similarly, and partly for the above reason, the Indian consumer demand for durable items increased but slowly over the short term and did not keep pace with the

TABLE 16

'An account of how and in what manner the factors are capable to give the company the overplus trade'

Trading goods	Company's standard valued as beaver			Factors' standard valued as beaver			Overplus gained beaver
Beads of sorts English	lb.	1 as	2	1	as	4	2
China		1 as	6	1	as	6	
Kettles brass of sorts		1 as	1½	1	as	3	1½
Shot of sorts		4 as	1	4	as	2	1
Powder		1 as	1	1	as	1	
Tobacco Brazil		¾ as	1	¾	as	1	
English roll		1 as	1	1	as	2	1
Virginia leaf		1 as	1	1	as	2	1
Vermilion		1	as 16	1	as 32		16
Fish hooks of sorts	No.	10 as	1	10	as	2	1
Brandy English	gallon	1 as	4	1	as	8	4
Strong waters		1 as	4	1	as	8	4
Baize	yards	1 as	1½	1	as	3	1½
Blankets	No.	1 as	7	1	as	8	1
Cloth broad	yards	1 as	3	1	as	4	1
Flannel		1 as	1½	1	as	3	1½
Duffles	yard	1 as	2	1	as	4	2
Gartering worsted		1½ as	1	1½	as	1½	½
Lace ditto		2 as	1	2	as	2	1
Lace orris		1½ as	1	1	as	1½	½
Awl blades	No.	8 as	1	8	as	2	1
Bayonets		1 as	1	1	as	1	
Combs		1 as	1	1	as	1	
Fire Steels		4 as	1	4	as	2	1
Files		1 as	1	1	as	1	
Flints		16 as	1	16	as	1⅜	⅜
Guns		1	as 14	1	as 14		
Pistols		1 as	7	1	as	8	1
Gun worms		4 as	1	4	as	2	1
Glasses burning		1 as	1	1	as	1	
looking		1 as	1	1	as	1	
Handkerchiefs		1 as	1½	1	as	2	½
Hats laced		1 as	4	1	as	4	
Hatchets		1 as	1	1	as	1	
Ice chisels	No.	1 as	1	1	as	1	
Hawks bells brass	pair	12 as	1	12	as	2	1
Knives	No.	3 as	1	3	as	1⅓	⅓
Net lines		1 as	1	1	as	1	
Medals		12 as	1	12	as	2	1

TABLE 16 cont'd.

Trading goods		Company's standard valued as beaver			Factors' standard valued as beaver			Overplus gained beaver
Needles		12	as	1	12	as	2	1
Powder horns		1	as	1	1	as	1	
Rundlets		1	as	1	1	as	1	
Rings stone		3	as	1	3	as	1	
Scrapers		2	as	1	2	as	2	1
Trunks		1	as	4	1	as	4	
Twine	lb	1	as	1	1	as	1	
Scissors	pair	2	as	1	2	as	2	1
Spoons	No.	2	as	1	2	as	2	1
Shirts stocking shoes and pumps each	No. and pair	1	as	2	1	as	2	
Sashes worsted	No.	1	as	1½	1	as	2	½
Thimbles brass		6	as	1	6	as	2	1
Tobacco boxes		1	as	1	1	as	1	
Total			116½			$169\,^{17}\!/_{24}$		$53\,^{5}\!/_{24}$

The Comparative

Trading goods	by company skins as beaver	by factor skins as beaver
Whole parchment moose valued	1 as 2	1 as 2
Half ditto valued	1 as 1	1 as 1
Whole dressed ditto valued	1 as 1½	1 as 1
Old bears valued	1 as 2	1 as 2
Cub ditto valued	1 as 1	1 as 1
Wolverenes valued	1 as 2	1 as 1
Wolves valued	1 as 2	1 as 1
Cats valued	1 as 1	1 as 1
Wejacks valued	2 as 1	3 as 1
Otters valued	2 as 1	2 as 1
Black foxes valued	1 as 3	1 as 1
Gray ditto valued	1 as 2	1 as 1
Red foxes valued	1 as 1	1 as 1
White ditto valued	2 as 1	3 as 1
Martens valued	3 as 1	3 as 1
Jackashes valued	3 as 1	3 as 1
Wenusks valued	2 as 1	2 as 1
Musquashes valued	6 as 1	12 as 1

SOURCE: Williams, pp. 277-9.

TABLE 17

Gallons of brandy traded and expended

	1700	'01	'02	'03	'04	'05	'06	'07	'08	'09	'10	'11	'12	'13	'14	'15	'16	'17	'18	'19	'20	'21	'22	'23
Fort Albany-Eastmain																								
Traded	17	0	17	0	40	6	32	30	4	122	155	286	224	30	20	158	99	128	89	130	101	129	100	173
Expended	53	0	3	11	81	6	33	43	21	79	160	72	60	60	37	34	40	36	36	40	40	40	38	42
Total	70	0	20	11	121	12	65	73	25	201	315	358	284	90	57	192	139	164	125	170	141	169	138	215
Moose Factory																								
Traded																								
Expended																								
Total																								
York Factory																								
Traded																	0	—	—	40	125	169	302	171
Expended																	0	—	—	41	130	75	118	79
Total																	0	—	—	81	255	244	420	250
Fort Churchill																								
Traded																			0	—	—	0	0	28
Expended																			0	—	—	0	0	35
Total																			0	—	—	0	0	63
Traded all forts	17	0	17	0	40	6	32	30	4	122	155	286	224	30	20	158	99	128	89	170	226	298	402	372
Expended all forts	53	0	3	11	81	6	33	43	21	79	160	72	60	60	37	34	40	36	36	81	170	115	156	156
Total all forts	70	0	20	11	121	12	65	73	25	201	315	358	284	90	57	192	139	164	125	251	396	413	558	528

TABLE 17 cont'd.

	1724	'25	'26	'27	'28	'29	'30	'31	'32	'33	'34	'35	'36	'37	'38	'39	'40	'41	'42	'43	'44
Fort Albany-Eastmain																					
Traded	69	244	131	239	285	286	373	357	323	325	299	307	263	204	403	192	395	295	244	255	320
Expended	112	48	30	38	48	41	45	50	52	54	80	95	108	89	100	116	115	75	57	73	178
Total	181	292	161	277	333	327	418	407	375	379	379	402	371	293	503	308	510	370	301	328	398
Moose Factory																					
Traded										49	107	117	—*	33	167	118	142	162	101	139	227
Expended										135	178	176	—	110	41	40	37	33	48	69	78
Total										184	285	293	—	143	208	158	179	195	149	208	305
York Factory																					
Traded	226	185	195	205	205	272	368	362	326	309	250	312	298	233	204	348	374	420	475	457	418
Expended	87	64	393	61	64	64	71	73	70	72	63	72	71	70	79	88	66	126	92	185	195
Total	313	249	588	266	269	336	439	435	396	381	313	384	369	303	283	436	440	546	567	642	613
Fort Churchill																					
Traded	96	99	80	71	27	87	18	93	72	148	58	90	106	73	103	122	83	150	45	250	273
Expended	40	49	63	49	45	46	48	51	88	110	139	128	127	181	116	129	130	136	103	160	168
Total	136	148	143	120	72	133	66	144	160	258	197	218	233	254	219	251	213	286	148	410	441
Traded all forts	391	528	406	515	517	645	759	812	721	831	714	826	667	543	877	780	994	1027	865	1101	1238
Expended all forts	239	161	486	148	157	151	164	174	210	371	460	471	306	450	336	373	348	370	300	487	619
Total all forts	630	689	892	663	674	796	923	986	931	1202	1174	1297	973	993	1213	1153	1342	1397	1165	1588	1857

* Post destroyed by fire

TABLE 17 cont'd.

	1745	'46	'47	'48	'49	'50	'51	'52	'53	'54	'55	'56	'57	'58	'59	'60	'61	'62	'63
Fort Albany-Eastmain																			
Traded	273	232	223	318	156	149	363	252	273	168	117	58	139	233	271	278	258	359	186
Expended	117	127	116	104	2	155	101	152	124	126	107	6	164	134	167	163	165	177	156
Total	380	359	339	422	158	304	464	374	397	294	224	64	203	367	438	441	423	536	342
Moose Factory																			
Traded	280	274	311	373	160	64	193	175	204	169	135	126	64	91	88	69	31	29	123
Expended	80	78	95	147	219	180	79	158	135	140	138	136	144	115	138	129	153	146	161
Total	360	352	406	520	379	244	172	333	339	309	273	262	208	206	226	198	184	175	284
York Factory																			
Traded	598	407	416	513	483	388	616	753	834	537	548	422	558	499	584	574	600	389	369
Expended	180	181	302	314	176	166	318	383	444	436	381	423	415	409	464	480	430	384	379
Total	778	588	718	827	659	554	934	1136	1278	973	929	845	973	908	1048	1054	1030	773	748
Fort Churchill																			
Traded	203	50	250	169	50	186	177	124	195	95	147	125	127	143	142	171	183	128	302
Expended	199	144	139	100	99	108	99	98	129	133	156	150	152	162	179	180	181	166	175
Total	402	194	389	269	149	294	276	222	334	228	303	275	279	305	321	351	364	294	477
Traded all forts	1354	963	1200	1373	849	787	1349	1304	1506	969	947	731	888	966	1085	1092	1072	905	980
Expended all forts	576	530	652	665	496	609	597	791	832	835	782	715	875	820	948	952	929	873	871
Total all forts	1920	1493	1852	2038	1345	1396	1846	2065	2348	1804	1729	1446	1663	1786	2033	2044	2001	1778	1851

FIGURE 11

FORT ALBANY: BRANDY TRADED

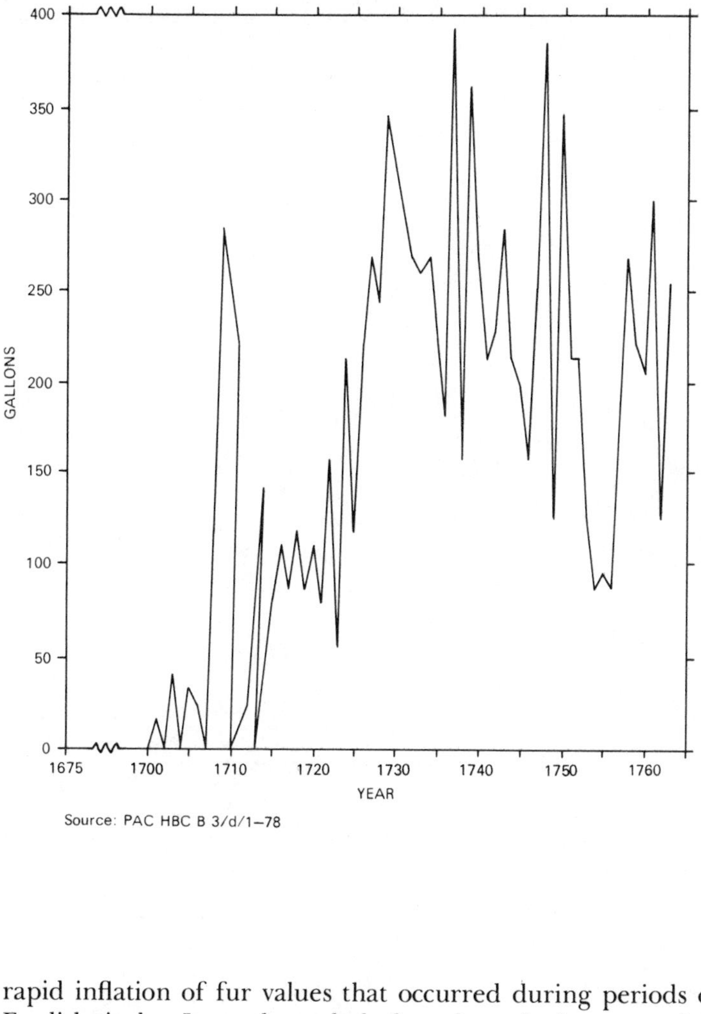

Source: PAC HBC B 3/d/1–78

rapid inflation of fur values that occurred during periods of French–English rivalry. It was through the brandy trade that some of the Indians' excess purchasing power could be absorbed.[9]

Of importance to the overplus trade of the Hudson's Bay Company, the growing volume of brandy that was being traded meant that the factors had a greater opportunity to apply their unofficial standards by diluting their stocks with water. The procedures that were followed ap-

FIGURE 12

FORT ALBANY: BRANDY USED

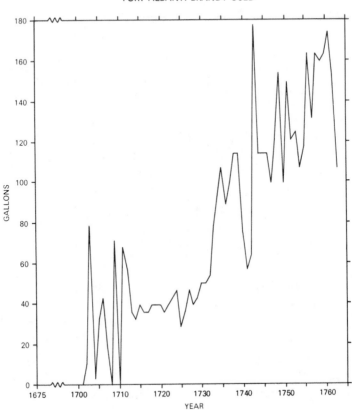

Source: PAC HBC B 3/d/1—78

pear to have varied somewhat from post to post.

At Moose Factory the 'watering ratios' differed depending on whether the brandy was being used to pay local hunters for their provisions (this would be an expense and recorded in the 'used' section of the accounts) or whether it was being traded to upland Indians coming from areas where the French were known to be present. Concerning these practices, Richard Staunton and George Howy reported that at Moose Factory:

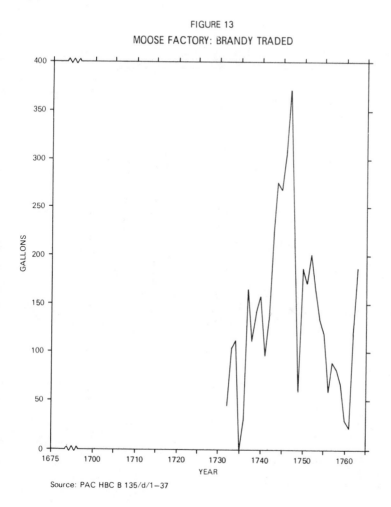

FIGURE 13

MOOSE FACTORY: BRANDY TRADED

Source: PAC HBC B 135/d/1−37

'What water we mix with brandy is very uncertain for when we mix it for our hunters the usual quantity is one-third because it is become a custom he that shoots five pounds of powder must have a bottle of brandy, or else no Indian hunters, which I think is an evil custom now brought up, and when I am sure that an Indian comes from the French I sometimes let them have it neat, but at other times for martens or small furs not above one-quarter water.'[10] Thus, it appears that at Moose Factory in the 1730s

FIGURE 14

MOOSE FACTORY: BRANDY USED

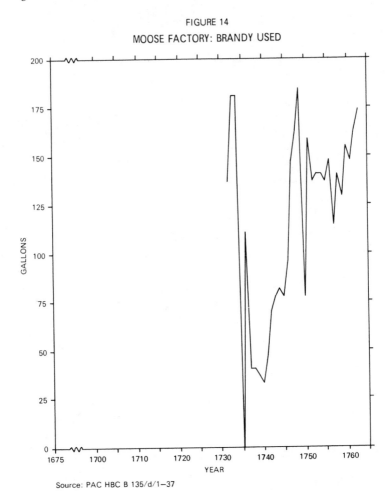

Source: PAC HBC B 135/d/1–37

and 1740s the factors were diluting the brandy with water by one-quarter to one-third depending upon the level of competition. Occasionally, it was traded undiluted as a special inducement. In all probability a similar practice was followed at Fort Albany, but unfortunately the Albany traders were vague in their discussion of the subject in their 1738 letter to London. In this letter they were supposed to give the governor and committee detailed information regarding their use of brandy in the

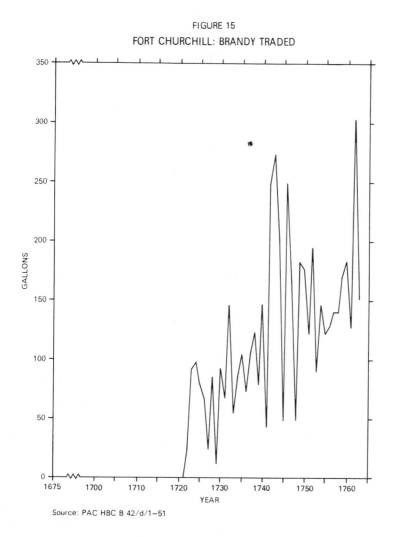

FIGURE 15

FORT CHURCHILL: BRANDY TRADED

Source: PAC HBC B 42/d/1—51

trade and their procedures for collecting overplus.

James Isham was more precise in his response to the question of how much water was put in the brandy. He indicated that at York Factory a dilution ratio of somewhat less than one-third was used.[11] He gives no indication that the ratio was flexible as it was at Moose Factory. Using Isham's figure and applying it to the annual volume of brandy traded at York Factory, it is possible to obtain some idea of the importance of

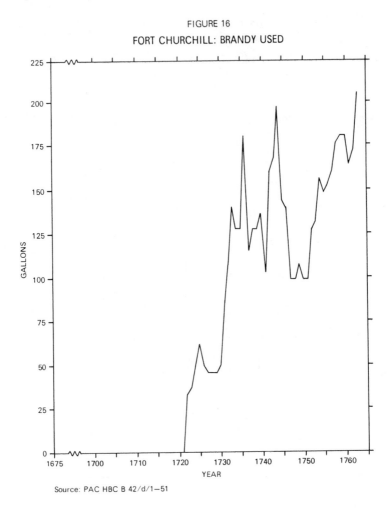

FIGURE 16

FORT CHURCHILL: BRANDY USED

Source: PAC HBC B 42/d/1—51

alcohol as a source of overplus. Figure 19 shows the estimated quantity of alcohol overplus that could have been obtained at York Factory if the one-third ratio had been applied every year. If the annual brandy over-plus figures are in turn divided by the annual overplus totals, we can obtain an idea of the relative significance of this one source. This is shown in Figure 20. This graph is revealing in that it indicates that as competition escalated and the factors were forced to relax their unofficial standards on

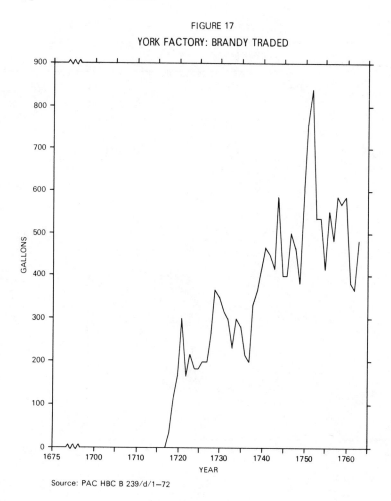

FIGURE 17

YORK FACTORY: BRANDY TRADED

Source: PAC HBC B 239/d/1—72

many items (as will be demonstrated subsequently), they were able to take more overplus in brandy due to the increased levels of consumption. Thus, as competition intensified, the percentage of total overplus that was derived from trading alcohol also rose sharply. Given this fact, the temptation on the part of the traders to encourage the Indians to purchase brandy must have been great.

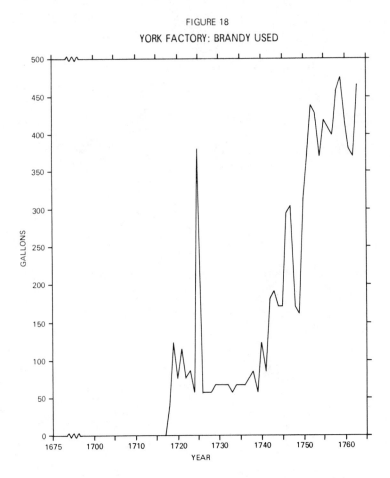

FIGURE 18

YORK FACTORY: BRANDY USED

VARIATIONS IN OVERPLUS

The total quantities of overplus (valued in MB) which were derived by various means at major Hudson's Bay Company posts are shown in Figures 21 to 24. These figures reveal that substantial quantities of overplus were always obtained, although considerable variability in amounts is in evidence. For example, at York Factory, the most important post in

FIGURE 19

ESTIMATE OF YORK FACTORY
OVERPLUS DERIVED FROM THE BRANDY TRADE*

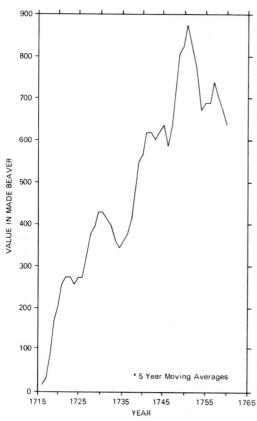

Source: PAC HBC B 239/d/1—72

terms of volume of trade, the overplus varied from a maximum of about 20,000 MB in 1729 to less than 2000 at the end of the first century of trade (1770). It will be noted that, in all graphs, the first twenty years of a post's operations were the most successful in terms of increasing volume of overplus gained. Thereafter the volume faltered and declined, sharply at some posts (e.g., Moose Factory) but more gradually at others (e.g., York Factory). The significance of the decline at various posts will become

FIGURE 20

ESTIMATED PERCENTAGE OF TOTAL YORK
FACTORY OVERPLUS CONSISTING OF BRANDY OVERPLUS *

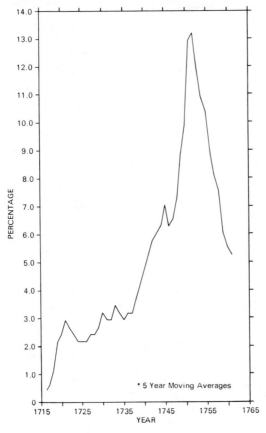

Source: PAC HBC B 239/d/1—72

apparent when questions of price and competition are introduced.

At a general level, *total overplus gained* can be considered a measure of gross fur price variation. This derives from the nature of the overplus, which was the result of the factors' varying their rate of mark-up over the relatively unchanging official standard of trade. Its use as an index of actual price variation is, however, limited by differences in volume of trade among posts, and it is incapable of showing the effective rate of

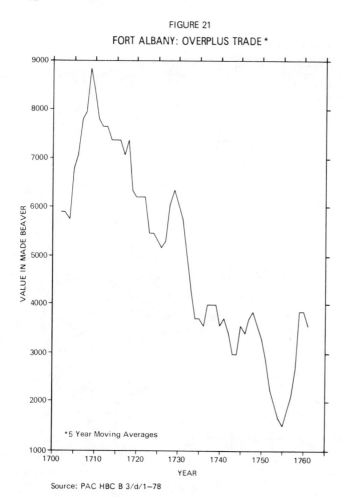

FIGURE 21
FORT ALBANY: OVERPLUS TRADE *

*5 Year Moving Averages

YEAR

VALUE IN MADE BEAVER

Source: PAC HBC B 3/d/1–78

mark-up on goods traded to the Indians.

This deficiency can be overcome by computing a ratio of the value in MB of goods traded for each unit of overplus gained. This ratio then becomes a measure of variation in the effective terms of trade, or the extent to which the factors advanced the rate of exchange above that specified in the standard of trade. According to this measure, a ratio of 2 units of goods to 1 unit of overplus would be the equivalent of an over-all 50 per

FIGURE 22

FORT CHURCHILL: OVERPLUS TRADE*

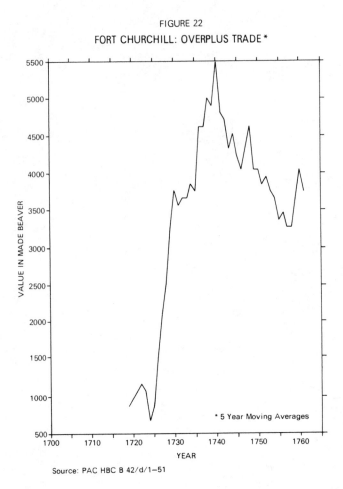

* 5 Year Moving Averages

VALUE IN MADE BEAVER

YEAR

Source: PAC HBC B 42/d/1–51

cent mark-up on the prices of goods over the official standard of trade, or an equivalent devaluation of the Indians' furs below the official standards. At this ratio, an article priced officially at 1 MB would have actually cost the Indians 1½ MB. Similarly, an index value of 1:1 would be the equivalent of a 100 per cent mark-up, in which case an article priced at 1 MB under the standard of trade would really have cost the Indians 2 MB. In short, as the value of the ratio increases, the effective price levels for European goods

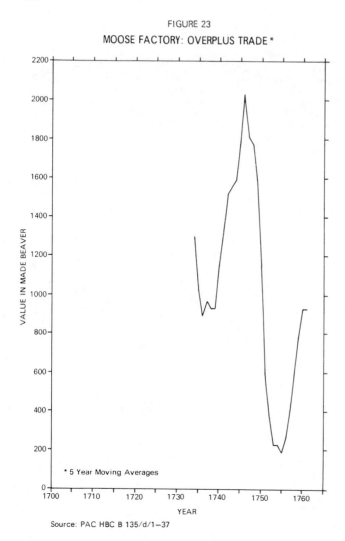

FIGURE 23

MOOSE FACTORY: OVERPLUS TRADE*

* 5 Year Moving Averages

YEAR

Source: PAC HBC B 135/d/1–37

to the Indian decreased, and, conversely, the price of Indian furs to the traders increased.

THE RATIO OF GOODS PER UNIT OF OVERPLUS AS AN INDEX OF ACTUAL PRICE VARIATION

Figures 25 to 30 show the temporal variations in the actual price levels of

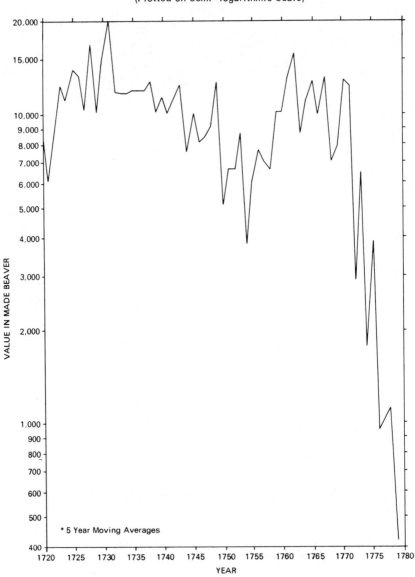

FIGURE 24

YORK FACTORY: OVERPLUS TRADE *
(Plotted on semi-logarithmic scale)

* 5 Year Moving Averages

Source: PAC HBC B 239/d/1–72

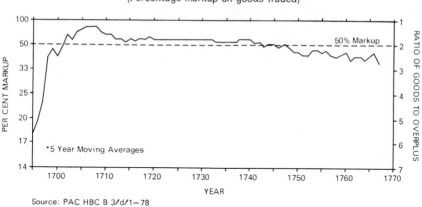

FIGURE 25

FORT ALBANY: INDEX OF ACTUAL PRICE VARIATION
(Percentage markup on goods traded)

Source: PAC HBC B 3/d/1—78

goods at the various posts (i.e., in the goods-to-overplus ratio). Two scales
are shown on the graphs: an ascending scale (left margin) of the percentage mark-up on the standard of trade and a descending scale (right
margin) of the ratio of goods to overplus used to calculate the rate of price
advances over the standards. To guide the reader, a dashed line has been
placed on each graph to indicate the 50 per cent mark-up level.

The graphs reveal two important trends. First, they show that the
factors were unable to raise the prices of European goods much in excess
of 50 per cent over the standards for any length of time. The profile of
Fort Albany is the principal exception in that a mark-up of over 75 per
cent was achieved between 1705 and 1710, and prices remained above the
50 per cent level from 1700 to 1740. Secondly, the graphs suggest that
there were three broad phases in the pattern of actual price variation at
many of the posts (Fort Albany, Fort Churchill, Moose Factory, and York
Factory), although they vary somewhat in clarity.

An initial period of adjustment of about ten to twenty years' duration is
evident following the establishment of each post. During this phase prices
fluctuated considerably, varying between 10 to 35 percentage points, or
up to 8 points on the ratio scales on the graphs. Fort Albany showed the
greatest range of variation and York Factory the smallest. No interpretations can be drawn for this early phase for Eastmain because gaps in the
data for the period 1696 to 1713 make it impossible to plot meaningful

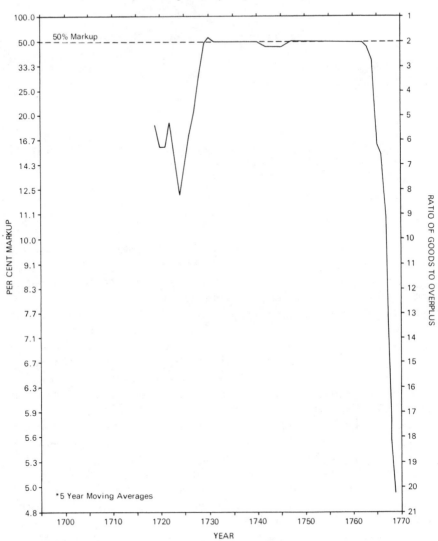

FIGURE 26

FORT CHURCHILL: INDEX OF ACTUAL PRICE VARIATION
(Percentage markup on goods traded)

Source: PAC HBC B 42/d/1–51

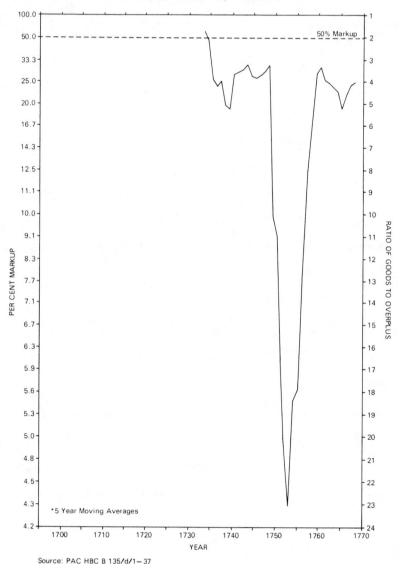

FIGURE 27

MOOSE FACTORY: INDEX OF ACTUAL PRICE VARIATION
(Percentage markup on goods traded)

Source: PAC HBC B 135/d/1 – 37

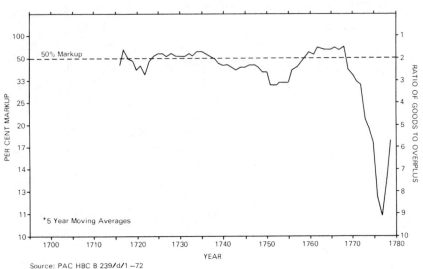

FIGURE 28

YORK FACTORY: INDEX OF ACTUAL PRICE VARIATION*
(Percentage Markup on Goods Traded)

Source: PAC HBC B 239/d/1 –72

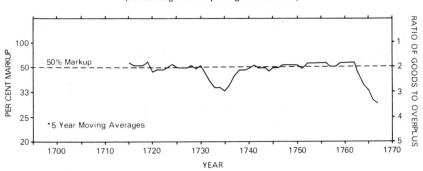

FIGURE 29

EASTMAIN: INDEX OF ACTUAL PRICE VARIATION
(Percentage markup on goods traded)

Source: PAC HBC B 3/d/4 – 78

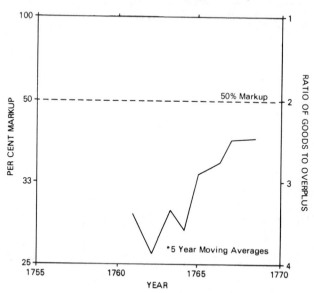

FIGURE 30

FORT SEVERN: INDEX OF ACTUAL PRICE VARIATION
(Percentage markup on goods traded)

Source: PAC HBC B 198/d/1–13

moving averages. For this reason no data were plotted for this post prior
to 1715.

The closing years of this early phase are generally characterized by an
upward movement in prices of trade goods as the factors advanced their
unofficial standards. Thereafter followed a longer period of somewhat
greater price stability during which time prices remained close to, or
slightly above, the 50 per cent level except at Moose Factory. At the latter
post there were wide variations in prices. At the other posts the principal
deviations from fairly stable prices occurred during the period from
1730–5 to 1750–5. Fort Albany was an exception in this case in that prices
remained reasonably steady until the early 1740s, when an erratic downward trend began.

A third period may be discerned from the graphs, beginning in the
mid-to-late 1760s when a dramatic relaxation of the factors' or unofficial
standards took place. This is especially evident on the graphs of Fort

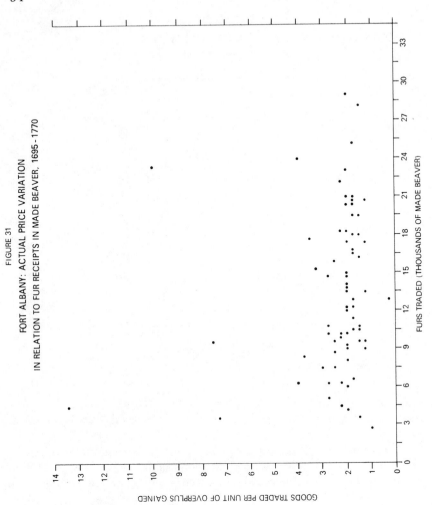

FIGURE 31
FORT ALBANY: ACTUAL PRICE VARIATION
IN RELATION TO FUR RECEIPTS IN MADE BEAVER, 1695-1770

Churchill, York Factory, and Eastmain. At Fort Albany and Moose Factory, no sharp drop in prices is indicated.

EXPLANATIONS OF VARIATIONS IN TRADE GOOD PRICES

In any explanation of the temporal variation of overplus and its relation to goods traded at various Hudson's Bay Company posts, a number of related aspects of the problem need to be considered. At the outset, we must consider the possible reasons for price variation over time. Economic theory postulates that changes in market price usually reflect changing relations between supply and demand. Evidence concerning these relations within the Hudson's Bay Company fur trade and their effect on variations in actual prices of trade goods is contained in a series of scattergrams (Figures 31 to 35) of fur receipts valued in MB at the comparative standard rate against the ratio of goods to overplus. As noted previously, given that the comparative standard that was used to calculate fur returns was held constant, these returns can be used as a rough surrogate measure of the total volume of pelts received. The scatter of points on the graphs for most posts is aligned with the horizontal axis, and does not in any of the graphs indicate a significant relationship between the volume of furs (as shown by the MB value according to the comparative standard) and actual prices paid for pelts in any given year. Thus, large volumes of furs offered do not appear to have driven down the actual prices paid for them. Conversely, there is no evidence of a positive response of fur supplies to changing fur prices (e.g., higher prices do not seem to consistently call forth larger supplies of furs).[12]

Since fluctuations in fur supplies do not seem to be clearly correlated with actual price variations, an explanation for the latter must be sought through an examination of demand conditions. In this connection it should be mentioned that, as far as the Indian was concerned, the European demand for his furs was virtually unlimited, since the Hudson's Bay Company factors regularly accepted all of the furs offered in trade. The factors had no choice in the matter because the Indians insisted that all of their furs be accepted or none would be forthcoming in the future. Traders did, however, attempt to encourage Indians to supply more of certain higher quality furs, but this was always done through exhortation and positive encouragements rather than by refusing to accept lower quality furs. To have refused the latter might well have jeopardized the entire trade at a post.

For this reason, although changes in the consumer demand for furs in

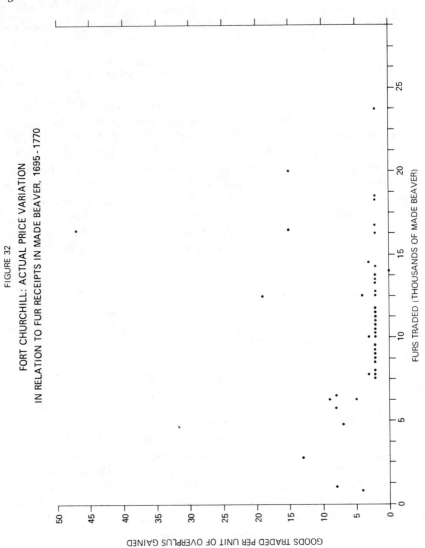

FIGURE 32

FORT CHURCHILL: ACTUAL PRICE VARIATION
IN RELATION TO FUR RECEIPTS IN MADE BEAVER, 1695-1770

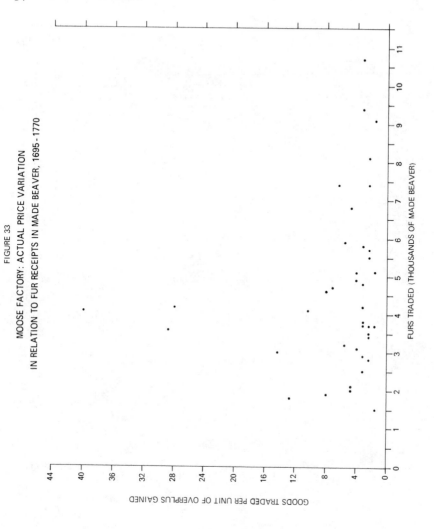

FIGURE 33

MOOSE FACTORY: ACTUAL PRICE VARIATION
IN RELATION TO FUR RECEIPTS IN MADE BEAVER, 1695 - 1770

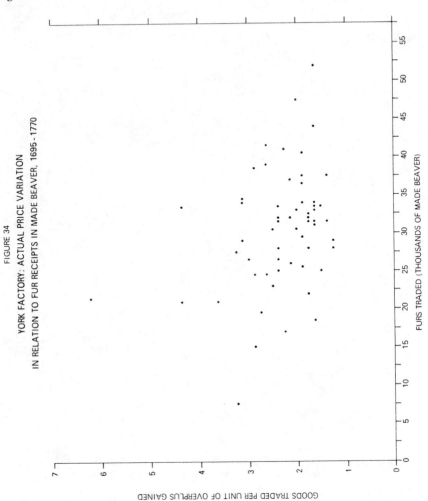

FIGURE 34

YORK FACTORY: ACTUAL PRICE VARIATION
IN RELATION TO FUR RECEIPTS IN MADE BEAVER, 1695-1770

Europe occurred, influencing prices accordingly, the company was in the awkward position of not being able to regulate the quantity and variety of furs that were brought to its posts by the Indians. The problems that the company had to face because of this predicament can be illustrated by considering its supplies and sales of coat beaver in the late seventeenth century.

In the 1690s the demand for coat beaver, which hitherto had been the staple of the trade, declined sharply, while sales of parchment beaver increased. The governor and committee found that, as a result of this change in the market, stocks of coat beaver were accumulating in the warehouse. To remedy the situation, they tried to get the factors to persuade the Indians to stop bringing coat beaver to their posts, and instead increase the number of parchment beaver. For example, in their letter of 31 May 1697 to Governor Knight and his council at Fort Albany, the governor and committee wrote: 'Relating to our Trade & Begin wth that which is our greatest grievance viz the quantity of Coate Beaver the Indians Bring to the Factory. Wee have about 70 thousand of them upon our hands & can not sell them soe that wee referr it to yor Principall Care to Supress by all wayes Imaginable the Indians from Cloggin us there-with.'[13] The same instructions were sent to Governor Baley at York Factory that year, but after pointing out that they could not sell their supplies of coat beaver in ten years, the governor and committee added: 'it is therefore our positive order that you doe not allow above one halfe for Coate wch you doe for Parchment nor Meddle wth any that hath not bin Worne at least two years.'[14] Thus, coat beaver was devalued relative to parchment beaver.

The London committee realized that a shift in emphasis in the trade from coat beaver to parchment beaver would have considerable implications for traditional native dress, in that beaver skins could no longer be worn before they were sold. To deal with this problem, the governor and committee hoped that the Indians could be persuaded to adopt certain articles of European clothing as substitutes. It was hoped that Henry Kelsey could use his considerable influence amongst the Indians to carry out their plan at York Factory. In a letter to Kelsey dated 31 May 1697 the governor and committee wrote: 'Wee recomend to yor Perticular care to Endeavr to ease us from the great burthen of Coate Beaver you being well Experienced and Knowne to the Indians may the better prevaile wth them to use our Sheape Skins, or to weare our Cloth Lined with Bayes, which will be warme & answer the End of Beaver, and to let ym Know how little wee value small Beaver Skins you may have in their presence Cutt the smallest

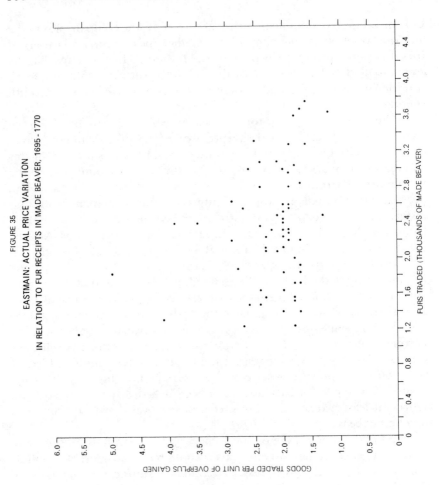

FIGURE 35

EASTMAIN: ACTUAL PRICE VARIATION
IN RELATION TO FUR RECEIPTS IN MADE BEAVER, 1695 - 1770

Skins into 2 or 3 peices & if that be not Sufficient to Convince them you may burne some of the Coate Beavr in their Sights at Severall times upon occasion if you burne 40 or 50 skins to Convince them how little we value their Coate Beaver.'[15]

The company's efforts were unsuccessful. The following year the governor and committee complained that they now had 80,000 coat beaver in the warehouse. In their 1699 letter to Governor Knight they expressed regret at the fact that Indians would not accept sheep skins for clothing as a substitute for coat beaver. And, they acknowledged that Kelsey was probably correct in his decision not to burn coat beaver skins in front of the Indians since the latter might take offence at such actions and refuse to trade in the future.[16] Thus, the coat beaver continued to accumulate in the company's warehouse. Their only immediate short term solution to the problem was to order the traders to keep their stocks at their respective posts and not ship any coat beaver to London until ordered to do so.[17]

Besides having difficulty in attempting to match Indian supplies of furs with European demand for those articles, the Hudson's Bay Company had to cope with varying intensities of demand competition for the Indians' peltry in the hinterlands of its posts in North America. This competition was offered by the French. Previous writers, such as H.A. Innis, have drawn attention to the general relationship in the fur trade between competition and prices, although the specific nature and extent of this relationship has not previously been examined using quantitative data.[18] The evidence contained in Figures 25 to 35 supports the view that demand competition for Indians' furs holds the key to an understanding of price variations in North America, and, indeed, may explain much of the economic history of the fur exchange during the first century of trade in Hudson Bay. Conceivably, the existence of a competitive fur market in North America may help explain one facet of the graphs of price variability at Hudson's Bay Company posts: namely, the existence of a fairly constant upper limit of approximately 50 per cent advance over the standard which is evident in figures 25 through 29. It would appear that the limit of Indian tolerance to the factors' practices of marking-up trade goods prices was reached near this level. If advances beyond this range were attempted, the Hudson's Bay Company men ran the risk of having the Indians desert to the French.

Given the nature of the Indian mode of transport, the canoe, it is not surprising that the Indians would have resisted price increases beyond a certain level. Hudson's Bay Company traders reported that Indian canoes could carry the equivalent of 150 MB of furs per man fully loaded. They also reported that the consumer demand of the Indians was fairly rigid, amounting to approximately 100 MB goods (valued at the official rates) per year per man of which 70 MB were for necessities and the remainder for luxuries.[19] If the factor's standard was set at about the 50 per cent mark-up level, in effect devaluing the Indians' furs by that amount, they would have been able to purchase no more than 100 MB of goods per man valued according to the official standards. This would have approximated their normal demand. At points beyond that price level, it would not have been feasible for individual Indians to satisfy their usual desire for goods. Faced with such a situation, it would have been tempting for the Indians to turn to the company's competitors or cease to trade entirely if no alternative was available.

Besides suggesting that there was an upward limit to the Indians' willingness to permit price advances on trade goods, figures 25 through 29 also suggest that the Indians, while insensitive to European market conditions as conveyed to them by the factors, were very perceptive to the advantages that English–French economic rivalry offered to them. The figures suggest that the Indians exploited this competition to improve the terms of trade in their favour. In effect, when fur demand was weak the Indian refused to decrease the supplies they offered, but when it was strong, they drove harder bargains and, as we will discuss below, tended to reduce the supplies they offered on a per-capita basis. The ways in which competition influenced European–Indian interaction at the various Hudson's Bay Company posts will now be considered in detail.

12

Variations in exchange rates
and levels of competition

In the foregoing discussion it was suggested that there was a strong connection between effective price levels and changing intensity of competition between the Hudson's Bay Company and its French rivals. This suggestion will now be explored, using both statistical evidence and contemporary letters dealing with problems of competition.

An examination of the early records of the Hudson's Bay Company clearly shows that the governor and committee in London responded to French trade rivalries along lines which formal economic theory would prescribe: i.e., they attempted to set prices in accordance with the need to meet competition and stimulate regular trade. For example, when discussing the setting of standards at York Factory in 1688, the committee instructed Governor Geyer to: '... keepe, to the Standard, that Mr. Radisson agreed to, but withall to give the Indians all manner of Content and Satisfaction and in Some goods Under Sell the French that they [Indians] may be incouraged to Come to our Factory's and to bring their Nations Downe, for *Wee are in your minde in that particular, that Wee ought to Trade with the Indians, Soe as that Wee may Trade with them againe, and to make them willing to Come to us and not for Once and never See them more.*'[1] Even during inflationary periods, such as the war years or the late seventeenth and early eighteenth centuries, the setting of prices in response to French opposition overrode the need to raise prices to cover mounting costs. For instance, in 1693, the London directors wrote to Governor Knight and urged him to raise the standard to cover costs which had trebled during the war, but added a cautionary note saying: 'As to the standard of Trade wee cannot precribe you rules therein But however we offer you our reasons as followeth, first we are of an oppinion that you Exact not upon the Indians to make them leave you and goe to the French ...'[2]

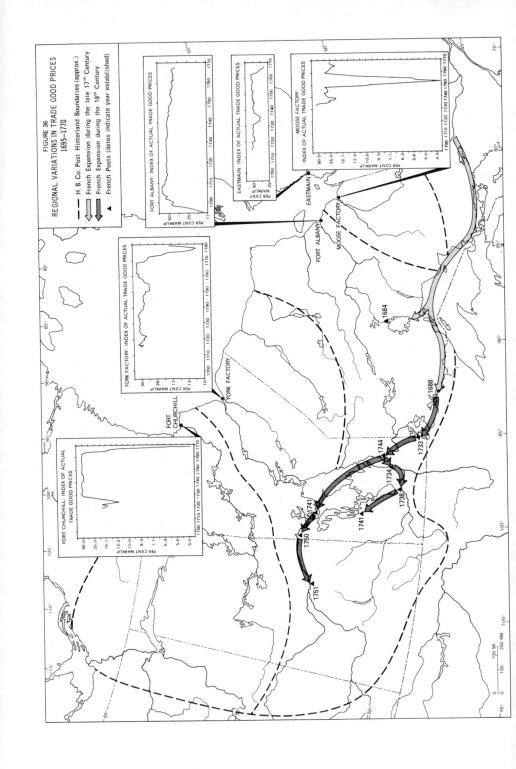

FIGURE 36
REGIONAL VARIATIONS IN TRADE GOOD PRICES
1695-1770

- - - H. B. Co. Post Hinterland Boundaries (approx.)

⇨ French Expansion during the late 17th Century

⬇ French Expansion during the 18th Century

▲ French Posts (dates indicate year established)

FORT ALBANY: INDEX OF ACTUAL TRADE GOOD PRICES

EASTMAIN: INDEX OF ACTUAL TRADE GOOD PRICES

MOOSE FACTORY: INDEX OF ACTUAL TRADE GOOD PRICES

YORK FACTORY: INDEX OF ACTUAL TRADE GOOD PRICES

FORT CHURCHILL: INDEX OF ACTUAL TRADE GOOD PRICES

EASTMAIN

MOOSE FACTORY

FORT ALBANY

YORK FACTORY

FORT CHURCHILL

1684

1688

1733

1744

1734

1738

1741

1741

1750

1751

PER CENT MARKUP

0   100 MI
0 100 200 KM

REGIONAL VARIATION IN FUR PRICES

Apart from general price variation over time, which evidence given below shows to be related to changing competition from the French, and under the pressure of inflating costs of operating the trading system, the Hudson's Bay Company experienced regional variations in prices which could also be ascribed to the proximity of individual posts to their French rivals. The patterns of such variations in both space and time are illustrated in Figure 36.

The information displayed in Figure 36 is a synthesis of data on the locations and hinterland characteristics of the Hudson's Bay Company posts, the previously introduced data on price variation (which, as will be shown subsequently, forms a very useful index of fur trade competition), and the routes and progress of French penetration into the bayside posts' hinterlands.[3] It will be seen that, at various periods, each post experienced phases of relative quiescence in which prices fluctuated very little, reflecting conditions of virtual Hudson's Bay Company monopsony/monopoly in the purchase of furs and dispensing of goods. At other times, the fluctuations on the graph reveal severe disturbances or imbalances in the terms of trade as a consequence of changing competition with trade rivals.

As Figure 36 shows, during the first hundred years of the English fur trade in central and western Canada, the posts located at the 'bottom of the bay' (James Bay) lay closest to the main trade routes of the French and their successors, the peddlers, and were the first to feel the effects of the efforts made by the French traders to isolate the English posts from their hinterlands. Other posts felt similar competitive effects at a later date.

PROFILES OF COMPETITION AND PRICE VARIATION
AT BAYSIDE POSTS

Fort Albany

Of the Hudson's Bay Company posts located in the James Bay region, Fort Albany was the most important. It was the centre of the company's operations, and the post located on the Eastmain River was subordinate to it. Similarly, when Moose Factory was established in 1730, men were dispatched from Albany to set it up, and they were instructed to pattern their operations after those of Fort Albany.[4]

As Figure 36 shows, during the early years of operation of Fort Albany, trade good prices were relatively low but on the increase from 1695 until 1710. This reflects a basic change in the nature of French–English competition. During the late seventeenth century, the French had pressed

FIGURE 37

FORT ALBANY: TOTAL VALUE OF FURS TRADED *

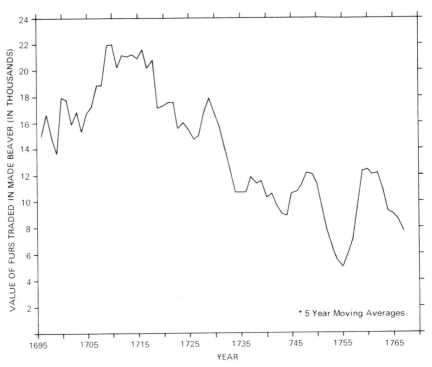

Source: PAC HBC B 3 / d / 1–78

their opposition to the English on two fronts. In the bay area they vied with the Hudson's Bay Company by using force, and control of the bayside posts changed hands frequently as each side launched repeated naval attacks. Meanwhile, in the interior the French pushed their network of posts westward from the St Lawrence Valley, reaching as far as Lake Nipigon and Rainy Lake, thus tapping the inland margins of the hinterland of Fort Albany.

Consequently, during the late seventeenth century, the traders at Fort Albany had to guard against attack by sea and, at the same time, lure the Indians down to the bay and away from the French in the interior. In order to do the latter, they made generous gifts to the Indian leaders and initially offered them favourable terms of trade. This is reflected in the low mark-up percentages used by the factors in the 1690s. Once regular trade was established, however, the factors began to drive harder bargains and make less generous gifts to the Indians.

In 1703 war was declared between England and France, and the French were forced to withdraw their posts in the West in order to defend their possessions in the east. Thus, the Albany traders were in the advantageous position of being unopposed in the interior, and they were able to further tighten their standards.[5] As Figures 25 and 36 and the Appendix show, between 1701 and 1715 mark-ups well in excess of 50 per cent were achieved before the Indians seemingly forced prices down to more acceptable levels. Table 18 lists the returns of the most important pelts for the various posts and Figure 37 shows the MB value of the fur receipts for Fort Albany. Significantly, the table and the figure show that while the factors were tightening their terms of trade, the volume of the fur trade was increasing at Fort Albany nonetheless. This suggests that the Indians were willing to accept less favourable terms of trade for short periods when they had no other choice except to stop trading altogether.[6]

Eastmain

The situation at the outpost of Eastmain appears to have been somewhat different during the early years of the period under study. The lands lying to the east of James Bay were always somewhat marginal to the fur trade, and competition between the French and English and later between the Hudson's Bay Company and the North West Company was always more intensive in western Canada where the prime fur territories were found. It is not surprising, therefore, that initially the Hudson's Bay Company traders applied the factors' standard more rigorously at Eastmain than they did at Fort Albany. Although it was not possible to graph the early ratios of goods to overplus on Figure 38 because of gaps in the record, the scattered data which does exist for the period before 1715 indicates that mark-ups were in the range of 50 per cent, or were roughly equivalent to what they were at the post between 1715 and 1730. In other words, it appears that the company traders did not believe that it was necessary to offer the Indians generous terms of trade at the outset to lure them to the post.

York Factory

In 1713 the Treaty of Utrecht brought hostilities between France and England to an end and gave the English exclusive control of Hudson Bay.

TABLE 18

Beaver and marten returns, Hudson's Bay Company posts, 1701-63*

	1701	1702	1703	1704	1705	1706	1707	1708	1709
Fort Albany									
Whole parchment beaver	4486	9330	7000	10,028	4422	9618	8508	10,296	18,003
Half parchment beaver†	675	1377	749	400	785	1420	918	1712	2355
Coat beaver	7316	8591	5062	8935	2496	5757	6835	5636	3039
Beaver as % of total return	92	95	93	84	86	92	93	93	93
Marten‡	305	123	273	875	519	840	641	736	795
Marten as % of total return	2	.6	2	4	6	5	4	4	3
Fort Churchill									
Whole parchment beaver	—	—	—	—	—	—	—	—	—
Half parchment beaver†	—	—	—	—	—	—	—	—	—
Coat beaver	—	—	—	—	—	—	—	—	—
Beaver as % of total return	—	—	—	—	—	—	—	—	—
Marten‡	—	—	—	—	—	—	—	—	—
Marten as % of total return	—	—	—	—	—	—	—	—	—
Eastmain									
Whole parchment beaver	966	750	1740	1750	—	—	1347	1054	1950
Half parchment beaver†	208	167	437	394	—	—	382	327	390
Coat beaver	1065	430	895	449	—	—	430	262	411
Beaver as % of total return	92	94	95	93	—	—	87	96	83
Marten‡	137	69	49	82	—	—	216	27	247
Marten as % of total return	6	5	2	3	—	—	9	2	7
Moose Factory									
Whole parchment beaver	—	—	—	—	—	—	—	—	—
Half parchment beaver†	—	—	—	—	—	—	—	—	—
Coat beaver	—	—	—	—	—	—	—	—	—
Beaver as % of total return	—	—	—	—	—	—	—	—	—
Marten‡	—	—	—	—	—	—	—	—	—
Marten as % of total return	—	—	—	—	—	—	—	—	—
York Factory									
Whole parchment beaver	—	—	—	—	—	—	—	—	—
Half parchment beaver†	—	—	—	—	—	—	—	—	—
Coat beaver	—	—	—	—	—	—	—	—	—
Beaver as % of total return	—	—	—	—	—	—	—	—	—
Marten‡	—	—	—	—	—	—	—	—	—
Marten as % of total return	—	—	—	—	—	—	—	—	—

*Returns rounded off to nearest whole number. All valued in MB.
†Valued at ½ MB.
‡Valued at ⅓ MB.

1710	1711	1712	1713	1714	1715	1716	1717	1718	1719
10,241	11,920	18,480	13,380	10,606	14,447	11,440	19,840	12,800	12,320
1000	1255	3363	1645	1514	1752	2000	2560	2000	1680
4871	4155	4587	4074	2750	3844	2050	3664	3000	2982
93	95	94	91	92	90	86	92	91	87
560	312	553	900	713	1245	1341	1097	816	1790
3	2	2	4	4	6	8	4	4	9
—	—	—	—	—	—	—	—	320	—
—	—	—	—	—	—	—	—	75	—
—	—	—	—	—	—	—	—	175	—
—	—	—	—	—	—	—	—	84	—
—	—	—	—	—	—	—	—	10	—
—	—	—	—	—	—	—	—	1	—
—	—	715	—	1114	648	1775	1648	—	1381
—	—	157	—	186	174	375	325	—	320
—	—	497	—	204	187	229	183	—	144
—	—	73	—	71	81	77	77	—	72
—	—	400	—	508	144	519	401	—	361
—	—	21	—	24	12	17	14	—	14
—	—	—	—	—	—	—	—	—	—
—	—	—	—	—	—	—	—	—	—
—	—	—	—	—	—	—	—	—	—
—	—	—	—	—	—	—	—	—	—
—	—	—	—	—	—	—	—	—	—
—	—	—	—	—	—	—	—	—	—
—	—	—	—	—	11,120	7804	12,080	20,340	8880
—	—	—	—	—	1040	1233	1840	2520	1560
—	—	—	—	—	3250	3358	4601	4441	4177
—	—	—	—	—	73	72	82	80	76
—	—	—	—	—	516	512	178	688	667
—	—	—	—	—	2	3	1	2	3

TABLE 18 cont'd.

	1720	1721	1722	1723	1724	1725	1726	1727
Fort Albany								
Whole parchment beaver	8800	13,403	6944	13,900	13,600	9306	6269	7534
Half parchment beaver†	1290	1850	992	1935	1954	1396	880	1177
Coat beaver	2241	2834	1289	2446	2428	2111	2137	1993
Beaver as % of total return	83	87	88	87	88	86	86	83
Marten‡	1559	1186	812	1468	1508	1097	582	1325
Marten as % of total return	10	6	8	7	7	7	5	10
Fort Churchill								
Whole parchment beaver	–	5880	4080	3360	2880	3440	3520	5120
Half parchment beaver†	–	748	420	480	320	320	400	560
Coat beaver	–	2222	1199	1092	708	1233	1624	1742
Beaver as % of total return	–	89	88	86	83	89	90	94
Marten‡	–	217	340	300	400	40	70	0
Marten as % of total return	–	2	5	5	9	1	1	0
Eastmain								
Whole parchment beaver	1456	1056	1200	656	1140	1120	1334	1055
Half parchment beaver†	313	212	243	208	305	367	365	321
Coat beaver	112	110	185	46	69	133	180	117
Beaver as % of total return	67	66	72	59	67	70	76	75
Marten‡	318	278	288	225	532	543	403	306
Marten as % of total return	11	13	13	15	24	24	16	15
Moose Factory								
Whole parchment beaver	–	–	–	–	–	–	–	–
Half parchment beaver†	–	–	–	–	–	–	–	–
Coat beaver	–	–	–	–	–	–	–	–
Beaver as % of total return	–	–	–	–	–	–	–	–
Marten‡	–	–	–	–	–	–	–	–
Marten as % of total return	–	–	–	–	–	–	–	–
York Factory								
Whole parchment beaver	21,060	18,000	21,680	17,920	23,920	20,000	16,480	27,280
Half parchment beaver†	2940	2960	3040	3200	3920	2800	2560	4960
Coat beaver	5747	8071	7388	7001	8419	9357	7884	9092
Beaver as % of total return	90	85	89	85	89	86	91	94
Marten‡	495	894	100	1433	1216	633	532	600
Marten as % of total return	1	26	.02	4	3	2	2	1

1728	1729	1730	1731	1732	1733	1734	1735	1736
11,420	9875	9009	12,006	10,907	6810	7600	3600	7920
1756	1517	1581	1957	1876	1467	1040	640	1120
2588	2493	2558	2536	3190	2202	1400	1658	1716
87	83	80	84	88	85	83	74	89
1725	2206	2663	2158	1266	1166	1300	1216	300
9	13	16	14	7	9	11	15	2
6880	5440	4320	8800	6240	5000	5200	4160	9840
1040	800	480	1200	880	640	640	560	1360
2813	2057	124	2899	2908	2535	3497	2464	3566
96	90	66	91	79	86	88	89	88
116	333	250	266	566	416	266	116	366
1	4	3	2	4	4	3	1	2
706	1380	1245	1711	1514	1853	879**	879**	800
184	404	323	499	363	484	277	277	240
49	156	118	190	134	90	54	54	25
60	64	67	65	65	67	50	50	49
337	625	510	738	342	353	388	388	266
21	21	20	20	11	10	16	16	12
—	—	—	—	—	3120	2160	2480	1440
—	—	—	—	—	880	560	560	240
—	—	—	—	—	432	479	444	237
—	—	—	—	—	81	63	72	81
—	—	—	—	—	700	1483	766	167
—	—	—	—	—	13	29	15	7
16,720	27,226	30,000	20,352	14,880	16,560	14,800	15,375	15,180
2880	4800	5120	3168	2480	2640	2720	1825	2320
8000	10,857	11,130	8961	6747	9333	9808	10,172	9742
91	90	89	88	71	89	84	87	88
1350	2566	3666	2233	4600	1166	1600	566	900
4	5	7	6	14	4	5	2	3

** Same figures both years

TABLE 18 cont'd.

	1737	1738	1739	1740	1741	1742	1743	1744
Fort Albany								
Whole parchment beaver	4465	6320	6416	6427	4010	5255	2511	6600
Half parchment beaver†	1471	1190	1294	1280	1025	1042	517	1404
Coat beaver	1655	2173	2180	2400	1738	1984	1151	2558
Beaver as % of total return	82	79	83	74	72	81	71	77
Marten‡	754	1631	1533	2000	1166	967	1167	1800
Marten as % of total return	8	13	13	15	12	9	19	13
Fort Churchill								
Whole parchment beaver	5280	14,320	5120	5600	9280	7630	7640	5048
Half parchment beaver†	880	2240	560	960	1493	1129	1065	737
Coat beaver	2784	5050	2824	4352	3796	6316	4202	3051
Beaver as % of total return	82	91	85	82	87	81	79	84
Marten‡	183	250	250	366	716	600	900	467
Marten as % of total return	2	1	2	3	4	3	5	4
Eastmain								
Whole parchment beaver	896	653	640	544	630	505	769	1080
Half parchment beaver†	266	249	250	146	175	158	317	356
Coat beaver	45	30	87	76	68	159	79	144
Beaver as % of total return	52	57	42	45	52	45	45	48
Marten‡	186	212	752	583	373	733	1133	1200
Marten as % of total return	8	13	32	34	22	40	43	37
Moose Factory								
Whole parchment beaver	1983	2160	2401	2720	2723	2320	3120	4080
Half parchment beaver†	544	480	695	640	720	542	880	1120
Coat beaver	561	610	665	1128	1184	676	755	831
Beaver as % of total return	91	80	79	77	60	85	84	82
Marten‡	67	617	633	938	850	333	633	950
Marten as % of total return	2	29	13	16	14	8	11	13
York Factory								
Whole parchment beaver	15,618	15,494	20,402	11,988	19,853	20,560	12,320	16,640
Half parchment beaver†	2745	3010	2718	8962	3267	2880	1600	2480
Coat beaver	10,636	9718	10,402	10,557	12,404	11,340	6942	13,024
Beaver as % of total return	86	88	86	83	86	85	83	83
Marten‡	1750	1000	2350	2383	1333	1400	1400	1333
Marten as % of total return	5	3	6	6	3	3	6	3

1745	1746	1747	1748	1749	1750	1751	1752	1753	1754	1755
3363	2338	4406	6041	5020	3755	2937	2448	2853	1809	905
879	705	1007	1314	1160	960	698	636	631	456	264
1635	1301	2083	3524	3696	2529	1736	1421	1587	924	818
66	70	79	77	68	63	46	51	50	62	48
2088	984	617	1300	2451	1834	2400	3091	3467	1200	766
23	16	6	9	17	16	29	35	34	23	19
2960	8830	5281	6080	6080	5920	3680	6243	3800	7828	5920
480	1562	907	1040	1280	1139	800	1165	720	1550	1401
2144	1794	4007	2853	4080	3261	2024	2322	2065	2624	1914
70	67	74	88	84	83	68	73	73	89	91
633	466	500	267	367	450	1266	1166	500	233	167
8	3	4	2	3	4	13	9	6	2	2
1080	1125	1274	1521	540	885	1200	1262	1517	1307	1495
440	375	433	449	200	240	349	324	354	306	376
78	136	247	227	57	125	228	408	460	407	281
60	72	66	58	56	76	81	77	71	68	76
783	316	666	1033	533	166	169	341	600	434	987
30	14	22	27	38	10	8	20	18	15	35
4260	3460	4000	5848	5258	1920	1600	1600	1920	1640	1900
1020	1020	1040	1520	1322	480	277	442	462	414	420
1055	1063	1273	1478	1139	568	464	462	502	429	612
78	82	85	83	84	80	63	61	67	70	72
1166	633	583	933	634	350	840	1116	1166	0	440
14	9	8	9	7	9	23	27	25	0	10
9120	9040	11,962	12,449	5788	8880	11,527	8060	5305	7083	6895
1600	1984	2038	1711	1225	1590	1085	1605	1146	1821	1950
10,631	9884	11,760	11,048	7402	8328	9809	8605	6691	7936	1252
77	80	82	76	74	71	81	60	63	69	38
900	433	450	1066	0	1353	2010	1883	757	1116	730
3	2	1	3	0	5	7	6	4	5	27

TABLE 18 cont'd.

	1756	1757	1758	1759	1760	1761	1762	1763
Fort Albany								
Whole parchment beaver	1085	1692	3066	3870	2965	5994	6699	2910
Half parchment beaver†	310	431	671	701	509	1306	1595	688
Coat beaver	760	1229	1516	1694	1772	3308	3835	1609
Beaver as % of total return	62	73	71	63	51	67	68	69
Marten‡	766	583	1395	2348	2014	1400	1056	883
Marten as % of total return	22	13	19	24	20	9	6	12
Fort Churchill								
Whole parchment beaver	4564	4806	3120	3840	2560	4880	5680	3720
Half parchment beaver†	880	788	778	948	640	1680	1381	960
Coat beaver	2218	2270	2610	2000	2690	2390	3788	2003
Beaver as % of total return	91	88	53	66	55	66	76	79
Marten‡	150	300	1867	1617	1305	917	333	206
Marten as % of total return	2	3	15	16	12	7	2	2
Eastmain								
Whole parchment beaver	835	858	1102	1040	1051	1446	1861	903
Half parchment beaver†	250	230	251	265	275	374	484	219
Coat beaver	239	369	180	613	144	168	292	136
Beaver as % of total return	76	76	72	90	67	83	72	49
Marten‡	139	216	350	432	352	105	460	666
Marten as % of total return	8	11	17	20	16	4	13	26
Moose Factory								
Whole parchment beaver	1286	746	880	1040	1200	965	1088	1600
Half parchment beaver†	340	184	240	320	280	395	432	503
Coat beaver	539	476	488	457	449	552	539	455
Beaver as % of total return	72	78	75	57	51	54	56	50
Marten‡	185	33	190	0	1226	716	650	1350
Marten as % of total return	6	2	9	0	32	20	18	26
York Factory								
Whole parchment beaver	9805	6075	3616	5212	5820	5880	3280	5038
Half parchment beaver†	2177	1307	1123	1487	1560	1878	1280	1682
Coat beaver	10,133	7694	6295	8422	9032	10,566	6640	8430
Beaver as % of total return	75	62	44	45	49	49	44	48
Marten‡	600	709	1245	1354	925	368	400	339
Marten as % of total return	2	3	5	4	3	1	2	1

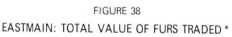

FIGURE 38

EASTMAIN: TOTAL VALUE OF FURS TRADED *

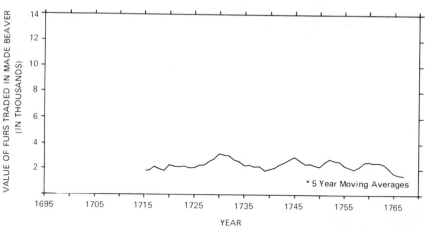

In 1714, James Knight took over control of York Factory ending the twenty-year occupation of that post by the French. Knight's first task was to re-establish Hudson's Bay company contacts with the Indians of the interior. Following the earlier pattern at Fort albany, he and his successors made substantial presents to the Indian leaders who came down to the post and sent gifts inland with various Indian groups to entice other bands to make the trek in subsequent years. Also, initially the factors' standard was not rigorously applied to provide a further encouragement to the Indians. Thereafter trade good prices rose, and from the late 1720s to the early 1740s, the York Factory traders advanced the standard by slightly more than 50 per cent (Figures 28 and 36).

Fort Churchill

In 1717 Fort Churchill was founded, and James Knight was placed in charge of operations during the first two years, being replaced in 1719 by Richard Staunton, a man who had had prior experience in trade at Fort Albany. Once again, as the traders at Albany and York had done, they attempted to develop the trade of Fort Churchill by lavish gift-giving and easy terms of trade (Figure 26). As Figure 39 shows, these efforts were successful, and the volume of furs being traded at the post increased rapidly.

In June 1723, the relatively inexperienced Richard Norton replaced

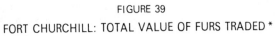

FIGURE 39

FORT CHURCHILL: TOTAL VALUE OF FURS TRADED *

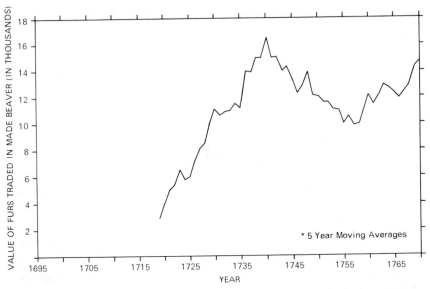

Source: PAC HBC B 42/d/1−51

Staunton as commander of the post. After he assumed control, the prices of trade goods began to decline (Figure 26). This suggests that Norton was not as skilful a bargainer as were his predecessors.

In any event, Anthony Beale was dispatched to Fort Churchill to replace Norton. Beale was an experienced trader who had served the company for many years in the James Bay area, including three years as governor of Fort Albany between 1711 and 1714.[7] While Beale was in command of Fort churchill, the terms of trade were tightened substantially until the trading standard leveled off at the 50 per cent mark-up level (Figure 26).

HINTERLAND COMPETITION BY THE FRENCH

Being barred from the bay by the Treaty of Utrecht, the French renewed their opposition in the interior after 1713, adopting the strategy of attempting to encircle the bay, thereby completely cutting off the Hudson's Bay Company posts from their hinterlands. The major thrust of the

French expansion is shown on Figures 3 and 36. As early as the summer of 1716, Thomas McCliesh, chief factor at Fort Albany, reported that the French had built two posts inland and were trading with the Indians who had been accustomed to come to Fort Albany by travelling down the Moose River and along the shores of James Bay. In all probability, the Frenchmen to whom McCliesh was referring were *coureurs de bois* who reached Lake Abitibi by voyaging up the Ottawa from their post at Timiskaming.[8] Thus, a period of renewed competition began at the bottom of the bay, affecting prices and fur volumes noticeably after 1730, although being blunted before that date by English counter-strategies.

The graph of total furs traded at Fort Albany in Figure 37 suggests that the French had little serious effect on the volume of furs at the post until the early 1720s, although they were trading with the Indians living in the hinterlands of Fort Albany as early as 1716. By that time they had completed the encirclement of the fort by reoccupying their establishments at Michipicoten and Lake Nipigon. Initially, the traders at Albany hoped to counter the French competition by making presents to leading upland Indians. Accordingly, Joseph Myatt, McCliesh's successor at Fort Albany, wrote the company directors in London during the summer of 1722 informing them: 'I have not failed to make some presents to the two leading Indians of Moose River by a Moose River Indian, being in great hopes that will induce them to come here again; if not we must refer it to your honours most serious consideration to resolve upon the best courses for the recovery of that trade that is so material ...'[9] Myatt's response was thus a modest one at best and there is no evidence that he made any effort to counter the French by relaxing the factors' standard at the post (Figure 25).

Richard Staunton, who replaced him the next year, exhibited the same caution. He was of the opinion that 'good goods and kind usage must be the only method to advance your honours' trade which I do assure you shall not be wanting in me to my utmost ability.'[10] It is uncertain exactly what Staunton meant by 'kind usage,' but he clearly did not envisage making lavish presents to the Indians or relaxing the unofficial standard. Figures 25 and 36 reveal that neither course of action seems to have been pursued at the post before the 1740s. Rather, the factors placed great stress on the importance of maintaining an abundant supply of trade goods of a quality superior to those stocked by the French.

The failure of the Fort Albany traders to rigorously counter the French by cutting prices, either officially or unofficially, appears to have been partly the result of the attitude of the company directors in London to such courses of action. For example, during the 1720s the directors strongly urged the factors to make every effort to encourage the Indians to bring 'small furs,' especially marten, down to trade. During his last year at Fort Albany, Richard Staunton attempted to pursue this policy by apparently promising to pay the Indians more for their marten skins than had previously been the practice. When Joseph Myatt resumed command at the fort in the summer of 1726 he was unsure whether or not he should honour Staunton's promise. Thus, he wrote to London: "'Tis certain the wood-runners take all opportunities to ruin your trade by discouraging the natives from coming to us, and how to prevent it I fear will be a very difficult task, if all be true as is reported; for I am creditably informed the French trade the martens at one per beaver [the company valued them officially at 3 per beaver] and Mr. Staunton tells me, to encourage the natives, he promised, them to trade martens at two per beaver the next year, therefore hopes your honours will not take it amiss if I should trade them so.'[11] In responding to Myatt's letter, the governor and committee in London informed him that he was not to alter the comparative standard. In explaining their position, they wrote that they had also learned that the French charged the Indians three times as much for their trade guns as the Hudson's Bay Company did.[12]

Being thus prohibited from lowering the official standards, the traders presumably could have relaxed the factors' standard if they thought it was necessary. However, it must again be recalled from Norton's experience at Fort Churchill that the London directors expected a certain amount of overplus each year even though they were not entirely certain how the factors obtained it. Therefore, the factors' ability to adjust their unofficial standard was initially rather limited.

Being at first rebuffed in their attempts to lower the standards of trade, the factors at the bottom of the bay apparently accepted the point of view of the governor and committee and attributed the French success to reasons other than better prices. For example, in Myatt's letter to the company in the summer of 1727, he explained the declining trade at Albany in the following manner:

... the primest of the leading Indians had left this place long since and traded with the French; ... 'Tis certain they are a people that may be wrought upon sometimes by way of presents; I have a strong opinion the French have drawn them away by those means. Not but I have reason to believe this part of the country was never so pestered with the wood-runners as at this time, for by all report they are daily among the upland Indians. I don't suppose the French trade so largely as we, but notwithstanding the natives being a people naturally inclined to laziness, they choose rather to trade the goods up in the country than have the fatigue of coming down here, and are grown so nice and difficult in the way of trade that I admire to see it, a true sign as I take it that they have a glut of goods up in the country.[13]

Thus, Myatt expressed the view that gift-giving and locational advantages for the purposes of trade were enabling the French to make significant inroads into the Hudson's Bay Company trade.

Although the French were siphoning off some of the trade of Fort Albany by these tactics, as shown by the graph of furs traded at this post in Figure 37 and Table 18, the *coureurs de bois* apparently also resorted to force and the threats of force to further their goals. For instance, in 1729 Myatt claimed that his trade would have been considerably better: '... if the French had not spread a report that they had engaged great numbers of Mowhawkes (who are in their interest) to come against this factory in order to cut us off, which discouraged the upland Indians from coming here to trade.'[14] In 1732, Joseph Adams, who had succeeded Myatt at Albany in 1730, reported that the French had built three new posts in the interior and that they were forcing the Indians who passed by them on their way to the bay to trade with them whether they wanted to or not.[15] Significantly, all of these reports regarding the alleged use of force by the French came from the Indians. Granting that there probably was substance to these stories, it is equally likely that the Indians exaggerated them to excuse themselves for having taken advantage of the opportunities which rival trading parties offered to them. As Myatt himself had noted in 1727, as evidenced in the passage cited previously, the Indians had become adept at exploiting the English–French competition.

In short, the renewal of opposition at the bottom of the bay between 1713 and 1730 did not result in serious direct price competition, even though the Indians attempted to initiate it by informing the English that the French paid them better prices for their small furs. The lack of an inflationary price spiral for furs, or lowering of prices on trade goods, can be attributed to the unwillingness of the directors of the Hudson's Bay Company in London to alter their prices, and the belief on the part of the factors in the James Bay area that the French success was largely due to the fact that their posts were located in the hunting territories of the Indians. Also, they accepted the stories of the Indians that the French were forcing them to trade.

FIGURE 40

YORK FACTORY: TOTAL VALUE OF FURS TRADED *

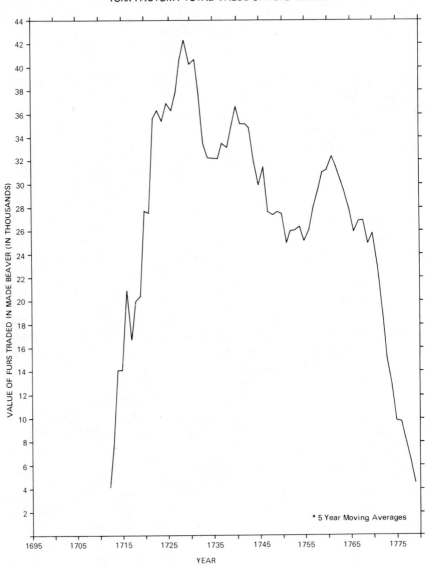

Source: PAC HBC B 239/d/1–72

York Factory

Along the western shores of Hudson Bay at York Factory and Fort Churchill, the effects of French competition on fur volume were felt at a later date, and in the case of Fort Churchill, to a much lesser degree as is shown by Figures 4, 39, and 40. Indeed, the letters despatched from York Factory to London make no mention of the French being in the interior until 1728. In the latter year Thomas McCliesh reported that they were four days' travel from Lake Winnipeg, and that 40 canoes of Indians who came to York Factory that summer were dressed in French clothing which they had obtained from the Frenchmen the previous year.[16] However, in spite of these initial incursions, the total volume of furs being traded at York Factory continued to rise until the late 1720s. Thereafter, it began to decline (Figure 40).

As was the case with the factors at the James Bay posts, McCliesh initially hoped to counter the French threat by maintaining a large inventory of superior trade goods. Consequently, he was quite disturbed by the poor quality of his stocks of powder, kettles, and hatchets. Accordingly, in 1728 he wrote to London: '... I affirm that man is not fit to be entrusted with the Company's interest here or in any of their factories that does not make rather more profit to the Company in dealing in a good commodity than in a bad. For now is the time to oblige the natives, before the French draws them to their settlement ...'[17] Of the various trading goods kept in stock at the post, the Hudson's Bay Company traders regarded Brazil tobacco as one of the most important. They hoped that by keeping a large supply on hand for the purposes of trade and making presents, they would be able to lure the Indians to the bay even as the French expanded their operations. Thus, after a record year in 1731, McCliesh forecast that the trade of the subsequent year would be low because he had only thirty pounds of '... that cursed bewitching weed' left in the warehouse.[18] Yet, in spite of occasional shortages and shipments of poor quality, the company did manage to keep the factories well supplied with Brazil tobacco, which the Indians preferred to the tobacco offered by the French.

Nonetheless, the trade at York Factory was being undermined by the French. Apparently, the traders at York did not feel that the French were undercutting them in price since they did not adjust the factors' standard at the post to any significant extent before the late 1730s, judging from Figure 28, nor did they urge the London directors to lower the official standards. Rather, they attributed the decline in their trade to poor harvests, threats by the French that they would kill those Indians who traded with the company, and a series of Indian wars in the interior, primarily between the Assiniboine–Cree group and the Dakota Sioux. According to the men at York Factory, the French had a hand in fomenting these hostilities to disrupt the Hudson's Bay Company trade. If the company believed that these events were responsible for the decline of trade, there was little reason to alter the terms of trade.[19]

Fort Churchill

At Fort Churchill, because of its more northerly location, the French had no significant impact on the volumes of furs being traded until the early 1740s (Figure 39 and Table 18). Not surprisingly, therefore, little mention is made of them in the Churchill letters to London before that time. Indeed, the activities of the French in Manitoba are not discussed until 1736. In that year Richard Norton, who had returned as commander of the post five years earlier, wrote that the French in the Lake Winnipeg region were forcing the Indians to trade with them.[20]

Since the French success with the Indians was seen to be largely the result of their use of force and intimidation, and the impact of this campaign was not felt at Churchill until the early 1740s, there was little need to relax the standards until the latter date. Indeed, Figures 26 and 36 suggest that the factors' standard varied only slightly from the 1730s to the early 1760s. However, the graph for Fort Churchill at this time must be viewed cautiously since the relatively fixed index which is portrayed was partly the result of Richard Norton's accounting methods. It should be recalled that Norton was relieved of command at Fort Churchill in 1727 for failing to obtain a sufficient overplus trade. After serving his apprenticeship at York Factory he resumed command at Churchill when Anthony Beale died in 1731. Beale had operated the post to the company's satisfaction, and when Norton replaced him he seems to have adopted Beale's factors' standard since the price index changed little with the succession of chief factors.

As discussed in chapter 9, in reporting the overplus which he gained from applying this standard, Norton apparently adopted the practice of averaging his returns to balance out short-term variations of a minor nature in order to present to the company as favourable a picture as possible. While Norton thus averaged his data, and therefore distorted somewhat the profile of the index for Fort Churchill, the index nevertheless is indicative of fairly stable price conditions since Norton would have had difficulty balancing one year with another if extreme fluctuations were taking place.

Although the Hudson's Bay Company traders' responses to the French incursions to the interior were rather limited before 1730, being largely oriented towards offering the Indians an abundant array of superior quality merchandise, it was becoming clear that more rigorous courses of action would have to be pursued in order to offset any further erosion of their trade. This was particularly true at the bottom of the bay. Accordingly, in 1730 the company decided to build Moose Factory in order to shorten the distances which Indians living to the south of James Bay had to travel to trade. Also, it eliminated the difficult leg of their trip along the shore of the bay which was frequently blocked with ice and where food was often difficult to obtain.[21] It was hoped that this move would bolster the trade from that quarter.

Moose Factory
When establishing Moose Factory, the London directors intended that the Indians should be dealt with by the same standards as used at Fort Albany, and in 1732 they sent a Fort Albany account book to William Bevan at Moose Factory telling him to use it as a model for his books. Bevan assured the directors that he would follow their instructions carefully. However, almost as soon as trade commenced at the new post, it became clear that some competitive price cuts would be necessary since the hinterland of Moose Factory had been heavily infiltrated by the French. For example, in a letter to London written in 1732, Bevan pointed out that the French were obtaining most of the Indians' martens because they valued a prime marten equal to a beaver, whereas the Hudson's Bay Company listed it at three per beaver.[22] Mindful of the company's exhortations to all the factors to obtain as many 'small furs,' such as marten, as was possible, Bevan wanted to know what course of action he should pursue.

The company held fast on its position that the standard was not to be altered. The London committee still believed that its charges for trade goods were substantially lower than those of the French, and apparently they were.

In this instance it is clear that the local Hudson's Bay Company traders' perceptions of the nature of the French opposition and the courses of action which should be taken to counter it differed from those of the directors living in London. Bevan seems to have remained convinced that a lowering of his prices was necessary. Being unable to alter his official

FIGURE 41

MOOSE FACTORY: TOTAL VALUE OF FURS TRADED *

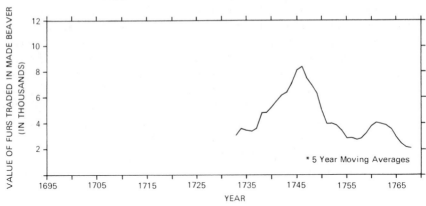

Source: PAC HBC B 135/d/1-37

standard from that of Fort Albany, he decided to relax the unofficial factors' standard. Being no doubt familiar with Norton's difficulties at Fort Churchill, and of the fact that the company expected a certain amount of overplus from each post, he wrote in August of 1734 that he hoped '... your honours will not expect so much overplus as you have at your northern factories.'[23] Thus, in effect, he notified the governor and committee in London that the traders were going to 'unofficially' reduce prices. As Figures 27 and 36 show, although mark-ups on the prices of trade goods at Moose Factory began at roughly the same level as those current at Fort Albany (i.e. 50 per cent over the official standard, Figures 25 and 27), they declined rapidly thereafter, and between 1735 and 1745 fluctuated between 20 to 33 1/3 per cent above the standard of trade. Apparently the London directors accepted this decision, since no orders were subsequently sent to the men at Moose Factory instructing them to obtain a larger overplus trade.

The relaxation of the terms of trade at Moose Factory appears to have achieved the desired effect, since the total value of furs being taken in trade at Moose Factory rose substantially between 1735 and 1745 (Figure 41). However, after that date, a decline set in. Initially the slump in trade was said to have been the result of the Indians frequently being unable to obtain all of the goods they required at the post because of insufficient inventories. Also, according to Robert Pilgrim, illegal private trade (by

Hudson's Bay Company men) at Moose Factory and trade practices at Fort Albany (they were unspecified) were hurting the trade of Moose Factory.[24]

By the late 1740s, the London committee apparently was no longer certain that the company's standards of trade were better than those of the French, and in 1749 they sent instructions to the various posts ordering the factors to obtain as much information as they could from the Indians concerning the prices which the *coureurs de bois* were demanding for goods and paying for furs. Pilgrim replied that he would relay the information as soon as was possible. However, the next year he was still unable to provide it and wrote, 'We are not able to give you any Satisfaction With Respect to the French Standard [.] the Natives are so Perfidious a Set of People that we Can Not find any Two of them to Agree in Any One Article Except that they Trade one Marten for one Beaver.'[25] Considering that the Indian was in the advantageous position of being the primary source of price information which the two European groups had to depend on, the above response is of interest and suggests that the Indians were attempting to exploit the situation. They were freely telling the Hudson's Bay traders about those prices offered by the French that were higher than the company's, while at the same time were being vague and confusing, no doubt deliberately, about those items for which the English prices were better. Perhaps it was for this reason that the demand for price information at Moose Factory was never fully complied with, and the subsequent letters from the post to the London directors do not contain any additional information about the French standards.

WIDENING OF ENGLISH INITIATIVES IN RESPONSE TO INCREASED FRENCH COMPETITION

As the French opposition intensified and the fur trade at Moose Factory suffered further declines, new courses of action were pursued in the early 1750s by Thomas White, who had replaced Robert Pilgrim as chief factor. White was convinced that the Indians would respond to more favourable prices and he therefore proposed to further relax the factors' standard. Indeed, judging from his correspondence with London, he appears to have considered that the use of the factors' standard was one of the principal reasons for the decline of trade at Moose Factory. Accordingly, in his report to London dated 17 August 1752 he wrote: '... Your Honours may depend upon my best endeavours to promote your Honours Interest and although the Trade this Year has not answer'd to my wishes as yet, but do expect several Indians down this fall and have given all those which have been here very great encouragement by trading with them more to their Advantage and by keeping up to the Standard which has not been practis'd here lately and has been the Principal Cause of the Decay of your Honours Trade at this place ...'[26] An examination of Figure 27 shows that White did pursue his intended policy of trading close to the official standard of trade and the rate of exchange at Moose Factory declined further than it did at any other post. Initially, the governor and committee of the company seem to have approved this course of action, since White subsequently wrote in 1753 that he was gratified that they were pleased with his conduct.[27]

Besides drastically reducing the overplus at his post, White also hoped to combat French influence amongst the Indians by making rather lavish use of credit. The practice of extending credit to the Indians in an effort to tie them to a particular post was a long established custom. An Indian was generally given credit up to a limit set by the value of furs which, in the eyes of the factor, he could reasonably be expected to bring down to the post next year. If such returns were not forthcoming on his next visit to the post, the Indian's credit would be reduced by the amount of the difference between MB expected and MB received. By controlling an individual's line of credit in this fashion, factors held abuses of the credit system to tolerable levels.[28]

The London directors had some misgivings about the use of credit since many of the debts were never collected, but they could not eliminate it. Rather, from time to time, orders went out to curb the use of credit as much as possible to prevent credit abuses from getting out of hand. In the 1750s, when the French influence was at its peak, the line of credit being extended to the Indians increased substantially, especially at Moose Factory. Yet, in spite of lowering prices for goods and making liberal use of credit, White had little success in recovering the trade which the French had taken away from the post. As Figure 41 shows, the value of furs taken at Moose Factory continued its downward trend until the late 1750s when the French were forced to withdraw because of military pressures in the east.

Not only did White's policies fail to achieve the desired effect, they left the post with the heavy liability of unpaid debts when he departed in 1755. Commenting on this subject, Henry Pollexsen, White's successor at Moose Factory wrote in 1757:

In Your Honours last Years Book of Accots it is stated that the Outstanding Debts due from the Indians amounted to 307 Beaver & which at that time I imagin'd to be the whole but when I came to examine into the Affair I found by Mr. White's own Book that the outstanding Debts at the time he left the Factory amounted to no less than the sume of 800 Beaver, 46 of which were due from Indians that died the Winter before, ... tho I am satisfied Mr. White did it with a very good Intention in order to encourage the Indians as your Honours direct & if possible to produce a Trade, but it had unfortunately a contrary effect and this he was too sensible of before he left this place, after expressing himself to me in this manner, 'These Villains knowing I am to go home will not come in to pay me a skin,' meaning the Eastern & Upland Indians [Cree], so that your Hons may very well be assured that if they would not come in to pay it to him from whom they receiv'd it, that they would not come to pay it to another ...[29]

Thus, it was clear to Chief Factor Pollexsen that the company was going to have to write off the debts which the Indians had accumulated in the heat of competiton.[30]

Pollexsen himself was in a quandary as to what course of action should be pursued at the post to regain the trade, since White's ideas had failed. Thus he wrote: 'I hope your Honours do not imagine that I send you this Accot [that cited above] as any ways reflecting upon the Character or Conduct of Mr. White, who I believe & am satisfied is a very honest Man, & did every thing he could for the promoting of your Honours Interest, but as my reason for the loss of the Trade which he nor no [one] else could perceive, for if Encouragement which your Honours direct to be given will have no Effect and this Credit I think was a very great Encouragement, I am really greatly at a Loss to conceive what will.'[31]

Fort Albany

At Fort Albany, the Hudson's Bay Company traders felt the effects of French competition as strongly as they had at Moose Factory, and, as Figure 37 shows, the volume of furs being traded continued an erratic downward trend until the mid-1750s. However, unlike Moose Factory, the Albany traders do not appear to have responded to this problem by lowering the factors' standard to any marked extent. As Figure 25 reveals, throughout the period between 1730 and 1763, prices of trade goods declined only gradually and the factors' standard never dropped below an overall markup of one-third.

In part, the differing response of the Albany traders to French opposition may have been the result of their more successful efforts in obtaining information from the Indians about the prices which the *coureurs de bois*

TABLE 19

A comparison of French and Hudson's Bay Company prices in the Fort Albany hinterland*

	1748 (French)†	1750 (French)‡	1750 (H. Bay Co.)**
Cloth	6 per yd.	1 per 5 or 6″	2 per yd.
Gun	25-40	40	10-12
Hatchets	4	4	2 per beaver
Knives	½	½	8 per beaver
Twine	3 per skane	3 per skane	1 per skane
Kettles	3 per lb.	3 per lb.	1 per kettle
Blankets	NA	12	6
Powder	NA	1 per ¼ lb.	1 per 1½ lbs.
Marten	2 per 1	2 per 1	3 per 1
Shot	NA	1 per 10 loads	1 per 5 lbs.

* Prices demanded or paid in numbers of Beaver.
† Correspondence Inward, PAC HBC A 11/2, pp. 136-40
‡ *Ibid.*, pp. 144-6
** PAC HBC B 3/d/58

were charging for goods and paying for furs. As at Moose Factory they had been ordered to obtain this intelligence, and forwarded it to London in 1748. These prices are listed in Table 19 above along with the official prices being demanded by the Hudson's Bay Company. Allowing for the fact that the Albany traders were marking-up the prices on cloth, powder, and shot by 33 1/3 to 50 per cent above those listed in the table, it is clear nonetheless that the Hudson's Bay Company prices were substantially better than those being offered by the French. Clearly, in the immediate area of the post, the success of the French in drawing off part of the company's trade had little to do with current price levels. Indeed, judging from the fragmentary information which was obtained from the Indians, the prices quoted may have been the lowest prices which the French offered. According to the Indians, the *coureurs de bois* adjusted their prices according to local supply-and-demand conditions, and when there were many Indians present and but few goods they gave short measure to ensure that all of the Indians received some goods. Thus, in many years, the prices offered by the Hudson's Bay Company may have been substantially better in a comparative sense than those indicated in the table.

The Albany traders believed that the French were successful largely because their posts were located closer to the Indian homelands, making it unnecessary for the Indians to undertake the long, dangerous trek down to the bay, and because the posts were strategically located along the waterways leading to James Bay so that the French could intercept the canoes of those Indians who were willing to make the trip, rather than because the French prices were better. Before 1763, the factors believed that the practice of intercepting canoes was particularly effective, and they claimed that the French frequently forced the Indians to trade with them as they had before La Vérendrye. Whether this was in fact the case is difficult to determine, since the Hudson's Bay traders had again based this conclusion on reports by the Indians. However, these reports were no doubt in part a justification by the Indians to the company traders for having traded with the *coureurs de bois*, a practice which they knew displeased the Englishmen.

In any event, the master of Fort Albany in the early 1740s, Joseph Isbister, decided to counter the French by building a post inland, and in 1743 he erected Henley House, 120 miles inland from James Bay on the forks of the Albany River. In this strategic location the post was to operate as a way station for Indians travelling down to the bay. There the Indians could obtain a few trade goods and see the line of merchandise which was available at Fort Albany. Also, the post served to protect the Indians en route from intimidation by the French. According to E.E. Rich, the establishment of the Henley outpost served to temporarily increase the trade at Fort Albany, and this is suggested by Figure 37, but it was also said to have had a detrimental effect on the trade at Moose Factory.[32] Figure 41 shows that average returns rose until 1746 when a downward trend began. Thus, if the construction of Henley House did affect the trade at Moose Factory, the impact was not immediate. This may have been one of the unspecified trading practices that the Moose Factory traders claimed the Albany factors were pursuing which served to undermine the trade of the former post. Eventually, the French built a post in the vicinity of Henley House and the Indians began to pressure the Hudson's Bay Company to establish Henley as a fully fledged trading post in opposition to it.[33] The London directors resisted this pressure, however, and continued to insist that trading operations could be most successfully and economically pursued by continuing to centre their operations on the shores of the bay.

Eventually, in 1755, the post was pillaged by the Indians and the Englishmen stationed there were killed. It was not re-established until 1759. Before that time the trade of Fort Albany began to rebound (Figure 37) and it is doubtful that the re-opening of the inland post played a major role in the recovery of the Fort Albany trade. Rather, as at Moose Factory, the upsurge in trade was largely due to the French withdrawal.

York Factory

At York Factory, the volume and value of the fur trade reached a peak about 1730, just prior to the invasion of the post's hinterland by La Vérendrye and his men. Fur receipts began to decline thereafter until the mid-1730s when a short-term rebound occurred which lasted until about 1740 (Figure 40). Curiously, during the 1730s there was little mention in the letters sent from York Factory to the governor and committee in London that the French were in any way responsible for the decline in trade. Rather, periodic shortages of goods (particularly tobacco) and hardships suffered by the Indians (usually severe winters and food shortages) were cited as the major reasons, even though the York traders were aware that *coureurs de bois*, moving in advance of La Vérendrye, had penetrated into northern Ontario and southeastern Manitoba as early as 1728. Apparently not having perceived the French as being a major threat to their trade at that time, they made little effort to counter them either by relaxing the factors' standard (Figure 28) before the late 1740s or by sending men inland. Credit had been extended to the Indians as at other posts, but in 1740 the traders at York indicated, without reservation, that they would comply with the London directors' orders to retrench their practice of extending credit to the Indians in the future.[34] This suggests that they did not regard it as an essential weapon in their economic war with the French at that time.

About 1740 the outlook of the fur trade at York Factory changed considerably. In particular, a rapid decline began in the value of furs being traded, as shown in Figure 40. The factors at the post no longer explained these reverses in terms of goods shortages or Indian hardships, but rather had come to the conclusion that the inroads which the French had made into the hinterlands were largely the cause. For example, in 1747, James Isham wrote to London:

I am Very sorry our Cargoe this year, will not answer your honor's Expectations ... I do assure your Honor's I have done the uttermost of my power to promote & Encrease itt. Itts not their going to warr yt is the occation of ye small trades intirely – its true their has been a sickness amongst the Natives yt carried off a Great many this Last Year, But its the french yt is our Cheifest Obstical they increasing more yn ever, – stop all the Indians yt comes to trade – takes ye best & Lightest of the natives goods & send us ye Remainder ...[35]

In response to the perceived threat of the French in the interior, Isham and the other traders at York Factory began to counter-attack more vigorously. This counter-attack largely took the form of price cutting and more lavish gift giving. As at Moose Factory, these courses of action led to a decrease in the rates of exchange for goods at the post during the period 1750 to 1755. However, the amount of adjustment which took place was much less at York Factory. As Figure 28 shows, beginning in the late 1730s the effective prices which the Indians had to pay for goods at York Factory fell below the 50 per cent mark-up on standard and remained below that level until the late 1750s.

This policy achieved only limited positive results. In 1752 James Isham reported that he had more Indians down that year than he had in the previous four years and that judging from the 'Quantity of small Furs it appears the Natives has not dealt with the French our way this season.'[36] Despite this reported success, the fur returns of the post continued their erratic downward trend until the early 1750s (Figure 40). Additional measures were clearly called for. At York, the response to this renewed problem involved sending men inland for the purposes of obtaining first-hand information on the French operations. Also, these men were to encourage the Indians to come down to the bay. The first of the men to make the trip to the interior was Anthony Henday, who travelled to the Blackfoot area of what is now eastern Alberta in 1755. Other company men made trips to the Manitoba and Saskatchewan areas in subsequent years. While these expeditions did achieve some success, the rising volume of trade in the late 1750s was largely due to the French withdrawal which began after the outbreak of warfare between England and France in 1756.

Fort Churchill

Fort Churchill, lying the farthest to the north, did not feel the impact of French opposition to the same degree as did the other Hudson's Bay Company posts. This is suggested by fur returns shown in Figure 39. Although there was a downward trend in trade after 1740, the magnitude of the decline was much less than that experienced at York Factory, Fort Albany, or Moose Factory. Figure 4 shows that most of the trade which the French may have drawn from Fort Churchill would have been from the southern peripheries of the post's hinterlands. In particular, the French would have had a considerable advantage in siphoning off the trade of groups living in the southwestern limits of the hinterland, the upper Churchill and Beaver River areas, since their presence would have saved these Indians the necessity of making a very lengthy and difficult trip. Indeed, it is unlikely that any efforts at the fort on the bay could have seriously undermined the position of the French manning the houses on the Saskatchewan River.

As Figure 26 shows, at this post there was a very slight adjustment of the factors' standard and the quantities of gifts given away in the 1740s. Although the traders at Fort Churchill 'averaged' the data, and thus probably minimized the extent of the price reductions that had occurred, it is nonetheless clear that the adjustments made at Churchill were substantially less than those made at the other posts until the early 1760s. Also, no attempts were made to send men inland or establish interior posts, and Ferdinand Jacobs, chief factor at Churchill, was openly skeptical about the value of such trips. For example, when James Isham was making plans to dispatch Anthony Henday to Blackfoot territory to increase the trade from that quarter, he received the following comment from Jacobs: '... pardon my freedom in saying, [I] am of Opinion those Earchethinues [Blackfoot] Indians, will never be brought to Trade at either of these Factorys. (I say never) and my reasons stand Good, they being a very Timerous People, and makes no use of Canoes, nay, nor wants to be persuaded to Venture in one, besides the Indians which trades Yearly with us gets great Quantitiy's of Furrs ... from the above said Earchethinues ...'[37]

In short, the effects of French opposition at Fort Churchill were slight, compared to the other posts, and consequently the reactions of the company traders at the post were of a rather limited nature.

TRADE DURING THE 1760S: THE INVASION OF THE NOR' WESTERS

During the late 1750s and early 1760s, the Hudson's Bay Company enjoyed a short-lived monopoly between the withdrawal of the French and the appearance of their successors, the peddlers from Montreal. As the graphs from the various posts indicate, during this time the volume of furs being traded rose. As well, the factors took advantage of the situation and drove harder bargains. Reflecting these efforts, prices of trade goods returned to the levels which had been characteristic at each post prior to the French invasion, with the exception of Fort Albany. At the latter post, there was a gradual lowering of the unofficial standard over time. Curiously, the Albany traders do not appear to have been as responsive to changing competitive conditions, in terms of price adjustments, as the other company factors were. Unfortunately, the correspondence from Fort Albany sheds little light on the reasons why the traders at the latter post pursued their somewhat different course of action.

Even before the Treaty of Paris was signed in 1763 extinguishing French claims in Canada, the Hudson's Bay Company was confronted with a new group of competitors, the traders from Montreal called the

Nor' Westers, who replaced the French in the interior. Although the fur trade of this later period lies largely outside of the scope of this study, it is nonetheless instructive to examine the initial reactions of the Hudson's Bay Company traders and the Indians to the renewal of competitive conditions, since the economic rivalries of the late eighteenth century were more intense than those experienced during the first hundred years of the English fur trade in central Canada. Also, many of the policies and practices which were developed during the 1760s were carried on in later years.

Moose Factory

As in earlier years, Moose Factory was the first post to feel the effects of the resumption of competition. As early as 1762, a year prior to the signing of the Treaty of Paris, Henry Pollexsen, who was in charge of the post, wrote to London:

... it gives me great Concern to think the returns from Moose Fort this year must fall so vastly Short of your Expectations; And that I cannot with Justice and Knowledge say, I entertain a thought of its amendmt my reasons for which are fully explained in my Journal of 26 of July. There you will find how we are already encroach'd upon to the Southward and SE by Interlopers who will be more Destructive to our Trade than the French was. The French were in a manner settled, Their Trade fixt, Their Standard moderate, and Themselves under particular regulation and restrictions, which I doubt is not the Case now.[38]

Thus, Pollexsen emphasized that the threat of the Montreal peddlers was different from that posed by the French in earlier years. Initially there was no central coordination of their effort, as there had been during the French period when men such as La Vérendrye were in charge of the posts. Equally important, their mobility was increased, since they did not operate out of a series of fixed posts, but rather sought out the Indians in their villages.

The economic threat that this new form of organization posed to the Hudson's Bay Company was succinctly stated in Pollexsen's 1762 letter to the company. Elaborating on the likely consequences of the lack of regulations or restrictions on the peddlers, he suggested that:

... every Party in view of increasing their Trade and Interest amongst Indians, will endeavour to draw them from each other, by the allurements of considerable Presents and Trading with Them upon easier Terms than their Neighbours. The

Indians perceiving this, the Trade will become an auction, and carried by them who bid most; thus for a Time these Settlements are like to Suffer, and none more so than Moose Fort, but I apprehend and hope it will not continue long, for as the result of such proceeding must be, the ruin of many, those who remain, in order to reimburse Themselves for Their former great expenses will be obliged to Contract their Standard of Trade, and then it is a morral impossibility but the Indians drop off from them, the nature of the Indians being such that when They have been once used to a Custom, there is no breaking it with Safty.[39]

Indeed, Pollexsen's prediction that the trade would amount to little more than an auction between competing groups of traders proved to be essentially correct. His only error lay in his assumption that the rival peddlers would not be able to survive prolonged economic warfare. Through subsequent amalgamations of rival groups, the Montreal-based traders eventually organized themselves into the North West Companies of a later date which enabled them to challenge effectively the power of the Hudon's Bay Company.

Fort Albany
The initial success that the peddlers had in opposing the Hudson's Bay Company is evident in Figure 4, which shows that after 1763 the value of the furs being traded at all the Hudson's Bay Company posts, except Fort Churchill, began to decline. As has been noted, Pollexsen at Moose Factory was quick to attribute this downward trend in trade to the Nor' Westers. At Fort Albany, no mention was made of the influence of the peddlers in the correspondence to London until 1766 when Humphrey Marten wrote that his post was surrounded by them. He claimed that these peddlers were stopping all of the Indians coming down to the fort and forcing them to trade.

York Factory
At York Factory, the letters to London make no mention of Nor' Wester opposition until 1768. The traders at York Factory obtained their information regarding peddler movements from their own men, whom they continued to send inland to encourage trade, and from the Indians. The latter source of information proved to be unreliable, however, because the Indians were in the difficult position of wanting to avail themselves of the opportunities which the presence of the Nor' Westers offered to them, but, at the same time, not wanting to antagonize their English trading partners. Thus, when the quantities of prime furs which the Indians were

bringing to York Factory began to decline, Ferdinand Jacobs asked the Indians if they were trading them with the peddlers. The Indians responded negatively. However, after having sent men into the interior, Jacobs' suspicions were confirmed, leading him to comment in his 1768 Letter to London:

With very great Concern Gentlemen I acquaint you of a great Fall in your Trade at this Place ... The Canada Pedlers are got in the very heart of the Trading Indians Country ... and have Sent Severall very Large Cannoes Loaded with the best of the Furrs down to Canada ... this affair has Effected me more than any thing that Ever happen'd to me, and what Grieves me most is, its not Possible to put a Stop to it unless they are Compel'd by Force to retreat from off your Lands. I was Deceiv'd Last year by the Indians telling me a Lye of there being no Pedlers amongst them. I have this year talked very Smartly to the Leading Indians how ungreatfull it was of them to Trade with those Pedlers.[40]

Jacobs' response is of interest in that it underscores the fact that the changing trading allegiances of the Indians affected the company's traders in more than a strictly economic sense. The latter prided themselves on their ability to deal with the Indians, and they often developed what amounted to a possessive attitude to certain Indian groups. Letters between company posts often contained references to 'my' Indians and 'your' Indians when the factors discussed their respective trades. Consequently, the factors tended to take declines in the trade rather personally. This attitude was perhaps most clearly manifest in the letter which Theodore Hopkins, who was stationed at Fort Albany, wrote to London in 1769. On the subject of the trade and the influence of the peddlers he wrote: 'It is a great unhappiness to us, Gentlemen, that we must inform You of the Farther Decrease of the Trade of Albany Fort, we have no other reason to assign for it, than the still increasing Feuds of the Natives, and the very great interruption the Leaders meet with from the Cursed Pedlars up Country, they are very numerous, line every Creek, River & Lake, use great force and are said to have killed several Indians who were coming to Trade with us. We most faithfully promise to exert ourselves in promoting Your Trade, not only as it is our Duty so to do, but also as our Honour is nearly touched in regard to Our Influence over the Natives ...'[41]

One of the first actions the company's traders took in their attempts to regain their influence over the Indians involved relaxing the factors' standards and more lavish gifts, especially of tobacco and alcohol. These

TABLE 20

Hudson's Bay Company and peddler prices in the York Factory hinterland, 1769-70

Items of trade	Peddler price*	HBC price†
Guns	20 beaver	14 beaver
Ice chisel	4 beaver	1 beaver
Knife	2 beaver	3 or 4 beaver (by size)
Ball	10 (no.) per beaver	1 lb. per beaver
Powder	¼ lb. per beaver	1 lb. per beaver
Cloth	1½ yds. per 10 beaver	1 yd. per 3 beaver
Blanket	10 beaver	7 beaver
Tobacco	¼ lb. per beaver	¾ lb. per beaver (Brazil)
Value of furs		
Marten	2 = 1 beaver	3 = 1 beaver
Fox	1 = 1 beaver	**
Wolf	2 = 1 beaver	1 = 2 beaver
Bear	traded few of them	1 = 3 beaver††
Otter	1 = 1 beaver	1 = 1 beaver‡‡
Wejack‡	1 = 1 beaver	2 = 1 beaver

* SOURCE: 'A Journal of the most remarkable Transactions and Occurrences of a Journey Inland Commencing 15th July 1769 and Ending 18th July 1770 kept by William Tomison,' PAC HBC 239/a/64, p. 21. These were the prices paid and charged by the peddlers in western Manitoba and eastern Saskatchewan.

† SOURCE: York Factory Account Book, 1769-1770, B 239/d/60, p. 7

‡ Fisher

** Company prices varied by type and were as follows: black fox = 4 beaver; silver fox = 3 beaver; red fox = 1 beaver; brown fox = ½ beaver; and white fox = ½ beaver.

†† This price was for a full grown bear. Cub bear was valued at 1 = 1 beaver.

‡‡ Cub otter was valued at 1 = ½ beaver.

moves are reflected in Figure 36 by the sharp decline in the index of trade good prices at all of the posts except Fort Albany. Only a slight decline was registered at the latter post.[42] Thus, by the late 1760s the bidding war which Pollexsen predicted had begun.

As trade rivalries escalated, the Indians were in an increasingly favourable position and became more difficult to deal with. Ferdinand Jacobs at York Factory complained of this problem in his 1769 letter to London, writing: '... the overbearing Demands of the Trading Indians who having So ready a Supply from the Pedlers are now Prodigeous hard to Please and if their unreasonable Demands are not complied with, or you deny them one Article, they then Immediately tell one they will not come to the Factory but trade with the Pedlers.'[43] Indeed, not only were the Indians becoming increasingly difficult to deal with, it was also apparent that price reductions at the bayside posts were not going to achieve the desired results even though the company's prices were well below those of the peddlers (Table 20). Many Indians were willing to pay higher prices and avoid the necessity of making the long trek to the Hudson's Bay Company posts. Their visits therefore became less frequent. Instead of coming every year, many Indians came only once in a two-to-three year period, as guns, kettles, or other articles were worn out. These were articles which the peddlers did not carry on their inventories in large quantities.

Again, it was the traders at Moose Factory who first brought this problem to the attention of the directors in London. John Favell, who had been in charge of Moose Factory since 1762, became suspicious of the reasons for the infrequency of the visits of certain Indians at his post. In airing his views on this subject, he wrote to London on 24 August 1766:

This is very Surprizing in my Opinion Gentlemen that 2 Indians shall come down & only Trade each of them a Gun, some Tobacco & a Nett, it is impossible to think that those Indians can Subsist the whole Winter, without any Powder & shot or a Blanket or a Piece of Cloth and as They did not Trade those things here. They must get them at other Places, or else, They cannot live till next Year. This hath been the manner in which several Indians have Traded their Goods at this Place this Summer, & they have really told me, We shall not come again till our Guns are worn out; I Ask'd them, Why so? Because our Families are so far off, and the several places where the English [peddlers] are now, are so very convenient for us that we can go to them at any time of Year either Summer or Winter & get what we Stand in need of; These are my Thoughts & fears Concerning it ...[44]

Thus, it had become clear to Favell that the locational advantages which the peddlers had for contacting the Indians would be difficult if not impossible to overcome, as long as the Hudson's Bay Company continued to limit its trading activities to the posts on the bay. The company was thus forced to abandon its long-standing policy of 'sleeping by the frozen sea' and, in 1774, built Cumberland House on Cumberland Lake in eastern Saskatchewan. This signaled the beginning of a program of vigorous inland expansion by the Hudson's Bay Company, a program which was matched by the Nor' Westers, and the proliferation of posts throughout central and western Canada which occurred fundamentally altered the character of the fur trade.

13

Trade expenses, factors' gains, and competition

Competition between the Hudson's Bay Company and the French affected the costs of carrying on the fur trade. These costs were of two types: overhead or fixed costs that had to be paid irrespective of the volume of trade, and 'out-of-pocket' or variable costs whose level was a direct function of the quantity of furs obtained.

OVERHEAD COSTS

As H.A. Innis pointed out in his classic study of the fur trade, the fixed costs of operating the Hudson's Bay Company trading network made up a high proportion of total costs that the company had to bear.[1] These costs derived from the need to maintain an extensive administrative, storage, and sales apparatus in Europe, from the operation of a fleet of ships, and also from the provisioning, staffing, physical maintenance, and protection of the bayside posts. Consequently, capital costs, depreciation, and wages had to be paid irrespective of the income derived from the sales of furs in any year. The bases on which these costs were 'fixed' were varied and complex, as pointed out by I.M. Biss [Spry].[2]

In inflationary periods, such as the years of warfare between England and France in the late seventeenth and early eighteenth centuries, the company's overhead costs increased dramatically and were a constant concern to the company directors, as their letters to the posts on the bay indicate. In particular, transportation costs, especially seamen's wages and the costs of obtaining ships, escalated rapidly.[3]

VARIABLE OR OUT-OF-POCKET COSTS

The major components of out-of-pocket costs were: the expense of procuring goods of sufficient quality and quantity in Europe; the actual expense of shipping the goods (loading and unloading charges); and the expense of providing gifts to the Indians. All of these were directly associated with the volume of furs the company anticipated acquiring. As with overhead costs, prices of trade goods were subject to rapid increases during inflationary periods since the goods traded were often basic consumer items, such as cloth, kettles, and knives, or war material such as guns, powder, and shot. On the other hand, furs, especially beaver, were rated as luxury goods in Europe and their prices tended to be depressed at these times.

The costs of acquiring goods in Europe were largely (although not completely) outside the power of the company to control.[4] However, the company could, and did, attempt to minimize variable costs at the bayside posts. One of the most important of these expenses was the cost of gift-giving.

Gift expenses

Although, as we have already shown, gift-giving among Indians had traditionally been for purposes of cementing alliances and materially expressing friendships, the Europeans quickly perceived that this institution could be turned to economic ends. For example, they employed it as a tool to foster 'customer loyalty' as well as to induce a 'demonstration effect' by sending goods as gifts into the interior. Such presents, carried mostly by reliable Indians and occasionally by their own employees, served to display the range and quality of the wares available at the company's posts.[5] An attempt was also made to use gifts as a means of obtaining the compliance of trading captains with an increase in the official standards of trade, but, as shown earlier, this gambit was not successful.

Gift-giving and competition

Undoubtedly the most important use of gift exchanges was for the purpose of luring Indian groups away from rival European traders and retaining the loyalties of important trading partners. This could be very costly. Samuel Hearne cited an incident that had taken place at Fort Churchill which involved the famous Chipewyan leader, Matonabbee. According to Hearne, in October 1776:

Matonabbee, came at the head of a large gang of Northern Indians [Chipewyan], to trade at Prince of Wales's Fort; at which time I had the honour to command it. When the usual ceremonies had passed, I dressed him out as a Captain of the first rank, and also clothed his six wives from top to toe: after which, that is to say, during his stay at the Factory, which was ten days, he begged seven lieutenants' coats, fifteen common coats, eighteen hats, eighteen shirts, eight guns, one hundred and forty pounds weight of gunpowder, with shot, ball, and flints in proportion; together with many hatchets, ice chissels, files, bayonets, knives, and a great quantity of tobacco, cloth, blankets, combs, looking-glasses, stockings, handkerchiefs, &c. besides numberless small articles, such as awls, needles, paint, steels, &c. in all to the amount of upwards of seven hundred beaver in the way of trade, to give away among his followers. This was exclusive of his own present, which consisted of a variety of goods to the value of four hundred beaver or more. But the most extraordinary of his demands was twelve pounds of powder, twenty-eight pounds of shot and ball, four pounds of tobacco, some articles of clothing, and several pieces of ironwork, &c. to give to two men who had hauled his tent and other lumber the preceding winter. This demand was so very unreasonable, that I made some scruple, or at least hesitated to comply with it, hinting that he was the person who ought to satisfy those men for their services; but I was soon answered, That he did not expect to have been *denied such a trifle as that was*; and for the future he would carry his goods where he could get his own price for them. On my asking him where that was? he replied, in a very insolent tone, 'To the Canadian Traders.' I was glad to comply with his demands.[6]

Thus, in this one incident, Matonabbee demanded and received over 1100 MB in presents by simply threatening to trade with the opposition next year if Hearne did not comply with his wishes. Although Matonabbee was an exceptional leader and this episode was probably not typical of the generosity afforded to Indian captains by the company traders, it nonetheless does serve to illustrate the kinds of problems that the factors had to contend with when attempting to hold the line on gift-giving expenses during periods of European economic rivalry.

In the years before 1763, while French–English competition for the Indians' furs intensified, gift-giving expenses rose substantially, as the expenses sections of the post account books show. Although post expenses included items other than presents as noted earlier, an examination of the accounts indicates that the cost of gift-giving was the item that varied the most over time. Hence, variations in the figures for total expenses at the various posts were largely the result of the changing expenditures of gifts of trade goods to the Indians. The expense totals for the major posts have been graphed in Figures 42 to 45. These figures reveal that gift and allied expenses (valued in MB) increased by more than 300 per cent between 1725–35 and 1750–5. Inflation in the unit of account can be ruled out as having any influence on the trends shown, since the standards of trade did not change significantly during the period before 1763.

Whereas the general trends portrayed in Figures 42 to 46 can be readily explained in terms of changing competitive conditions and the need to dispense gifts with an appropriate degree of generosity, detailed movements of expense totals on the graphs are more difficult to account for. For instance, expenses appear to have increased in stages or steps. This is evident in the data for Fort Albany, Fort Churchill, and York Factory. At these posts periods of rising costs were broken by shorter phases when costs tended to level off, or even decline as is especially noticeable in the case of Fort Churchill (Figure 43). Between 1720 and 1750 there were three periods when a leveling off, or short-term decline in expenses took place at the various posts. The first such period occurred at Fort Albany between 1722 and 1730, at Fort Churchill between 1724 and 1730, and at York Factory between 1724 and 1735. A similar phase took place between 1737 and 1742 at Fort Albany, between 1736 and 1740 at Fort Churchill, and 1734 and 1740 at Moose Factory. This phase is not represented in the data for York Factory. A time of escalating costs was again followed by a period when the upward trend was temporarily halted or even reversed. This took place at Fort Albany from 1746 to 1752, at Fort Churchill from 1745 to 1748, at York Factory from 1744 to 1747, and at Moose Factory after 1745. Unfortunately, the company records provide no clues that might help account for the fluctuations in the data noted above.

Average fur costs associated with gift-giving
The serious impact of gift-giving expenses on the trade is further dramatized when the factors' expenses per MB unit of furs received in trade is considered. Figures 46 to 49 clearly reveal the acceleration in gift costs through time for each MB taken in trade. At Fort Albany, for example, expenses per MB gained rose exponentially (though erratically), from about 6 per cent per MB of fur in 1730 to nearly 50 per cent in 1753, before declining to around 20 per cent in the 1760s. Similarly, at Fort Churchill, expenses as a percentage of the average MB of furs traded oscillated upward from 11 per cent in 1720 to nearly 35 per cent in 1760. Steep rises in factors' costs were also recorded at York Factory and Moose Factory between the early 1730s to the mid 1750s. It is notable that York Factory (Figure 45), with its large turnover in furs, had very low average factors' costs per MB of furs before 1730 (in the vicinity of 4 to 8 per cent), but by 1755 expenses at the post represented 33 per cent of the value of each MB. Moose Factory recorded the highest factors' costs per MB of furs of any post in the late 1750s (over 60 per cent).

In this context, the role of brandy should be considered further. As

FIGURE 42

FORT ALBANY: EXPENSES *

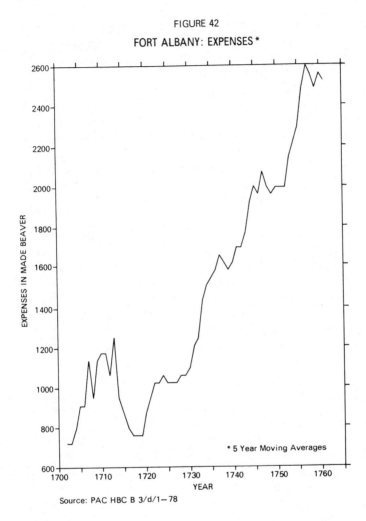

Source: PAC HBC B 3/d/1—78

noted in chapter 11, brandy figured prominently in gift exchanges. Since it was diluted before being given away, the factors were able to cut their expenses. The potential saving therefore must have served to encourage the traders to dispense brandy liberally instead of other gifts.

At all major posts, a drop in average factors' costs per MB is observable after 1755, coinciding with the withdrawal of the French at the outbreak of war between England and France.

Thus, besides influencing effective prices, European rivalries had a

FIGURE 43
FORT CHURCHILL: EXPENSES *

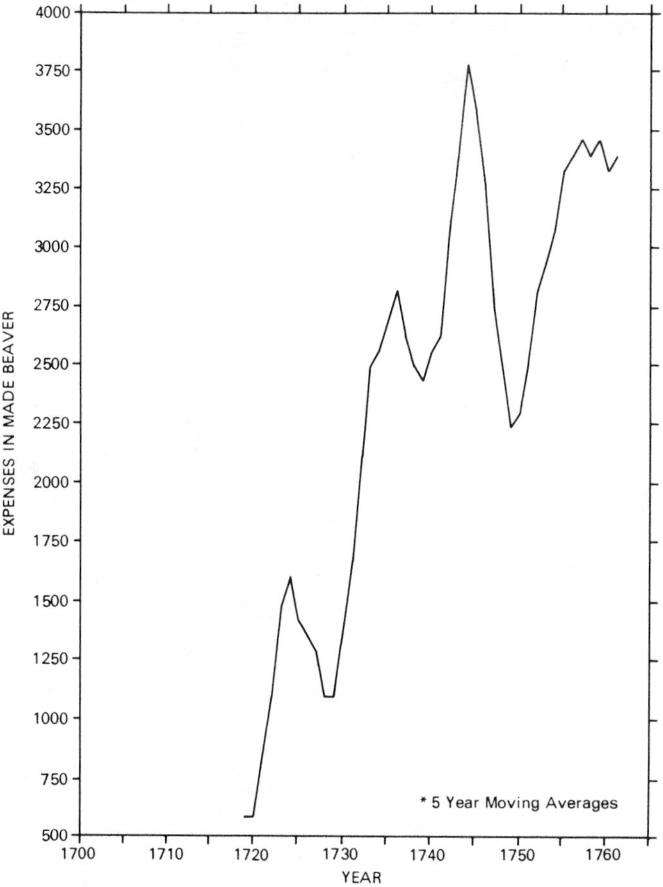

Source: PAC HBC B 42/d/1—51

strong impact upon costs. As the prices being paid to Indians rose, so also did the gift and allied expenses incurred at the posts as the factors were forced to be more generous in their gift-giving ceremonies in order to retain the loyalty of their Indian trading partners.

EXPENSES AND THE OVERPLUS TRADE

Considering that competition drove gift expenses upward and at the same

FIGURE 44

MOOSE FACTORY: EXPENSES *

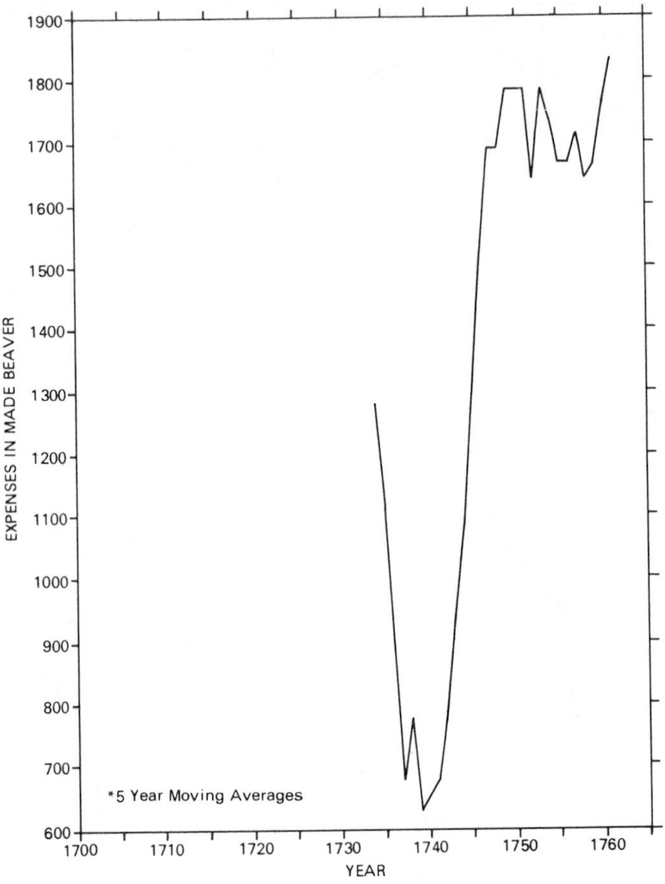

*5 Year Moving Averages

EXPENSES IN MADE BEAVER

YEAR

Source: PAC HBC B 135/d/1-37

time forced the traders to relax the unofficial standards, it is clear that the post traders were in a difficult position. Variable gift expenses and the overplus were the only two facets of the trade over which the local factors could exert any influence. In a sense, the expenses were their input or direct commitment to the trade, and the overplus was their return. Judging by the company's dismissal of Norton at Fort Churchill in 1727, the London directors also paid close attention to these two variables and, to a

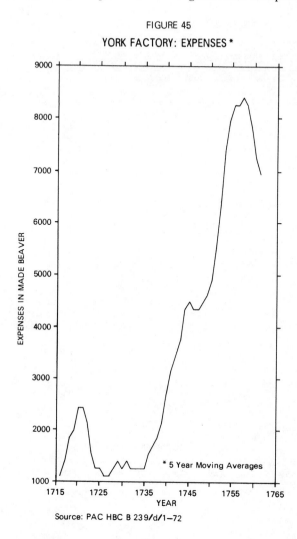

FIGURE 45

YORK FACTORY: EXPENSES *

Source: PAC HBC B 239/d/1–72

considerable extent, used them to evaluate the performance of their chief traders. A 'good' trader held expenses to a minimum and, at the same time, attempted to exceed, or at least cover, these costs, with the overplus gained through the application of the factors' standard. Thus by subtracting expenses from the overplus trade it is possible to measure the degree of success that the factors achieved, or, in other words, estimate their net gain on the standard. As noted earlier, the company used these two

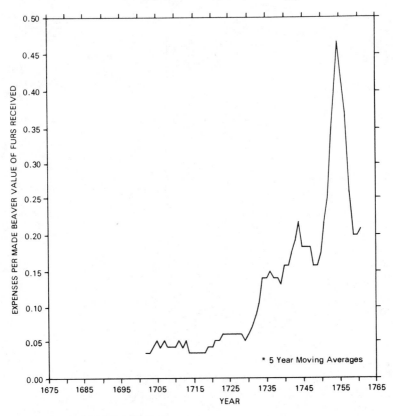

FIGURE 46

FORT ALBANY: AVERAGE FACTORS' EXPENSES PER MADE BEAVER
OF FURS RECEIVED *

(Excluding the value of stock traded)

* 5 Year Moving Averages

Source : PAC HBC B 3/d/ 1—78

variables in its profit and loss section of the early account books to calculate the positive or negative net return on each inventory of goods at the
various posts. Figures 50 to 54 display the relationship of expenses to
overplus at bayside posts. In effect, these graphs enable us to see the
degree to which the various factors' returns exceeded those they would
have obtained had they neither given the Indians gifts of goods nor
applied the factors' standard.

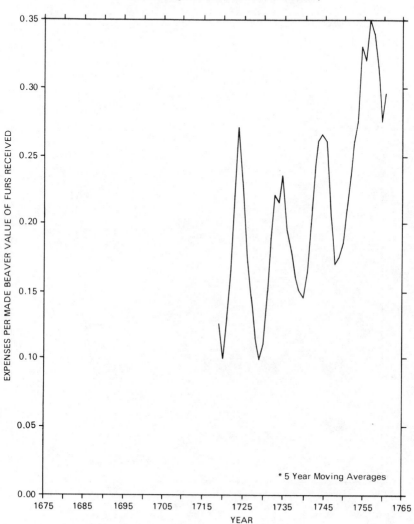

FIGURE 47

FORT CHURCHILL: AVERAGE FACTORS' EXPENSES PER MADE BEAVER
OF FURS RECEIVED *

(Excluding the value of stock traded)

Source: PAC HBC B 42/d/1–51

FIGURE 48

MOOSE FACTORY: AVERAGE FACTORS' EXPENSES PER MADE BEAVER
OF FURS RECEIVED *

(Excluding the value of stock traded)

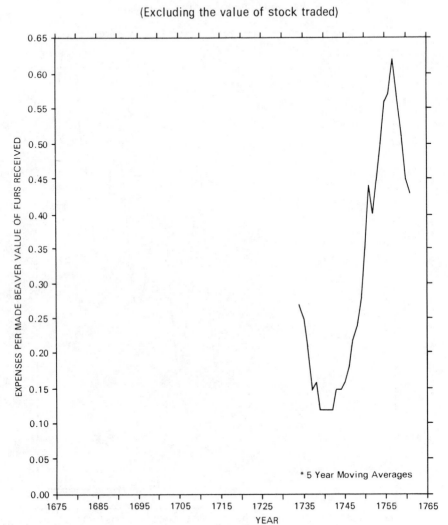

Source : PAC HBC B 135/d/ 1–37

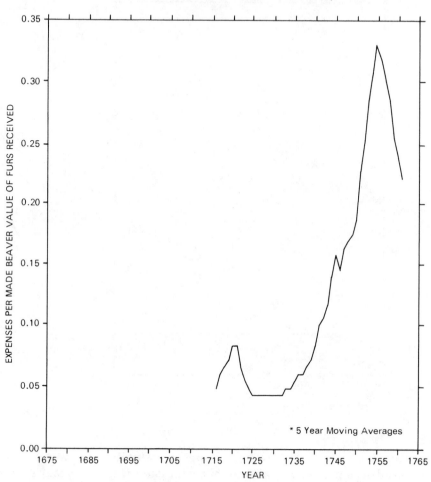

FIGURE 49

YORK FACTORY: AVERAGE FACTORS' EXPENSES PER MADE BEAVER
OF FURS RECEIVED *

(Excluding the value of stock traded)

Source: PAC HBC B 239/d/ 1–72

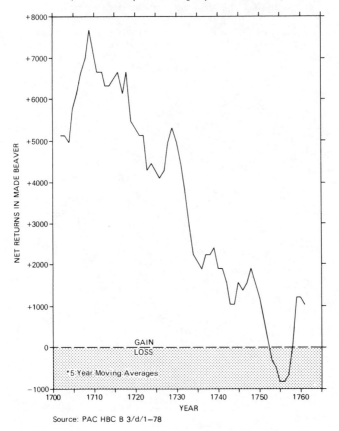

FIGURE 50

FORT ALBANY: FACTORS' NET RETURNS
IN RELATION TO OFFICIAL STANDARDS*

(Determined by subtracting expenses from overplus)

Source: PAC HBC B 3/d/1–78

An examination of these figures suggests why Richard Norton was relieved of command at Fort Churchill in the late 1720s. On 17 May 1723, Norton had been appointed to serve as chief trader at Fort Churchill. Nathaniel Bishop was then the factor at the post. On 30 June, Bishop died and Norton was appointed to take his place.[7] This means that the bulk of the 1722 stock of goods for Fort Churchill would have been traded while Norton was in command, given that the trading year usually began in August, and July was the most important trading month.

TABLE 21

Fort Churchill: expenses and overplus

	1721	1722	1723	1724	1725	1726	1727	1728	1729	1730	1731
Overplus	2826	696	630	567	634	601	2017	4135	3131	2650	4769
Expenses	1140	1747	1365	1341	1853	1722	908	898	896	894	1956
Net return	1686	−1051	−735	−774	−1219	−1121	1109	3237	2235	1756	2813

SOURCE: PAC HBC B 42/d/5-15

As Figure 51 shows, the year Norton assumed control the overplus trade declined sharply. More important, Table 21 reveals that expenses exceeded the overplus by 1051 MB in 1722 (this is not apparent in Figure 51 because of the use of the five-year moving averages). During the next four years Norton was unable to increase his overplus or to trim his expenses enough to bring the two items into balance. As noted previously, the governor and committee were not satisfied with Norton's performance and they decided to relieve him of command temporarily to give him time to gain more experience.

Examination of Figures 22 and 43 and Table 18 suggests that, although the governor and committee cited expenses as one problem, Norton's major difficulty stemmed from the fact that he was not obtaining enough overplus in comparison with his expenses and with the volume of overplus taken at Fort Churchill in earlier years. It may be that his inexperience as a factor and a trader meant that he was not sufficiently skilled in the application of the factors' standard.

Anthony Beale, who was Norton's replacement at Fort Churchill, had had considerable prior experience at the 'bottom of the bay' and at York Factory.[8] A glance at Table 18 shows that Beale quickly corrected the situation and the overplus began to exceed expenses again by a wide margin. It would appear that Beale's success related mostly to his ability to take in a large quantity of overplus. His overplus trade was more than three times that of Norton. Beale trimmed his expenses also, but not by the same margin.

After having established the trade on a sounder footing, Beale died on 13 April 1731. He was succeeded in that year by Thomas Bird who was in turn replaced by Richard Norton who returned to Fort Churchill in the summer of 1731.[9] Thereafter, Norton performed to the satisfaction of the company.

Figures 50 to 54 show that all of the traders were having difficulty attempting to obtain a sufficient amount of overplus to compensate for

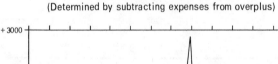

FIGURE 51

FORT CHURCHILL: FACTORS' NET RETURNS

IN RELATION TO OFFICIAL STANDARDS *

(Determined by subtracting expenses from overplus)

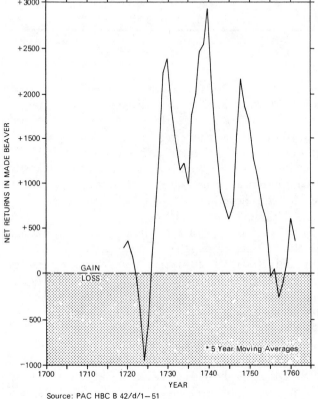

Source: PAC HBC B 42/d/1—51

rising gift-giving expenses during the 1750s. By the middle of that decade, French opposition had forced the company's traders to relax their
unofficial rates of exchange and to increase their generosity during gift
exchanges to the point that expenses exceeded the overplus trade at all
the posts except Eastmain. Moose Factory, the post closest to the French
route of expansion, was the first fort to show a loss, and it was the only
establishment that failed to make an adequate recovery during the late

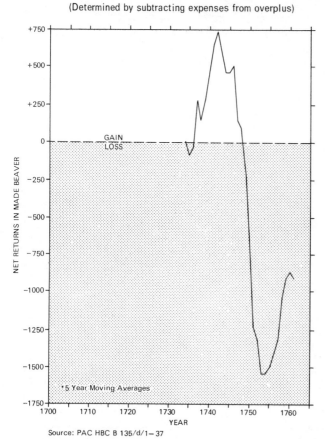

FIGURE 52

MOOSE FACTORY: FACTORS' NET RETURNS

IN RELATION TO OFFICIAL STANDARDS *

(Determined by subtracting expenses from overplus)

Source: PAC HBC B 135/d/1–37

1750s and early 1760s. At Forts Albany and Churchill, and at York Factory, the period of loss was much shorter, only four to five years in duration, and occurred between 1753 and 1758.

Whether these were real losses to the company is uncertain, because it is unknown if the official standards were originally set by the London directors with a built-in mark-up to assure a profit. The Royal African Company employed such a device in its ounce trade in West Africa, where

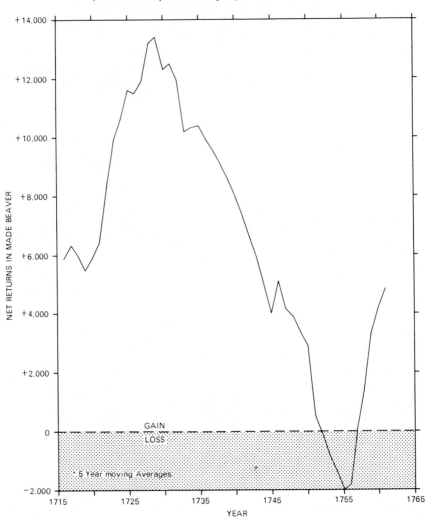

FIGURE 53

YORK FACTORY: FACTORS' NET RETURNS IN RELATION TO OFFICIAL STANDARDS *
(Determined by subtracting expenses from overplus)

Source: PAC HBC B 239/d/1—72

a 100 per cent advance was made, so a precedent for such a practice existed.[10] Certainly, according to the account of Joseph Robson in 1752, the company reaped large profits about that time from its operations, not all of which could have come from the overplus.[11] If such a mark-up was built into the Hudson's Bay Company standard of trade, then the overplus may have represented an additional profit over and above that obtained through its dealings in European markets. In this case the true break-even point could have been at such a level that factors' expenses might have exceeded overplus by a considerable margin before a real loss was sustained by the company.

Regardless of the true company profit or loss, the Norton episode suggests that the expense-overplus figures were the ones that the traders and the governor and committee used to gauge the factors' success in the Hudson Bay sphere of the trade, and to determine the need for changes in command or policy.

RELATIONSHIPS BETWEEN GIFT EXPENSES, COMPETITION, AND FACTORS' NET RETURNS

As suggested previously, a notable feature of the trade at several posts was that expenses and competition (measured by the constraints on the rate of overplus gained) acted in a pincer fashion to curtail factors' net returns and reduce their manoeuvrability in responding to worsening 'market' conditions. As competition for furs increased, and more goods had to be bartered under relaxed factors' standards for each unit of overplus taken in trade, a concurrent need for lavish gift-giving sent expenses spiralling. There was no possibility at most of these posts of cutting gift expenses as a means of restoring the factors' returns to their earlier levels. Under such circumstances, meeting the stated expectations of the governor and committee of the company must have taxed the ingenuity of even the most astute and experienced factors.

Evidence of the 'pincer movement' of gift expenses and actual prices under competition can be obtained from Table 21 which shows Pearson product-moment correlations between factors' returns, expenses, and prices at the posts under competitive conditions. The posts most affected by French competition (Albany and Moose Factory) have positive correlations (0.80 and 0.35, respectively) between expenses and the index of actual price variation (ratio of goods per unit of overplus). At Fort Albany, the high positive correlation suggests that gift-giving was a major weapon at this post in meeting French competition. That is, the behaviour of

FIGURE 54

EASTMAIN: FACTORS' NET RETURNS

IN RELATION TO OFFICIAL STANDARDS *

(Determined by subtracting expenses from overplus)

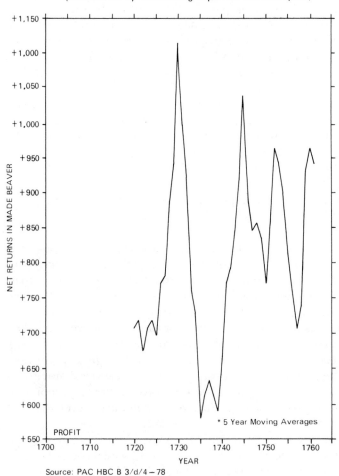

* 5 Year Moving Averages

Source: PAC HBC B 3/d/4 – 78

expense levels fairly closely parallels the variations in the level of competition (as indicated by variations in prices charged for trade goods). Indeed, as the discussion in chapter 12 revealed, Joseph Myatt at Fort Albany attributed French success in the hinterland to their gift-giving practices, and adopted more lavish presentation of gifts as his countermeasure. The lower correlation coefficient for Moose Factory precludes the drawing of a similar conclusion with the same degree of confidence. It should be recalled from chapter 12 that the Moose Factory traders believed that price competition was an important element and that effective prices were lowered in the 1730s by William Bevan and again in the 1750s by Thomas White. Thus, price competition may have been much more important than gift-giving competition at Moose Factory. This may account for the weaker correlation.

However, at the more northerly posts, the levels of expenses are not so closely governed by competition in the trade, at least as shown by the evidence in Table 21. At York Factory, this relationship is only weakly positive (0.25), while at Fort Churchill, expenses actually tend to decline as competition increases (i.e., goods expended in trade per unit of overplus gained increased). The inverse relation is moderately strong (−0.56), and may suggest that the factors at Fort Churchill were successful in following a policy of gift-expense curtailment (e.g., watering brandy or substituting less expensive goods for those previously given) despite the pressures of a competitive market. It should be recalled in this regard that Richard Norton who commanded the post in the 1730s and 1740s claimed that he always received more gifts from the Indians than he presented to them. Anomalously, expenses at Churchill were higher when factors' profits were large. This suggests that Norton's successors were not able to obtain more in gifts than they gave away. In any event, at all posts there is on the whole a strong negative correspondence between factors' net gain on the standard and what we have termed the index of actual prices.

14

The Indians' responses

Having considered the degree to which European traders managed to influence the trading allegiances of the Indians by gift-giving and by price and credit manipulation, we now focus attention in greater detail on the ways in which these trading practices influenced the supplies of furs the Indians offered to the traders on a per-capita basis. Also, the implications of various additional inducements that the Hudson's Bay Company, the French, and the peddlers offered to the Indians to encourage them to trade, and the Indian response to these, will be discussed in detail.

PER-CAPITA SUPPLY RESPONSES OF THE INDIANS TO INCREASED GIFT-GIVING AND PRICE AND CREDIT MANIPULATION

The previous discussion has shown that the Indians responded as individuals to demand competition in ways that may be called conventional economic behaviour (i.e., they drove harder bargains, as the above data have shown, and sought out better terms of trade amongst competing buyers). In certain other ways, however, the Indian reaction was the reverse of the conventional economic behaviour observable among suppliers in a competitive market who both control the amount they offer for sale and are motivated by a desire for profit. In particular, the increased rivalries among fur buyers which resulted in improved prices for the Indians (i.e., lowering of the factors' standard) did not induce them to increase the per-capita supplies of furs which they offered. Indeed, according to the scattergraphs of price and fur quantities (Figures 22 to 26) analysed previously, the anticipated relationship between price and supply variation is not evident for the trade as a whole. Rather, available evidence from the historical record makes it abundantly clear that the

TABLE 22

Relationships between factors' returns, expenses, and trade good prices

Post	Pearson's product-moment correlation coefficients	
	Factors' Returns	Expenses
Fort Albany		
Factors' return	—	
Expenses	−0.79	—
Index of trade good prices	−0.99	0.80
Fort Churchill		
Factors' return	—	
Expenses	0.66	—
Index of trade good prices	−0.96	−0.56
Moose Factory		
Factors' returns	—	
Expenses	−0.30	—
Index of trade good prices	−0.95	0.35
York Factory		
Factors' return	—	
Expenses	−0.29	—
Index of trade good prices	−0.99	0.25
Eastmain		
Factors' return	—	no data
Expenses	no data	—
Index of trade good prices	−0.97	no data

Indians' individual response to improved prices took the form of a classical backward sloping supply curve. That is, as fur prices became more favourable to the individual Indian traders, each Indian commonly offered fewer furs.

Although there are theoretical grounds for separating the expected individual response of suppliers in a competitive market from the aggregate response, it may be of interest to examine the data in Table 22 in the light of the above discussion about the backward sloping supply schedule of individual Indians. This table is designed to assess the strength of the aggregate Indian response at Hudson's Bay Company posts to changing prices (as measured by the trade good price index) in terms of changing

TABLE 23

The lagged effect of trade good price changes on the total furs traded

	0† Year			1† Year			2† Years			3† Years			4† Years		
	df r	r^2	Students' t	r	r^2	Students' t	r	r^2	Students' t	r	r^2	Students' t	r	r^2	Students' t
Fort Albany	−0.30	0.09	−2.45	−0.44	0.20	−3.85	−0.19	0.04	−1.53	−0.39	0.15	−3.21	−0.31	0.09	−2.45
Fort Churchill	−0.61	0.37	−5.12	−0.58	0.34	−4.76	−0.52	0.27	−3.96	−0.42	0.18	−3.02	−0.44	0.20	−3.17
Moose Factory	−0.30	0.07	−1.52	−0.26	0.07	−1.45	−0.22	0.05	−1.20	0.12	0.01	0.64	0.25	0.06	1.30
Fort York	−0.33	0.11	−2.41	−0.22	0.05	−1.57	−0.24	0.06	−1.65	−0.28	0.08	−1.99	−0.40	0.16	−2.91
Eastmain	−0.17	0.03	−1.14	0.16	0.03	1.07	0.33	0.11	2.25	0.33	0.11	2.23	0.14	0.02	0.93

* .05 level of statistically significant correlation

** .01 level of statistically significant correlation

† Number of years by which dependent variable is lagged

fur supplies offered for trade. It also tries to test whether this was a lagged response taking effect one or several years after prices schedules were introduced.

The predominance of negative correlations between prices and volumes of furs offered at all posts suggests that better prices for furs meant that fewer furs would be offered by the Indians (and the converse). There is, however, considerable variety among the posts in the strength of the relationship of price to supply. The strongest inverse relationship was recorded at Fort Churchill ($r = -0.61$). This may be interpreted as revealing a fairly consistent tendency to reduction in total furs supplied as prices improved. The response was weaker at the other posts, but seems sufficiently consistent to incidate a degree of generality in this aggregate Indian reaction to price changes.

However, the evidence for a lagged response is not strong, and no over-all pattern emerges that might indicate lagging at all posts (Table 23). At most posts, the correlation is weaker if the data for fur supplies are lagged one, two, or more years after the data for actual prices. This suggests that response of fur supplies to price changes did not involve extensive time lags. There are, however, several exceptions which may be worthy of note. At Fort Albany the correlation improves in the first and third years and weakens in the second and fourth years of the lag cycle, indicating that perhaps a one-year lag may exist in the negative response of fur supplies to better prices. On the other hand, the inverse correlation at York Factory is highest after a two-three-four-year lag, while at East-main, a two-to-three year lagged response appears possible from the data given. In the latter case, the response is positive, indicating that fur supplies actually showed an improvement at this post several years after each upward adjustment of actual prices. However, it should be stressed that the lagged correlations in the latter cases are relatively weak, and must be interpreted with caution.

The negative correlations between prices and fur returns shown in Table 22 can probably best be explained by considering two factors – Indian economic behaviour and the presence or absence of alternative trading opportunities. The record shows that individual Indians tended to reduce their per-capita supplies of furs whenever the prices being paid for these furs increased. This conduct which appeared inexplicable from the perspective of merchants in London, was not well understood by those who were not dealing with the Indians directly. Indeed, it was partly because the Indians responded individually to price changes in this fashion that the Hudson's Bay Company was vulnerable to the attacks of its critics who maintained that the company's monopolistic policies were detrimental to England's interests in the fur trade of Canada. For example, Arthur Dobbs, a contemporary critic of the Hudson's Bay Company, argued that the company's prices for goods (the official and factors' standards) were inordinately high, and, therefore, offered no positive incentives to the Indians to bring down larger volumes of furs. In fact, Dobbs maintained that if the Indians had not already become dependent on the company for certain goods, they would have ceased trading at the bay altogether.[1]

Dobbs' point of view clearly represents the traditional European conception of the supplier's behaviour in a competitive market. It was based on an unsupportable assumption concerning the attitude of fur suppliers to utility and profit, seeming to imply that Indians traded to maximize economic returns. On the evidence of its past experience, the Hudson's Bay Company countered this argument by pointing out that a relaxation of its standards would not serve to increase the per-capita volume of furs traded, but instead would in all probability lead to a further decline. The reason advanced by the company was that the individual Indian's demand schedule for goods was essentially rigid, in the short run at least. Andrew Graham was most emphatic on this point. Regarding the subject of lowering the prices of goods to encourage trade, he observed:

... if the trading standard was enlarged in favour of the natives, would ruin it all; for I am certain if the natives were to get any more for their furs, they would catch fewer, which I shall make plainly appear viz. one canoe brings down yearly to the Fort one hundred made beaver in different kinds of furs, and trades with me seventy of the said beaver for real necessaries. The other thirty beaver shall so puzzle him to trade, that he often asks me what he shall buy, and when I make an answer, Trade some more powder, shot, tobacco and hatchets etc., his answer is, I have traded sufficient to serve me and my family until I see you again next summer; so he will drink one half, and trade the other with me for baubles ...

Many people are of opinion that the Company would get more furs was the standard to be enlarged. With due deference to their judgement I cannot coincide with them for the following considerations. The natives are naturally indolent, and having food and raiment for the present never concern themselves for the future, until all is expended. Now if an Indian could furnish himself with necessaries for twenty beaver skins I dare aver from twenty-five years experience that he would not bring forty to the Factory.[2]

As Andrew Graham thus pointed out, the rigid demand for goods of the individual Indian was in part a function of basic cultural differences with respect to future planning and to the discounting of future as against present value of goods. The Indians purchased only enough goods to satisfy their immediate needs and did not buy extra items to replace goods which might be lost or broken during the course of the year. In part, this was no doubt due, as we have suggested, to the fact that the mobile lifestyle of the Indians set limits on the physical quantities of goods which they could carry with them or store. Furthermore, during the period before 1774 when the Indians were obliged to travel by canoe to and from the bay in order to trade with the Hudson's Bay Company, the cargo capacities of their canoes set upper limits on the quantities of goods which they could carry into the interior.

The Indians' lack of interest in the accumulation of physical property also would have served to limit their per-capita demand for goods. Whereas the primary motive for European participation in the fur trade was to make a sustained profit, evidence indicates that the Indians took part to meet their basic needs, to satisfy their love of adventure and ceremony, and to gain status amongst their fellows. The virtue of generosity so esteemed by the Indians has been amply illustrated in the earlier discussion of the roles of the factor and the trading captain. This attitude and the sanction against hoarding would have also served to check personal acquisitiveness.

In addition to the negative supply response of individual Indians to rising fur prices, the negative correlation between prices and fur returns at the Hudson's Bay Company posts undoubtedly reflects the effects of alternative trading opportunities during periods of competition. As the earlier discussion demonstrated, actual prices for goods declined (i.e., the Indians' furs were of greater value) at the company's posts when competition was strong. Therefore, since actual prices reflect the effects of competition, they are, in effect, also an indicator of alternative trading opportunities. As has been shown, some Indians traded convenience for price advantage and bartered with the French when the latter were present even though it cost the Indians more in furs to do so than would have been the case had they travelled down to the bay. Furthermore, as Henday's account of trade on the Saskatchewan River in the 1750s indicated, many of the Indians who continued to deal with the Hudson's Bay Company even after the French invasion, stopped at the French posts while en route to the bay in order to obtain brandy.[3] This practice would have served to further reduce the quantities of furs an individual Indian would bring to a Hudson's Bay Company post during competitive periods,[4] and also to reduce the number of Indians who arrived at the bay.

FIXED DEMAND LEVELS AS AN EXPLANATION OF INDIAN RESPONSE TO PRICE FLUCTUATIONS

Besides influencing the Indians' supply responses to more favourable prices for their furs, it is clear that the rigid Indian consumer demand was partly responsible for their relatively unresponsive attitudes to upward revisions in the official and factors' standards of trade. The Indian middlemen obtained only enough furs each year through their trading activities to satisfy their own perceived needs for European goods. The quantities of furs which would have been required to achieve this depended upon the prevailing prices at the posts, and generosity of factors during the gift exchange ceremony; and the Indian traders would have had to gauge the quantity of furs they needed on the basis of the treatment that they had experienced at the company posts the preceding year. Consequently, if the standards of trade were sharply raised from one year to the next and gift-giving sharply curtailed, the Indians would have been unable to obtain all of the goods which they required.

Given the fact that middlemen played a central role in the Hudson's Bay Company fur trade, accounting for over 70 per cent of the furs being traded at some posts, such as York Factory, the ability of the Indians to respond to price fluctuations would have been further dampened. Because these Indian middlemen visited the bay only once a year, and some even less frequently, information concerning market conditions often could not have been passed on to them until nearly a year had elapsed.[5] Since the middlemen in turn were unable to relay this information to their inland trading partners until the following spring when they met them in order to trade, another year would have elapsed before price changes could be brought into effect without placing either participating Indian group (trappers or middlemen) under undue economic stress. Therefore, even if the Indians had accepted European supply and demand conditions as the mechanism by which prices were established, a two- to three-year lagged response to European market conditions was the quickest reaction that could have been expected in many quarters because of the extensive nature of the trading system. As shown in Table 22, although some evidence for such a lagged response exists, it is inconclusive.

Furthermore, it may be hypothesized that it was the nature of the system coupled with the rigid character of the demand of the middlemen which encouraged the latter to resist any attempts by the Hudson's Bay Company traders to raise the factors' standard to more than 150 per cent of the relatively fixed official standard of trade on even a long-term basis.

We have seen that the limit on the numbers of furs which the middlemen could carry in their canoes constrained the effective per-capita demand for goods and similarly set upper limits on the prices which the Indians could have afforded to pay. Presumably, if the middlemen could have handled and transported greater per capita volumes they might have been in a position to tolerate wider fluctuations in the standards of trade.

In addition to the problem of rigid consumer demand, the central role which gift exchanges played in the fur trade served to accentuate the tendency of the Indians not to respond positively to reductions in the standards of trade, which could be interpreted as increases in the prices being offered for their furs. As noted, since generosity was regarded as a physical or tangible expression of goodwill and friendship by the Indians, English and French traders found it necessary to be more lavish in their preliminary gift-giving ceremonies in the hopes of convincing the Indians that they were better friends than their competitors. These actions favoured an upward spiral in the quantities of goods being given away prior to trade as the two European groups attempted to forestall the defection of their Indian clientele to the opposing party. The net effect of this practice would be that the Indian would receive more goods for essentially no greater output on his part. Consequently, gift-giving practices under competitive demand conditions for furs reinforced the Indian's tendency to bring down fewer furs in order to satisfy his relatively static demand for European goods.

EFFORTS TO INFLUENCE INDIAN BUYING HABITS

In an effort to counteract the falling per-capita volumes of furs being offered by the Indians, and thereby cut its escalating costs of operation, the Hudson's Bay Company resorted to a number of devices aimed at increasing the total quantities of furs being taken. First, the company endeavoured to induce the Indians to buy a wider variety of goods by introducing new commodity lines from time to time, i.e., they resorted to the so-called 'demonstration effect.' Generally these innovations did not achieve the desired results, however, for a number of reasons. In particular, the Indians commonly had a well-defined set of priorities for the list of goods which they required and a small number of items tended to dominate this list: articles such as guns, ammunition, knives, hatchets, files, kettles, cloth, and blankets. Only when the demand for these items was satisfied did the Indian traders show an interest in additional goods.

Rather than becoming interested in new articles of trade, the Indians were more attentive to innovations and improvements in the quality of their short list of staples. For example, the French introduced the short barrelled gun (later known as the northwest trade gun) which became popular amongst the woodland Indians at an early date because it was easy to handle in bush country and to carry in canoes. Shortly after its introduction, the Indians living in the Fort Albany hinterlands began to pressure the Hudson's Bay Company traders to stock these guns. In order to hold on to its share of the trade, the company had to respond to this pressure and began to import shorter guns (e.g., three-and-a-half and three-foot guns in addition to the older four-and-a-half and four-foot guns). Since guns were priced by length, the newer shorter guns were one to two MB cheaper than the older guns. Thus, this innovation actually meant a saving to the Indians.[6] Besides responding to changes brought about by the French, the Hudson's Bay Company made innovations in its own product line, the best known example of which was the high quality, striped Hudson's Bay Company point blanket of a later date. These blankets came to be highly prized by the Indians.

Regarding the quality of goods, it must be stressed that the Indians were discriminating consumers who quickly developed an eye for superior merchandise. Contrary to the popular view which often portrays the Indian as a dupe who readily parted with his furs for a few worthless trinkets or other cheap trade goods, Indian middlemen often refused to trade for articles which they perceived as being of substandard quality. Under competitive situations they were in a position to demand high quality and forced the English and French merchants to keep a close eye on the grade of each other's lines of goods. In fact, the Indians would often bring French goods to Hudson's Bay Company posts to show the factors items which they believed were of better quality than those being offered by the English company. For instance, in 1728 the chief factor at York Factory, Thomas McCliesh, wrote to London:

Never was any man so upbraided with our powder, kettles and hatchets, than we have been this summer by all the natives, especially by those that borders near the French. Our cloth likewise is so stretched with the tenter-hooks, so as the selvedge is almost tore from one end of the piece to the other. I hope that such care will be taken so as will prevent the like for the future, for the natives are grown so politic in their way in trade, so as they are not to be dealt by as formerly, for they value not giving a skin or two more than what is common provided the commodity be good and serviceable; ... For now is the time to oblige the natives, before the French draws them to their settlement, which is not above four days' paddling from the

Great Lake [Lake Winnipeg] that feeds this river ... for here came at least forty canoes of Indians this summer, most of them clothed in French clothing that they traded with the French last summer. They likewise brought several strong French kettles and some French powder in their horns, with which they upbraided us with, by comparing with ours ...[7]

McCliesh's experiences at York Factory were repeated at the other Hudson's Bay Company posts, and not surprisingly, therefore, many of the letters which the traders wrote to the directors in London during the early eighteenth century dealt at great length with the subject of Indian reactions to the quality of the company's merchandise. Indian complaints were recorded in great detail and the London directors usually tried to satisfy their demands. Frequently, the governor and committee in London asked their representatives in the bay if succeeding shipments of goods were more to the Indians' liking.

The ability of the Indians to perceive quality in merchandise, and their consistent demand for it, placed the European traders in a difficult position. They were forced to cater to these wishes and compete with each other in an effort to present the Indians with a superior line of goods. The Indians, on the other hand, did not necessarily equate better quality with higher prices. Thus, if they had agreed to pay 12 MB for a three-and-a-half-foot gun, they maintained that all three-and-a-half-foot guns should be traded at that price even if the quality had been improved. According to the Indian view, the European traders should never have traded poorer quality items in the first place. Therefore, in spite of the fact that the Hudson's Bay Company had to pay higher prices for better quality goods during periods of intensive trade rivalries, it had difficulty passing these added expenses on to the Indians.

A somewhat more successful attempt at increasing the fur volumes taken in at the posts involved the European manipulation of the Indian institution of gift-giving. Whereas in Indian society the giving of gifts had the connotations of affirming friendship and goodwill, the Hudson's Bay Company traders introduced another element – the presentation of gifts as rewards for services rendered. Graham's description of the pre-trade ceremony, outlined in chapter 6, shows that although gifts were initially given only to the band leaders prior to actual trade, by the latter half of the eighteenth century, chiefs were being given additional presents at the conclusion of their bands' trade. According to Humphrey Marten, a company factor, these presents were expressly given as rewards for the band leader's efforts on behalf of the company, and were given in proportion to the number of canoes which the band leader brought down to the bay in a given year. This practice appears to have achieved the desired end, for, as Graham pointed out, Indian captains made every effort to increase their following, knowing that more deferential treatment would be accorded them at the factories.

PART FOUR

EMPIRICAL EVIDENCE AND COMPARATIVE
ECONOMIC THEORY: SOME IMPLICATIONS OF
THIS STUDY

15

Trade and politics: a reinterpretation

Having presented a detailed analysis of fur trade operations in Part III, our task is now to relate the evidence we have presented to previous ideas about the trading system and, broadening the scope even further, to consider the relevance of concepts of trade and exchange in general. In doing so, we must navigate between the shoals of conceptual oversimplification, on the one side, and overestimation of the importance of specific details and 'unique' characteristics of the fur trade on the other side. Although our immediate goal is to evaluate the usefulness of existing conceptual frameworks in understanding the Hudson's Bay Company's fur trade, we cannot avoid entering the controversy which surrounds the use of some concepts in explaining cross-cultural trade. Consequently it will be necessary for us to consider possible modifications to existing frameworks for comparative economic analysis. At issue is the question of the extent to which Indian trade was 'embedded' in a socio–political system (i.e., economic decisions were made by political authorities or on the basis of custom and tradition rather than by property owners and entrepreneurs in pursuit of a profit), and the adequacy of concepts dealing with such kinds of exchange to classify and give perspective and insight into the trade.

THE POLITICAL CONTEXT OF TRADE: EXISTING VIEWS

Previous researchers have pointed out that in many non-western state or peasant societies trade and exchange seem always to have taken place in accordance with social or political norms. In such instances they represent, in effect, concomitants of political treaties, alliances, or cordial agreements rather than manifestations of conventional market behaviour.[1] Terms such as 'gift trade,' 'administered trade,' 'treaty trade,' or 'long-distance trade' have been used to categorize politically and socially embedded exchanges among different groups. (Trade which is not 'embedded' in this way may be classed as profit-oriented or market trade.)

Politically motivated trade (i.e., trade conducted as a concomitant of political interaction) has been identified as a predominant form in the case of many North American Indian groups before European contact. Some scholars, notably Rich and Rotstein, have categorized the Indian–European trade in furs as a form of treaty trade. Rotstein declares that the fur trade is a case of the subservience of economic motivations to political objectives, implying that without the conclusion of formal alliances between Indians and Europeans, no trade would have taken place. Trade, in effect, is interpreted as having been an occasion for the cementing of military–political alliances, wherein the things exchanged were of less significance than the symbolic strengthening of the alliance which the trade ceremony represented. This thesis, which underlies Rotstein's 'Fur Trade and Empire,'[2] is extended to the Hudson's Bay Company fur trade as well as the earlier trade of Huronia and the St Lawrence.

As we have attempted to show in this study, such an interpretation of the motivations underlying the Indian's participation in the Hudson's Bay Company fur trade does not accord very satisfactorily with available evidence. In particular, it is seemingly contradicted by the following aspects of the Hudson's Bay Company trade:

1/ The English, as Rotstein agrees, never entered into hostilities among Indian bands or aided one group militarily against another in their long sojourn on the shores of the bay. As a route to military advantage over their enemies, therefore, Indian groups would have derived little benefit from alliance with the English at the bayside posts. Yet the Hudson's Bay Company's trade grew and prospered over an extensive period. Likewise the French, after an early experimental alliance with the Sioux, quickly realized their mistake and neutralized themselves so that they could trade with the Assiniboine and Cree who were enemies of the Sioux.

2/ During the frequent hostilities between the English and French in the Hudson Bay area, the Indians showed no evidence of accepting the idea that previous trade with the English precluded them from dealing with the French or obliged them to take up arms against the latter, even though European pressures were exerted in this direction. On the contrary, as plentiful evidence attests, probably the majority of Indian bands around the bay traded freely and simultaneously with both English and French, and were clearly guided in their choice of trading partners by economic and not political considerations. That is, they were primarily concerned with the cost in furs of the goods they sought, and the relative quality of the merchandise at a given price, and, in their 'shopping around,' their behaviour was not unike that of any modern Western consumer. Their habit of flaunting French goods at English posts and reproaching the traders for their higher priced or poorer quality goods is reminiscent of the behaviour of consumers in any bazaar or market, and indicates motives on the part of the Indian that were far from being purely or even predominantly political.

3/ The 'leading Indians' who came to the bayside posts were not in any sense paramount chiefs or even political leaders endowed with authority to make binding alliances. As we have pointed out, they were trading captains whose authority was quite limited. The bands they came from did not possess the necessary political structure, size, and continuity to fulfil obligations if called upon by their European allies.

4/ The 'typical trade speeches' quoted earlier (page 66) do not make any reference to political or military alliances. In fact, they deal exclusively with the purely economic matters of fair measurement, quality and price of goods, and adherence to previously agreed upon terms of trade (on the part of the Indian trading captain), and to volume and quality of pelts and the need for greater diligence in the hunt for more furs (on the part of the factor).

In short, to conclude that alliances were a dominant feature of the Hudson Bay fur trade involves inferences about the Indian participants' motives and behaviour which are not supported by the evidence presented in this study. Such ideas are largely based on similarities between the pre-trade ceremony of the Hudson's Bay Company and those of Huronia and the St Lawrence where the alliance system was undoubtedly a significant factor in the trade. Records of the Tadoussac trade, however, indicate that economic motives may have been dominant here as well. At the bayside posts, it seems that the pre-trade ceremony with its gift exchanges was more social than political in nature, i.e., a reaffirmation of the friendship and goodwill that are prerequisites to fair dealings in barter trade. In short, the pre-trade ceremonies were probably more akin to the exchanges of courtesies or pleasantries which often precede business dealings in the modern Western world, rather than symbolic of the confirmation of military pacts or political alliances, even though they may have originally taken these forms in pre-contact times.

TRADE AND EXCHANGE IN 'BAND' SOCIETIES

The concept of administered trade or treaty trade as an explanation of the Hudson's Bay Company furs–goods exchange has other limitations. For instance, while this concept appears to have validity when applied to exchanges in a variety of *state* societies, it could be argued that it is inapplicable to exchange among *band* societies. The latter tend to have an egalitarian structure and frequently lack the hierarchical organization and centralization of authority necessary for administered trade to operate. Indeed, goods exchanges may not be a sufficiently common phenomenon in these societies for the elaborate norms of treaty trade to be well developed, notwithstanding the fact that exchange which does occur may indeed be strongly regulated by social customs and traditions.

The Hudson's Bay Company fur trade, of course, involved participants from state societies (the English and French) as well as from band societies. But still the concept of administered trade does not appear applicable to this exchange. This is because: (*a*) the Europeans attempted (within constraints imposed by the Indians) to conduct *market trade*, in which the actual exchange rates at the posts were set by cost–profit considerations and not by decree or tradition monitored by a central administering authority; and (*b*) the constraints we have mentioned brought the trade more into line with the customs of exchange in Indian band societies which, as outlined previously, did not resemble administered trade. Thus, although relatively fixed official exchange rates were established for the trade (which might on the surface appear to denote administered trade), these were, in practice, accorded only lip service by trade participants. The Europeans circumvented them via the overplus and gifts, and the Indians attempted to drive harder bargains (asking for 'more than measure') with the support of English–French competition for their furs.

Another inadequacy of the concept of administered trade as applied in the present context relates to the place of this concept in an overly simplistic dichotomy which splits trade into two mutually exclusive classes: (1) exchange between individuals *within* political units, and (2) exchange between individuals of *different* political units. The terms *short-distance* and *long-distance* trade are often used synonymously with the first and second classes respectively. Administered trade is conceptually linked by scholars who favour this dichotomy with long-distance or intergroup trade or exchange.[3] However, this conceptual scheme is not helpful and is, in fact, misleading when applied to the Hudson's Bay Company fur trade. For, as we have shown, both within-band and between-band exchanges were inextricably woven into the trade at an early stage in its development. The trading Indians, and especially the middlemen, were both *agents* (purchasing specific goods on behalf of their families and kin) and *merchants* (obtaining a stock of goods earmarked for eventual exchange with trapping bands not socially related to them). In the latter role, they also presented their Indian trading partners with gifts in pre-trade ceremonies. In short, the trade included transactions within *and* between Indian political units. Moreover, the fur trade does not fall easily into the dichotomy of long-distance versus short-distance trade for several reasons. First, by any measure, extremely long distances were involved in journeying to the bay. Second, the goods transported over such vast distances were subsequently distributed to close kin and other related as well as unrelated bands in the migratory cycle followed by most Indians in the hinterland. Clearly the fur trade is not amenable to the simple categorization outlined above.

Recently, scholars interested in comparative analysis of trade have begun to question the dichotomy of long distance–short distance trade. For instance, Renfrew, in an important theoretical treatise, adds a third category (intermediate trade) which identifies important forms of exchange among early state societies not accommodated by a simple dichotomy.[4] Gray and Birmingham[5] assert that distance bears no necessary correlation to the form or context of commodity exchanges and reject it as a classificatory concept.

To these general criticisms of the original conceptual dichotomy may be added another. The proponents of this scheme envisaged that different explanatory concepts governed long-distance and short-distance trade or exchange in traditional socieities. Long-distance trade required application of concepts of gift trade, administered trade, or market trade, while short-distance trade embraced reciprocity, redistribution, and local market exchange.[6] This implies that one must first decide whether a case being examined belongs in the long-distance or short-distance category before knowing which set of explanatory concepts to apply. To the present authors, this is not a relevant research paradigm. The primary value of conceptual frameworks should be their generality and broad validity under simplifying assumptions.

It is unacceptable to have a body of supposedly general concepts made dependent on fine distinctions as to the distance involved or type of exchange, which imposes a priori an apparently arbitrary classification on the researcher. What we must have is a set of general concepts of exchange capable of being applied in all contexts with appropriate *ceteris paribus* assumptions. Within this set of concepts should be more specific and elaborate concepts applicable to subsets of general types of exchange, these subsets being determined by relaxation of certain limiting assumptions, not by arbitrary and purely a priori considerations. A satisfactory theoretical framework should thus stress general similarities and relationships rather than be based on prior partitioning of a class of phenomena into fundamentally dissimilar and conceptually unrelated compartments.

To again stress the point of this chapter: existing conceptual dichotomies relating to the political context of trade are not helpful and even inhibit insight and possible explanations when applied in a rigid way to the Hudson's Bay Company fur trade. This trading system is impossible to label neatly as 'gift trade,' or 'administered trade,' or 'market trade,' since it embodies elements of all these forms. While all of the above concepts relate to 'long-distance' trade or exchange, they are not sufficient to describe or categorize the Hudson's Bay Company trade. Concepts of short-distance trade or bartering, socially based reciprocity, and redistribution must also be drawn upon to complete the picture, as our evidence suggests.

Our evidence in this study, matched with preexisting concepts, leads us to these theoretical conclusions: (1) that the consciously political aspects of the trade, both on the European and Indian sides, diminished in importance at an early point in the development of the exchange; (2) that, although retaining some important formal characteristics from earlier systems of 'embedded' exchange in traditional Indian society, the trade institutions were modified to reflect increasing dominance of economic considerations. New institutions and institutionalized roles, such as the middleman and the factors' standard, emerged as this transition gained momentum; (3) consequently, we must use concepts in explaining the trade that apply both to market institutions as well as socially embedded forms of exchange, that relate to institutions of state societies as well as band societies, and that do not attempt *a priori* to relegate the trade to some arbitrary category on the overly simple grounds of superficial similarities of the trade with different trading systems at other times or places. Since consideration of a suitable conceptual framework involves appraisal of existing concepts of comparative economics, these will be reviewed in the next chapter and their applicability to the present case assessed.

16

Economic dimensions of the trade

EVALUATING ECONOMIC CONCEPTS OF EXCHANGE IN
TRANSITIONAL OR CROSS-CULTURAL CONTEXTS

In the earlier chapters, it has been shown that many features of the Hudson's Bay Company fur trade are inexplicable unless a dominant economic rather than political basis for the trade is assumed. Yet, in the search for a suitable conceptual framework to apply to the trade, one cannot lose sight of the characteristics which derive from earlier 'socially embedded' forms of exchange in Indian society. Explaining trade between such strongly dissimilar groups as the Indian and European means blending and perhaps extending certain existing conceptual frameworks in economics and economic anthropology. These disciplines, in practice, keep largely separate and distinct those forms of exchange identifiable as market-oriented or 'Western,' and ceremonial or 'socially embedded' forms encountered in societies that are 'primitive and archaic.'[1] It will be readily appreciated that, in cross-cultural exchanges such as the Hudson's Bay Company fur trade, where social and economic transitions were underway, such conceptual dichotomies are not meaningful. However, in searching for an adequate set of concepts to apply in this case, our point of departure must be a closer review of the applicability of existing concepts of comparative economics.

CONCEPTS OF MARKET AND NON-MARKET EXCHANGE

To the present, the study of comparative economic systems as interpreted by economists has tended to stress analysis of modern *state* economies following variants of Western or Marxist ideologies. Market exchange tends to dominate economic interaction in such socieites, and concepts related to this form of exchange permeate the study of state economies.[2]

Market concepts

Economists and economic anthropologists are by no means in agreement on the minimal set of conditions which identify a transaction as being a form of market exchange. Some would specify that either or both a buying crowd and a selling crowd must be present for market exchange to occur. Others assert that markets are characterized by behaviour of exchange participants which features 'haggling' over prices or exchange rates. Still others would opt for a more general and cautious definition. For example, a market could be defined simply as 'a group of people in sufficiently close communication with each other for those disposing of goods freely to switch disposal from one prospective acquirer to another, or those wishing to acquire goods to switch their custom from one disposer of goods to another.'[3]

References to markets and market behaviour usually imply 'arm's-length' dealings between acquirer and disposer, as well as the establishment of relationships between schedules of goods and services offered (supplied) and sought (demanded) at each of a range of possible prices. These relationships between goods in demand (demand schedules) and goods offered for sale (supply schedules) are expressed through price. In barter markets, or transitional markets price may be expressed in units of other goods, while in more sophisticated markets a single medium of exchange, into which units of all goods may be translated, is commonly used.

Besides embodying particular exchange institutions and processes, markets also imply underlying motivations. For example, the act of switching custom from one disposer of goods to another is only rational if this entails some advantage to the acquirer. In economic terms, the primary advantage to be secured by such behaviour is gain in consumable or disposable goods through more favourable terms of trade or prices. Gain through market exchange also results from the efficiency of this system of redistributing goods, and from the fact that it permits specialization of production of goods by those enjoying comparative production advantages.

As defined in this admittedly very much simplified fashion, concepts of market exchange appear to have definite applicability to elements of the Hudson's Bay Company fur trade, including all three spheres of exchange: in the European auction markets, at the bayside posts (although not a perfect market as will be discussed below), and in exchanges among Indians within the hinterlands and trapping territories.

The activities in the fur markets of Europe and the markets in which goods for the trade were purhcased identify these institutions as being of the free-market type. There is evidence that the London fur market was relatively stable between 1713 and 1763, with prices remaining fairly close to an average that the company found acceptable. This may be inferred from the stability of the 'upset price' which the company set on the furs offered at auction during this period.[4] An added inference is that the volume of furs marketed by the company was not out of step with the quantities demanded at that price to any marked degree until 1750, after which the upset price increased, reflecting inadequate fur supplies (due to diversion of furs through the company's competitors to the somewhat separate Paris fur market). However, our main interest is in understanding the basis of the trade at the factories on Hudson Bay and in the hinterlands. Concepts of the market apply equally to institutions, institutionalized roles, procedures, and motivations of the participants in these theatres of the fur trade.

Thus, early in its development, the Hudson's Bay Company fur trade came to be characterized by a division of labour which saw certain individuals or bands specializing in trapping and preparing beaver skins, while others, the middlemen, specialized in the transportation and bartering of furs. It is significant that a large specialized Indian middlemen population did not exist as a functionally distinct group prior to the establishment of the bayside posts. The middlemen were truly creations of the fur trade and their function was predominantly an economic one. They represented an adaptation of Indian social and political structures to the circumstances and economic opportunities which the fur trade brought about.

The commodity exchange which took place at the bayside posts and among Indians in the hinterland had strongly monopolistic/monopsonistic characteristics during some periods, especially between 1720 and 1730. At other times competition intensified, and oliqopolistic conditions were in evidence. Again, the behaviour of these participating groups leaves little doubt that they were involved in a form of market exchange. Thus, Indian 'disposers' of furs readily switched their custom from English to French 'acquirers' when English prices (overplus taken per unit of goods bartered) were raised to unacceptable levels. The Indians also responded to opportunities which permitted them to reduce *costs* of trading, as when they opted to pay somewhat higher prices for goods from *coureurs de bois* in the hinterland rather than face the cost in time, effort, and physical risk entailed in covering the longer distances down to the bay.

Goods–furs exchange rates in the trade again bear a stronger relation to prices established by market forces (in this case, demand competition for furs and competition in the supply of trade goods) than to equivalences set by social tradition or by an administering authority. We have shown that, although MB equivalence was relatively fixed over a long period, de facto exchange rates varied substantially.[5] Both Europeans at the posts and Indian middlemen trading to trapping bands in the interior exacted mark-ups on the goods they offered in barter. The mark-up on goods at the posts, in the form of overplus minus gifts to Indians, has been dealt with at length in this study and is, in many ways, central to our interpretation of trade institutions and processes. This mark-up was a highly significant profit element for the company rather than simply a gift fund or 'slush' fund, as was previously thought by some scholars. The mark-up, however, is not, strictly speaking, a premium charged over and above the cost of trade goods to the company, but is rather an overcharging in furs on the official exchange rates accepted at the initiation of the trade by the Indian and European participants. The official standard, although an equivalence system applicable only to the North American sphere of activity, most probably already had a profit element built into it. But subsequent inflation of the cost of trade goods may have eroded this built-in profit to the point where the official standard of trade may indeed have been an approximation of the cost of goods to the company, in which case the overplus, after deduction of gifts to Indians, would have possibly been the major component (and perhaps also the most reliable component) in over-all profit from the company's operations.

The Indian mark-up does not permit such a straightforward explanation. Unlike the European *overplus* which was related to the official standard, the Indian's mark-up was based on his actual purchase price of the trade good. Certainly this mark-up represented in part an attempt to cover expenses of the trade (e.g., gifts in pre-trade ceremonies and in return for provisions), as well as losses through consumption and deterioration of goods over the time and distance travelled by the middlemen. Recompense for lost time in hunting or social pursuits may also have been a factor. The notion of negative reciprocity ('scoring' off one's opponent in barter through sharp trading) also may be relevant to an understanding of Indian mark-ups.[6]

Profit motives must also be considered in an attempt to explain the Indian middlemen's practice of advancing their trade good prices. This study has indicated that taking profits for the accumulation of personal material wealth was alien to the traditional cultures of the Indians dealing with the Hudson's Bay Company in the eighteenth century. The trading captains, for example, redistributed most of their gains on trade to their followers. However, this does not mean that the captains and their followers were not interested in making a profit in trade. By redistributing his profit amongst his followers, a trading captain was able to maintain or improve his social position. The trading captains' concern with their social status was manifest in their realtions with their followers and with the Europeans at the trading posts. For instance, Samuel Hearne noted that Indian leaders 'pride themselves much on the respect which is shown them at the Factory; to obtain which they Frequently run great risques of being starved to death in their way thither and back.'[7] As was noted earlier, the Hudson's Bay Company men learned to manipulate this behaviour to their own advantage by affording the greatest respect to the captains who brought the greatest number of canoes and furs to the posts. Under these circumstances, it would have served the interests of Indian middlemen to obtain as many furs as they could for the goods that they traded.

In sum, the Indians' motivation for participating in trade with the Hudson's Bay Company was complex. They traded to satisfy their own immediate demand for European goods and to acquire status through the redistribution of material wealth that they gained through exchange. The love of adventure, ceremony, and social contact were also factors which encouraged them to travel to the bay. The political dimension did not assume great significance in that exchange at the bay was not predicated on the negotiation of military alliances nor intended to cement political treaties. At the same time, however, it is clear that the Hudson's Bay Company was a valuable trading partner from the perspective of power politics because the company was a reliable source of firearms and ammunition. Hence, even though the company attempted to discourage warfare in the hinterlands of its posts and took no active part in conflicts, the arms it supplied to its trading partners undoubtedly served to upset the traditional balance of power in favour of Indian bands who had contact with the bayside posts.

Non-market concepts
We stressed in the previous chapter that elements of the fur trade institutions resembled and were derived from what have been termed 'socially embedded' forms of exchange which predominated in the pre-contact

period. The conceptual framework for interpreting such non-market interaction was systematized by Karl Polanyi.[8] This framework or paradigm was intended by Polanyi as an alternate conceptual scheme to formal market concepts (e.g., scarcity, economizing, profit maximizing, price, money) for comparing and explaining economic interactions in 'traditional' economies. It should be emphasized here that the Polanyi framework was intended for application under *static* conditions.[9] The present case of the Hudson's Bay Company fur trade comprises a *transition* in which 'traditional' exchange institutions of Indian band societies were modified and adapted to effect cross-cultural exchange with Europeans, who were also obliged to modify their exchange procedures. The economic and social change initiated by the fur trade had not, however, proceeded to the point where all elements of 'traditional' Indian trade were obliterated, but our evidence in this study suggests that some characteristics, although appearing to be the same (e.g., the pre-trade ceremony) had already taken on new significance and lost some of their original meaning.

Thus, as has been shown while *gift exchange* was a characteristic feature of the Hudson's Bay Company fur trade, its function altered as the trade developed. The Indians did not give status gifts to the European traders as they may have done with each other in pre-contact gift exchanges. Instead they offered furs, the staple of the trade, which had no status connotations to either Indians or factors, and country produce, which had practical rather than symbolic value. The Europeans, on the other hand, used gifts as lures to entice Indian bands to their posts. The gifts were of several kinds: consumable luxury items such as Brazil tobacco and brandy, utilitarian goods like guns and knives, and status adornments like captain's outfits. The latter were intended to enhance the trading captain's importance among his companions and hence induce more Indians to follow him to the bay in succeeding years. In later years, special gifts were added to those given during pre-trade ceremonies as rewards to trading captains. The value of these gifts was directly proportional to the number of Indians they brought with them to the posts. The European motives behind gift-giving, not surprisingly, were almost purely pragmatic. However, the practical rather than ceremonial nature of the Indian goods offered as gifts, and the fact that furs given to the traders (collected from band members by leaders as a kind of tax) were frequently poorer quality ones, suggests that the Indians also consciously began to use the traditional form of the gift exchange as a means to their own economic gain, especially as English-French competition for their furs intensified.

What the above discussion leads to is this: the concept of *gift exchange* applies to the Hudson's Bay Company fur trade in a formal or superficial sense only, since there is evidence that the spirit behind the gift exchange waned as the trade developed. The pre-trade ceremony became a tool which each participant used with the aim of introducing more flexibility (as required by a competitive market) into the terms of trade. In a similar way, the concept of *administered trade* is, as has been pointed out in chapter 15, not really applicable in the case of the Hudson Bay fur trade, since the exchange (from the Indian point of view at least) was not politically controlled. That is, the schedules of goods traded were not restricted on political grounds (e.g., weapons were not excluded), nor were there effective restrictions on those permitted to trade. Even the official fixed prices were not effectively enforced. The English, in their attempts to prevent Indian–French trade, had to use economic inducements, exhortations, and the cultivation of personal relationships, rather than political controls over the movement and interactions of the Indians. Moreover, the opposition of the Hudson's Bay Company to the French during outbreaks of hostilities between England and France was mainly of a defensive rather than militarily offensive nature.

Of the three 'long-distance' trade concepts of gift trade, administered trade, and market trade, therefore, the latter conceptual scheme appears to provide the most useful insights and the most accurate characterization of the Hudson's Bay Company fur trade in its first century of operation. The non-market trade concepts outlined above, however, contribute to a broader understanding of the exchange system once it is realized that the features to which they relate (especially gift-giving and fixed equivalence) were already in transition, having been modified and adapted for use in cross-cultural exchange. If applied at face value, these concepts may give (and, in the past, have given) an inaccurate idea of the economic character of the Hudson's Bay Company fur trade.

The concepts of *reciprocity* and *redistribution*, which relate to within-group (short-distance) exchange rather than between-group or long-distance trade, also have a place in an understanding of the fur trade. These concepts deal with forms of non-market economic behaviour in band or other aboriginal social organizations, and provide useful insights into aspects of the behaviour of Indians trading at bayside posts and in the post hinterlands.

The term *reciprocity* as commonly used by economic anthropologists covers several related forms of economic behaviour in which prestation, mutual gift-giving, or similar exchanges are involved. Usually the exchange takes place within or between closely related social groups, although long-distance gift trade could be considered a variant. *Balanced reciprocity* covers exchanges which involve virtually simultaneous giving and receiving of goods whose values are equivalent, but where the equivalence is not overtly regulated by supply–demand conditions. *Generalized reciprocity* does not necessarily involve immediate or direct mutual gift-giving, but may involve long-standing agreement among kinship groups or band members concerning equitable division of different goods produced.

Balanced and generalized reciprocity were undoubtedly important in pre-contact Indian exchanges. We have illustrated in this study the way in which Indians regarded surplus goods as theirs for the taking, and their acceptance of the practice of using the possessions of other band members when these were not in actual use by their 'owners.' This behaviour amounted to generalized reciprocity since, in the long run, as Umfreville pointed out, no band member would suffer a net loss from such 'borrowing.' However, these Indian attitudes to ownership of property and the disposition of surplus goods necessitated the institution of the 'hole-in-the-wall' at English trading posts, to prevent Indians from simply taking trading goods from the stores. Reciprocity of a more balanced or specific kind was expected in the pre-trade ceremony, which has already been dealt with as a transitional variant of gift trade. Equivalence in the value of gifts exchanged may at first have been conscientiously striven for, but was soon abandoned in favour of what may be termed *negative reciprocity*: the willful proffering of a gift of inferior value to that received or expected. On the European side, as Richard Norton's admission attests, negative reciprocity in gift-exchange ceremonies was a recognized way of taking overplus while he was in command of Fort Churchill. Indians were no less canny in offering inferior pelts as gifts and saving the better ones for barter exchange, and at York Factory, the traders gave away goods of greater aggregate value than they received.

Redistribution of goods through gift-giving as an exchange concept also provides insight into the Hudson's Bay Company fur trading system and illuminates behavioural patterns of Indian participants. We have discussed in detail the custom in which the factor's gifts to the trading captain were redistributed among the band members accompanying him after they left the post for the return journey to the hinterland. This redistributive action can be interpreted as a means of gaining status and approbation in a basically egalitarian society in which no political or social hierarchy existed to confer such status, where leaders were obeyed voluntarily or as a result of inducements rather than by command, and where wealth accumulation (hoarding) was almost impossible and was considered anti-social behaviour. We have pointed out that the Hudson's Bay Company authorities in London did not understand the implications of gift-giving to the trading captains and the practice of redistribution, since at one stage they suggested increasing personal gifts to these individuals to secure their compliance in raising the official standards of trade.

Redistribution of accumulated surpluses also helps to explain the unorthodox Indian response to price changes for furs. Since they clearly did not carry on the trade to amass personal wealth, Indians saw no reason to bring down larger volumes of furs when fur prices improved under English–French demand competition, but continued to trade in accordance with their usual needs. In this instance the behaviour of Indian traders contrasted strongly with 'expected' behaviour of suppliers in a (conventional Western) market, and thus we must turn to the non-market concept of redistribution to explain the motives behind this aspect of Indian behaviour.

17

The Hudson Bay fur trade
as a spatial system:
conclusions, and implications for
comparative economic geography

Spatial aspects of the fur trade have been shown to be indispensable to a full understanding of the trade as an integrated system. Consequently, a more explicit treatment is necessary at this point. Our objective in examining the spatial characteristics of the trade is to determine the usefulness of existing concepts to an understanding of the trading system in the Hudson Bay area.

A first question relates to the system of posts at which the institutions of European–Indian exchange took place. Our initial discussion of their relative locations and the development of their hinterlands in which centripetal consumer movement and centrifugal goods disbursement or diffusion occurred, leads us to enquire whether they shared the general characteristics of permanent market centres as envisaged in the framework of central-place theory,[1] or, if not, whether other concepts of location theory are applicable.

The second question concerns the specific effects of the costs or frictions of travel distance, risk, and difficulty on the evolution of the trading pattern and in the saga of Indian manipulation of French–English rivalry. We anticipate that, as with other spatial-economic systems, development went hand-in-hand with efforts to reduce the costs of movement within the system. However, as some evidence suggests, the European and Indian sectors of the trade complex appear to have responded differently to the evolving patterns of travel costs.

In attempting to answer these questions about the geography of the trade, we must try to visualize the spatial complex of posts, routes, and hinterlands as a whole. The maps presented earlier (Figures 2, 3, and 8) and the abstract spatial model (Figure 7) are an appropriate starting point for this exercise. However, in order to account for the configurations of posts and hinterlands which appear in these figures it is reasonable to first consider the existing stock of concepts relating to the pattern and function of settlements. We may endeavour, in other words, to examine the posts as a special form of market centre, and apply our knowledge of consumer movement to such centres to throw light on the spatial behaviour of their Indian clientele in the hinterlands.

SPATIAL CONCEPTS OF THE MARKET

Whereas the formal economist usually sees the market as an abstraction, i.e., an institutionalized mechanism of exchange between acquirers and disposers of commodities, the geographer seems more inclined to regard the market as a *locus* for the specific interaction of buyers and sellers of goods and services. In this regard, the geographer's approach is more akin to that of the economic anthropologist or archaeologist, as the work of Renfrew shows.[2] A comprehensive review of the geographical literature on markets in various cultural contexts is provided by Brian J.L. Berry in his book *Geography of Market Centers and Retail Distribution*.[3] In part three of his book, Berry synthesizes empirical and theoretical contributions of earlier scholars to provide an overview of the progressive elaboration of exchange systems through time and space. He envisages a three-stage sequence: (*a*) socially administered exchange, corresponding to Polanyi's notions of redistribution and reciprocity; (*b*) barter exchange, as in some peasant economies, together with simple money-based exchange, which is common in many periodic markets and fairs of less-developed regions; and (*c*) permanent market-centre hierarchies, based on specialization of production and a high degree of interdependence among localities, and among economic production and consumption units. Although Berry's book concentrates primarily on the latter form of exchange complex, whose relevant concepts are drawn from central-place theory, he also discusses some examples of geographic research which focus on more primitive spatial exchange systems, including periodic markets.[4]

These market variants have attracted significant research attention in recent years. Notable studies dealing with periodic markets are those of R.J. Bromley,[5] Polly Hill and R.H.T. Smith,[6] and Thomas Eighmy.[7] Bromley's paper is essentially a review of the literature on the market as a locus of exchange, whereas the work by Hill and Smith is more concerned with the geographic aspects of the synchronization and spacing of markets using detailed studies of northern Nigeria as examples.[8] The paper by Eighmy views examples of rural periodic markets in Nigeria as being 'understandable in terms of general spatial diffusion and central place theory as these are modified to reflect an indigenous African situation.' The approaches in these studies typify the strong concern of the geographer for developing and applying suitable models of the spatial organization of markets in a variety of cultural contexts. To date, however, conceptual treatment of the spatial implications of cross-cultural exchange, such as that represented by the fur trade, is not well developed, and consequently a cautious approach to the application of spatial concepts developed in other contexts is indicated.

HUDSON BAY POSTS CONSIDERED AS CENTRAL PLACES

Since the Hudson's Bay Company posts were permanent establishments, rather than seasonal or ephemeral centres, and dispensed a wide variety of goods and services to extensive hinterlands, it may be tempting to try to class them with other forms of market-points in the framework of central-place theory.

The basic postulate of this theory is that, given the amplifying assumptions of a uniform distribution of consumers, goods, and services on an isotropic plain, and the requirement that all consumers be served by establishments which dispense such goods and services, a pattern of retail centres will arise in which the latter are equidistant and their market areas hexagonal. Along the boundaries of market area hexagons, consumers are equidistant from alternate market centres and hence are indifferent as to which centre to patronize. The spacing of centres will be dependent partly on the tributary population needed to support a particular economic function (the threshold) and the distance consumers are willing to travel to acquire that particular good or service (the range of the good). Since the range and threshold of various goods differ (i.e., they are of different orders), centres which typically dispense these various goods are organized into a *hierarchy* of centres ranging from the very small rural nodes (with constricted market areas and dispensing low order goods) to the very large metropolitan centres (with market areas for their high-order services covering the entire central place system).

Relaxation of the stringent assumptions (e.g., the isotropic plain and the geometric perfection of the hexagonal market lattice) does not diminish the usefulness of this theory in illuminating the spatial organization of market centres.[9] The essential concepts of central-place theory (the range, threshold, and market hierarchy) have been applied to many systems of urban centres and rural settlements in many different cultural, economic, and historical contexts. However, these concepts are of doubtful applicability to the fur trading system centred around the Hudson's Bay Company posts during the period under examination. For instance, differences in size or economic importance of the posts did not denote the existence of a functional hierarchy as postulated in central-place theory, since all of the Hudson's Bay Company posts, as we have seen, offered the same variety of goods and services to the Indians. Thus the obvious predominance of York Factory was a function of its location on routes providing accessibility to a larger hinterland population and yielding a larger turnover in trade, and not to the availability there of any higher-order goods or services. Conversely the size of hinterlands could not really be ascribed to the dispensing of higher-order goods at any particular post. The concept of *threshold* of goods or services, i.e., a minimum hinterland population or radius for the dispensing of a particular item, likewise does not strictly apply in this case.

Inter-post relations

As the bayside posts were not organized into any functional hierarchy[10] and all offered the same variety of trade items and services, such as blacksmithing, gun-repairing, clothes-making, etc., they tended to act as more or less independent units. This tendency was fostered by overt policy of the company, which tried to establish each post under monopolistic conditions and hence strongly discouraged inter-post competition for Indian clientele.

Indeed, the factors stationed on the shores of the bay developed rather possessive attitudes to their Indian trading partners and jealously guarded against any encroachments on their trade by adjacent company posts. For example, when Fort Churchill was established for the purpose of trade with the Chipewyan and other northern Indian groups, it also attracted some Cree bands who had formerly traded at York Factory. This was in part the consequence of the practice of the Churchill traders of applying the factors' standard less rigorously in the early years than was the case at York Factory (Figure 36). Therefore, although the official standards at the two posts were nearly identical, the actual prices (in furs) of trade goods at Churchill were less than those at York Factory. The traders at the latter post were quick to object to this 'abuse.' James Knight, who was in charge at Fort Churchill at the time, responded to these complaints by saying that every effort was being made to discourage the 'York Factory Indians' from coming to his post.[11]

Similarly, at the bottom of the bay the company men kept as close an eye on the activities of their fellow traders as they did on the French. Many of the letters written to London by the traders at Moose Factory and Fort Albany charged that trade practices at the one post hurt business at the other. The London directors usually pursued these charges, since they wanted to keep disruptive inter-post competition to a minimum, and the accused factors found it necessary to defend themselves. For example, when Thomas White embarked on his plan of lowering the factors' standard in the 1750s, the Albany traders viewed this action with misgivings since they feared it would draw some of the Indians away from their post. Feeling obliged to justify his actions, White wrote to London in 1751 saying: 'I am very sensible of the bad consequences of endeavouring to draw away Indians from one Factory to another, nor did I ever in all my time act in any such manner, but I very well know under some of your peevish Factors formerly who for want of a proper knowledge or I believe I may rather Say, want of honesty to support your Interest when I have had some Trades larger than common to have thrown such Aspersions before your Honours I cannot help if Indians of their own Inclinations come to one or any other Master of your Honours Factorys to Trade, such Indians I presume are not to be sent away packing with their goods to perhaps the French because they have been slighted by us ...'[12]

White's rebuttal of the charges is fairly typical of those given by other traders and serves to illustrate some of the constraints within which the factors were forced to operate. Any efforts to counter the French by drastically relaxing the unofficial standard, or taking other lines of action, ran the risk of undermining the trade of other company posts even though such a result was not intended. In brief, the policy of the company and the avowed objectives of the various factors were opposed to competition among Hudson's Bay Company posts.

Hinterland patterns: effects of French and Nor'wester competition
The fact that the variety of goods at all posts was essentially the same implies that, under the monopolistic conditions aspired to by the Hudson's Bay Company, no particular good had a greater drawing power (or 'range,' in central-place parlance) than any other. However, as the previous discussion suggested, this was not the case under competitive conditions. Nor was it the case given the cultural and physical diversity of the hinterland areas. The French, and later their successors, the Nor'westers, did not have access to central and western Canada via the Hudson Bay. Rather, they were forced to ship their furs and goods by canoe to and

from Montreal through inland waterways and over numerous portages. Consequently, their transportation systems placed severe constraints on the quantities and types of goods which they could use in the trade. With respect to trade goods, the French *coureurs de bois* and the peddlers were unable to transport a sufficient range or quantity of bulky or heavy items to satisfy Indian demands (among the most important of these kinds of goods were kettles and guns). Instead, they relied on trade items which were lighter, less bulky, and thus more suitable to canoe transportation.

Indeed, following the invasion of the northwest by the peddlers in the 1760s, a curious pattern of trade developed at the bottom of the bay in which the Indians traded most of their small, high value furs with the peddlers for a variety of light-weight goods and visited the Hudson's Bay Company posts at more irregular intervals to exchange their bulkier furs for guns and kettles. Since the company continually urged the factors to obtain as many 'small furs' as was possible, the trading pattern which was emerging placed the latter men in a difficult position. They had to encourage the Indians to bring down these other furs, but they could not refuse to take their lower value furs in the interim since in doing so they would run the risk of losing the Indian trade altogether.

The letters of John Favell from Moose Factory in the late 1760s highlight these problems and indicate the delicate diplomacy which was required. Regarding his trade during the summer of 1767, Favell wrote: '... you will find the Trade still meets with interruptions. ... will Endeavour at all Opportunitys if possible to persuade the Natives to bring all their Goods here. Those mention'd in Journal having only ... Quantity of furrs & most of them but indifferent, I Traded their Goods & used them exceeding well; but at the same time/ in order to induce them to bring all their Furrs in future/ I told em if They did not bring Martens & Otters etc. as well as Beaver & Musquash, That They need not expect to be supplied by me with those particular Articles, such as Guns & Twine, for, Numbers of them only come for those very things & that perhaps but once in two Years or 2 & ½. All which went away very well Pleased. Some of them said They would come again next year, and bring all their goods & small Furrs, & Others plainly told me/ tho very well satisfied with my Treatment/ that they should not come here any more, till such time as They stood in need of those particular Articles again ...'[13] Thus, Favell mixed good treatment with threats and achieved partial success.

However, one of the problems with this course of action was that the peddlers were apparently using some of the Indians to obtain a supply of guns. The traders at Albany became suspicious of this practice and in a postscript to their annual report to London in 1770 stated: 'Whether Your Hons Trade hath been prejudiced by the Inland European Traders getting Possession of some of Your heavy Goods, is hard to determine. Your Council have Suspicions some what of this Nature. We imagine that the Inland Traders realy Employ Indians to bring to Your Settlements Old worn Beaver Coats and damag'd and Stage [summer] Furrs, as now & then a Cannoe doth come down with such sort of Goods, on such Bundles of Goods being Opend for Trade, Mr. Marten hath allways Strongly taxed the bringers with his suspicions that They were Inland European Property, which the Indians hath as strongly denied, Alledging that They ... belonged to great Families who were Obliged to dress the Chief part of what Beaver They kill'd for their Winter Wear, that if Mr. Marten did not chuse to Trade their Furrs, They would come no more and would inform others that We were grown bad at Albany and would not Trade Beaver Coats ...'[14] Although the Indians denied the charges made by Marten, there was nonetheless considerable evidence that they were in fact 're-trading' guns and other articles to the peddlers. Considering that the Hudson's Bay Company was trading firearms at the rate of ten to twelve beaver each at the bottom of the bay while the peddlers charged up to forty beaver for them, it is clear that both the Indians and the Nor'westers could have profited from such a trade.

Besides the greater drawing power or 'range' of guns and kettles under competitive conditions, the Hudson's Bay Company had large quantities of Brazil tobacco available for barter and gift-giving, and this was strongly preferred to that of the French. There is little doubt that this tobacco played a major part in the company's efforts to offset the influence of the French and later the peddlers. In fact, Anthony Henday reported in 1755 that, on the basis of his experiences inland, he believed the company would lose the trade to the French altogether without Brazil tobacco.[15] Granting that Henday exaggerated the case somewhat, his observations nonetheless underscored the significance which this luxury good played in the trade.

Thus, under competitive conditions, the Indians began using the rival trade networks of the English and French as central-place theory would predict. That is, they traded more frequently with the closer French 'posts' for goods in constant need, such as powder and flints, while they made much less frequent trips (only once every two to three years in some cases) to the more distant Hudson's Bay Company posts for certain luxuries and for bulkier goods like kettles and guns. As a rule these goods were more durable and did not need to be replaced each year. However, this pattern could not be construed as an indication that a true system of central places had arisen, since the primary attributes of such a system (hierarchical ordering of functions and locations, relationships between range and threshold of goods and umland radius) were absent.

LOCATION CONCEPTS: THE MERCANTILE MODEL

In view of the nature of the bayside posts as goods repositories frequented largely by middlemen, perhaps additional insight into the system can be obtained by viewing the spatial organization of the trade as an example of the location of wholesale establishments. The 'mercantile model' of wholesale trade developed by James Vance is of potential value in this context.[16] The essence of this model is that wholesale centres arise as link-places in a long-distance trade network connecting scattered, specialized producers with even more dispersed consumers. Unlike the central-place model, the mercantile model does not envisage the spatial organization of centres arising on the basis of proximity of services to tributary areas, but on the specialization and quality of these services. Hinterland size of wholesale establishments is based on the capacity of each establishment to provide a given quality of service and a particular level of specialization. Wholesale centres tend to emerge at locations which facilitate the collection and dissemination of goods in long-distance trade and become eventually the foci for the growth of central-place systems. The mercantile model was consciously applied by Vance to the explanation of evolving settlement patterns in the New World. Certainly, this model is capable of shedding light on the spatial organization and locational attributes of the Hudson's Bay Company posts.

Thus, the bayside posts fall readily into the category of link-places or 'places of attachment' envisaged by Vance. They were entrepôts and the quality of service they provided to specialized middlemen did indeed play a part in determining the hinterland size of individual posts. Competition among 'wholesale establishments,' as represented by the Hudson's Bay Company posts, and those of the French and Nor'Westers, hinged to a significant degree on the type and quality of goods stocked, and on readiness to provide the level of service demanded by their Indian clientele. This 'service' included satisfactory terms of trade, deferential treatment of Indian traders, and in some cases the provision of credit.

The mercantile model also illuminates certain aspects of the location of individual posts, for example, their transport orientation. The selection of tidewater sites on canoe routes was the most efficient locational solution from the company's point of view, since such locations were at a natural break-in-bulk point between relatively cheap ocean shipping and costly small craft transportation into the interior. Under earlier monopolistic conditions of trade, especially with the middlemen performing their redistribution and collection services to the interior, there was little economic incentive to the company to attempt to relocate closer to the actual fur sources. A minimal number of posts could cover a maximum area of fur-producing hinterland, and could be stocked and provisioned relatively easily by company ships. Under increasing competitive pressures, however, additional posts were built which not only tapped new supply areas but also, as has been shown, shortened the distances which many bands were required to traverse to reach a post, and otherwise improved services to the Indians. These newer posts represented a compromise between minimizing logistical costs of the system and increasing accessibility to the Indians for trade goods (and to the 'supply' of furs). The need to locate closer to the centre of fur trapping eventually led to the construction of inland trading posts after 1763. Thereafter followed a period in which the company and its reorganized competitors (the North West Company) engaged in a struggle for control over both routes for the movement of furs and access to the actual supply areas, which culminated in the construction of rival posts side by side in many locations. This activity is strongly reminiscent of the classic spatial duopoly case described by Hotelling.[17]

CONCEPTS OF SPATIAL INTERACTION

Some useful insights into the geography of the trade can be elicited from the application of general concepts of spatial interaction – complementarity, transferability, intervening opportunity, and substitutability – but again we need to preface this with the cautionary comment that such concepts lack adequate previous testing in transitional, cross-cultural interactions of the present type.

The concept of complementarity refers to the specific supply–demand relationship which comprises the condition necessary for movement of a commodity to take place. As originally defined,[18] the idea implies a market framework. There is difficulty in conceiving of complementarity as a precondition for gift trade, for example, since no specific demand for a gift need exist in order to generate its movement. However, in the present case, the concept seems to apply satisfactorily due to the elements of market behaviour present in this transitional form of exchange. Similarly, the notion of transferability is a market-based concept as originally de-fined, implying that all goods that move over distance have a value sufficient to overcome the costs of transportation. Again, the market cost of a gift may be considerably less in monetary terms than the cost of transporting the gift to a recipient. The 'real' value of the gift may be in its status qualities or associations (e.g., it may have 'sentimental value'). The concepts of intervening opportunity and substitutability do not necessar-ily imply market exchange, but they do assume rational economic be-haviour in which goods will not be transported over longer distances if they can be obtained in sufficient quantities from a closer source (inter-vening opportunity), and if it is more convenient to import the technolog-ical skills and materials needed for home production of the desired goods rather than importing them ready-made (substitutability).[19]

That a condition of complementarity existed as a basis for the fur trade is almost self-evident. There was a demand for Indian furs which could be satisfied by fulfiling the Indian demand for European goods. In both cases, the superior *qualities* rather than the *kinds* of goods were the prim-ary stimulus to trade. After all, European felt hats could be made from rabbit skins instead of beaver pelts; Indians already knew how to make hatchets, knives, utensils, and effective weapons, although they were quick to recognize the superiority of equivalent metal items produced by European technology. There was no possibility in either case of domestic production of the desired quality goods, nor (initially) any intervening location at which supplies could be obtained more conveniently. The spatial pattern of posts, trade routes, and hinterlands, therefore, evolved on the basis of these conditions as they were perceived by the parties to the exchange.

EFFECTS OF DISTANCE

The effect of distance on the diffusion of information and material goods within the hinterlands is a topic with much potential value, but at present insufficient empirical data exist for a detailed analysis to be presented here. Several points based on evidence in this study are, however, worth noting in connection with the effect of distance on diffusion. First, the trading system appears to have developed an efficient information net-work covering vast distances. This is evidenced by the responses of the Indians to the opening of new posts (e.g., 'York Factory Indians' diverting their trade to newly opened Fort Churchill), and their reactions to oppor-tunities and changing conditions opened up by English–French competition. The power of this information system is proven by the fact that traders generally took to heart the Indian threats to 'spread the word' about bad treatment or poor prices at posts such as Albany.[20] Second, it appears that diffusion of material goods and information was tightly controlled as long as the middlemen retained their crucial role and geographic position. They ensured that information on competitive terms of trade which filtered to the English traders worked to their own advantage, and stressed the perils of journeying to the bay in their dealings with trapping Indians to discourage them from attempting to make the trip. Goods filtered into areas beyond the middleman zone at a rate which was determined by the needs and movement patterns of trading bands, since most of these goods were passed on after having been used by the latter. It is interesting to speculate whether a distance decay effect operated on the diffusion pattern, since such effects are identifiable for many other forms of human interaction.[21] However, because of the nature of middleman activity, such a pattern is unlikely to be discernible from the archaeological record,[22] and no adequate alternative source of data on goods movement in the hinterlands is currently available.

Indian Perceptions of the 'Friction of Distance'
The evidence presented above concerning the spatial behaviour of Indians in the trade leads to some interesting conclusions concerning their perception of costs and benefits associated with the great distances frequently traversed in trading with the Europeans.

First, the existence of clear trade-offs between costs and gains from the journey to trade is suggested by their reaction to the price differences among Hudson's Bay Company posts touched upon earlier. If prices at Fort Churchill were sufficiently lower than at York, as was the case under James Knight's administration, the 'York Factory Indians' clearly considered this enough of an incentive to undertake what may have been a considerable increase in distance and difficulty of travel.

On the other hand, the Indian perception of 'trade-offs' under the competitive situation provided by the *coureurs de bois* shows their apparent willingness to pay higher prices for goods (from the French and the peddlers) in order to avoid the long and arduous journey down to the bay each year. Of course, their demand for bulkier items such as guns and kettles and for luxuries and high quality merchandise such as Brazil tobacco still drew them the extra distance to the bayside posts, but, as we have mentioned, at less frequent intervals.

TOWARD A CONCEPTUAL BASIS FOR COMPARATIVE ECONOMIC
GEOGRAPHY: SOME IMPLICATIONS OF THIS STUDY

The need for a comparative theoretical framework is increasingly being felt by economic and cultural geographers concerned with adequately explaining and assessing the significance of common phenomena such as market exchange in different types of societies. To date, however, the point has not been reached at which a body of spatial concepts, capable of being applied to patterns of economic activity in widely varied static and transitional societies, exists in a generally agreed upon form.

A problem with many existing spatial concepts is that they are not adequately geared to explanation of spatial phenomena in transitional (or even 'traditional') societies, nor in the special case of cross-cultural exchange. For example, concepts of location, spatial interaction, settlement formation, and regional development have mostly evolved and been tested in contexts of extant fairly evenly peopled 'Western' societies.[23] This is not to say that general spatial concepts, as a class, are inapplicable in non-Western contexts, just that the cross-cultural ramifications of these have yet to be fully thought through, and there is a possibility of ethnocentric bias in the interpretation of non-Western behavioural patterns, especially those of migratory peoples, in the light of these concepts.[24]

Many spatial concepts are actually based on the assumed existence of universal underlying processes which themselves are not necessarily spatial. For example, spatial diffusion is often regarded as a basic geographic process, and yet to say, for instance, that an innovation 'diffuses' is rather like saying 'the ink spilt': the causes or mechanisms are not specified in the concept itself. Yet, in the diffusion of innovations, basic differences in cultural attributes can radically affect the probabilities, processes, and hence patterns of spatial diffusion. Thus, *hierarchical diffusion* describes movement through an area in which human habitation is known or assumed to be organized on a central-place principle. *Wave diffusion* presupposes physical contact among carriers and potential recipients of the thing being diffused, i.e., a homogeneous medium for spatial diffusion.

In the practical application of these concepts and the ancillary techniques of analysis associated with them, some problems arise in the cases of traditional and transitional societies. For instance, a territory which is poly-cultural may have discontinuities in its diffusion probability surface which may or may not be revealed in the actual spatial pattern of diffusion: it may appear much as expected according to the conceptual representation. The problem may be revealed once interpretation or deeper analysis is attempted. For example, an area may display a hierarchy of settlements, but some levels of the hierarchy may not, in effect, service a portion of the area's population as expected, due to cultural differences in consumer travel.[25] To assume in this case that hierarchical diffusion will occur throughout the area in accordance with existing conceptualizations of this process may lead to serious error. Similarly, wave diffusion may take place in the usual fashion across a territory, but yet only touch certain *strata* in the culturally heterogeneous but uniformly distributed population. This situation is possible in some empirical cases of the diffusion of modernization.

Some of the drawbacks of existing conceptual frameworks in economic geography have been pointed out by a number of previous researchers. In discussing shortcomings of settlement concepts as applied to modernization, for example, Peter Gould has called for the development of a *dynamic* central-place theory capable of dealing with characteristics of transitional societies and explaining the evolution of systems of market centres.[26] But even this may not encompass all types of settlement (for example, agricultural villages in subsistence areas or special-purpose centres) where the principles of retail marketing of goods and services do not apply.

The point is, of course, that many of the concepts of economic geography are based on the assumed operation of market processes. Central-place theory as currently developed is one obvious example. Thunian agricultural location theory and the theory of manufacturing locations are others. Market-behavioural assumptions are particularly strong in normative location theories with their stress on transport cost minimization and market orientation. We have demonstrated earlier in this chapter that spatial interaction principles, particularly the concepts of complementarity and transferability, likewise carry this implicit assumption. Even in spatial concepts without specific dependence on the market principle, applications have in practice been overwhelmingly oriented towards market-based societies.

No doubt it is reasonable to argue that the great majority of cases which the economic geographer studies are market societies. However, the current upsurge of interest in periodic markets in various societies is leading researchers closer to situations where non-market behaviour is likely to be encountered. In addition, there are a significant number of past and extant societies of potential interest to geographers (such as the Hudson's Bay Company fur trade) where market concepts are not capable by themselves of giving a full account of the patterns and processes involved.

We do not advocate the development of separate spatial concepts to apply to non-market and market societies. In this respect, a useful lesson can be learned by examining the recent literature of economic anthropology, which contains a lively debate on the issue of whether such a dichotomy of economic institutions and motivations is or is not valid.[27] The present consensus of the leading protagonists in this debate seems to be that a single, unified set of concepts embracing both market and non-market forms of economic organization needs to be developed.[28] To date, however, a set of meaningful and truly universal concepts in comparative economics continues to elude practitioners in this field. Indeed, it may not be possible to develop such concepts. In geography, as we have indicated, a similar set of unified spatial concepts is equally desirable and elusive to this point. However, on the basis of findings in the present study, we venture to suggest some guidelines which may be employed in future endeavours towards the formulation of a conceptual framework for comparative economic geography. These guidelines relate to:

1/ The use of cross-cultural 'laboratories' for the testing of concepts. It will be difficult to fall into the trap of viewing exchange in 'Western' and 'traditional' societies as separate and discrete if attention is focused on the considerable amount of economic interaction, both past and present, that takes place between highly dissimilar cultures. There is a need for more empirical studies of such interaction, extending perhaps the kind of research undertaken in this book.

2/ The devotion of more attention to the cultural and economic bases of spatial processes such as diffusion, regional development, and urbanization. Generalizations about spatial processes may contain errors unless they look underneath at the non-spatial interactions and structures which house the mechanisms producing spatial organization, and, the relevant basic geographical features need to be carefully considered. While this is not a new idea, it is worth reiterating in view of the number of studies that apply concepts such as urbanization and diffusion without adequate consideration of this question.

3/ The need to develop dynamic rather than static models of location and spatial interaction, and to recognize that 'static' concepts may apply merely to the form or superficial appearance of patterns in transitional societies, while the function or social significance of the phenomena involved may have changed.

4/ The need to develop meaningful comparative concepts of structures and institutions as well as processes and behaviour. The conceptual dichotomy of normative versus behavioural is as unsatisfactory in dealing with the comparative study of spatial organizations as is the dichotomy of market versus non-market concepts.

To achieve the goal of devising a satisfactory conceptual scheme, it will be necessary for geographers to increase their familiarity with the work of economic anthropologists and historians as well as other scholars in the disciplinary borderlands which have as their focus the comparative analysis of economic activities in disparate cultures. The results will undoubtedly be of benefit to comparative economic geography and to neighbouring disciplines as well.

Appendix

Efforts to obtain a detailed picture of the sources of overplus have been hampered by the fact that the factors' standards were closely guarded secrets. The traders were reluctant to divulge this information even to the governor and committee. However, in 1715, the committee ordered Richard Staunton to send them an account of the factors' standard in use at Fort Albany. Staunton complied with this request and inserted it in the 1715 Fort Albany Account Book. Staunton's standard and the official company standard are included in Table 24 for comparative purposes. Tables 25 and 26 show the quantities and official values of the goods and furs that were exchanged at the post in 1715. Table 27 gives the official comparative standard and compares Staunton's standard to it. The difference in the estimated value of the returns derived by using the two sets of standards is given also. Table 28 compares Staunton's standard of trade to the official standard and provides an estimate of the overplus he could have derived from the different types of goods.

Regarding Table 28, it should be noted that the estimate of the total overplus gained amounts to 5698.97 MB. If 311 MB (the loss shown on Table 27) is subtracted, a net estimate of 5387.97 is obtained. This means that by not considering the marten trade we can account for 77 per cent of the overplus that Staunton reported in 1715 (Table 26). It is not possible to derive a more precise estimate because we do not know how the Indians spent the 4978 marten listed in Table 26. Presumably, the Indians would have avoided spending their marten, to the extent that they were able, on those goods for which the factor charged a marten premium (i.e., gun powder, kettles, beads, vermilion, guns, baggonets, fire steels, gun worms, twine, powder horns, painted boxes, broadcloth, and knives).

Since marten became one of the most prized furs, the low prices that

TABLE 24

The standards of trade at Fort Albany, 1715

'The Standard of Trade by Which I [Richard Staunton] have Traded By, to ye Best of my Knowledge Alby Fort July ye 25th 1716'	Official standard of trade, 1715	
Powder 1 lb. Pr Beaver & 1¼ pr 4 Martins	1½	lb. pr beaver
Shott 3¼ lb. Pr Beaver	5	lb. pr beaver
Kettles ¾ lb. Pr Beaver & 1 lb. pr 4 Martin	1	lb. pr beaver
Brazill Tobacco ½ lb. Pr Beaver & 1 lb. pr 4 Martin	1	lb. pr beaver
English Roll Tobacco 1 lb. pr. Beaver	1½	lb. pr beaver
Beads ½ lb pr Beaver & ¾ lb. pr 4 Martin	¾	lb. pr beaver
Vermillion ¾ of an Ounce pr Beaver & 1½ oz pr 4 Martins	1½	oz. pr beaver
Red Lead ¾ lb. Pr Beaver		(not listed)
Black Lead 1 lb. Pr. Beaver	1	lb. pr beaver
Thread ½ lb. Pr. Beaver	2	lb. pr beaver
Gunns of 3½ ft 8 Beaver Pr. Gunn or 32 Martins Pr. Gunn	8-10	beaver pr gun
Gunns of 4 ft: 10 Beaver pr Gunn	8-10	beaver pr gun
Flints 15 pr Beaver	20	pr beaver
Baggonetts 1 pr Beaver & 2 pr 4 Martins	2	pr beaver
Fire Steels 2 pr Beaver & 3 pr 4 Martins	4	pr beaver
Files 1 pr Beaver	1	pr beaver
Wormes [gun] 4 pr Beaver & 6 pr 4 Martins	4	pr beaver
Nett Lines 1 pr Beaver	2	pr beaver
Awle Blades 8 pr Beaver	12	pr beaver
Twine 1 Scaine pr Beaver & Ditto [1] pr 4 Martins	1	pr beaver
Spoones 2 pr [beaver]	4	pr beaver
Stockins 1 Pair Pr Beaver	1	pr beaver
Powder Hornes 1 pr Beaver & 2 Pr 4 Martins	2	pr beaver
Hatchetts 1 pr Beaver &	2	hatchets pr beaver
1 & 2 Knives Pr 4 Martins	8	knives pr beaver
Painted Boxes 2 pr Beaver & 3 pr 4 Martins	4	pr beaver
Shirts 1 pr Beaver	1	pr beaver
Combs 1 pr Beaver	2	pr beaver
Tobacco Tongs 1 Pair pr Beaver & 2 Pair pr 4 Martins		(not listed)
Tobacco Boxes 1 pr Beaver		(not listed)
Pewter Buttons 60 pr Beaver	12	doz pr beaver
Rings 6 pr Beaver		(not listed)

were being paid to the Indians for it in 1715 warrant a brief comment. It appears that marten were abundant around the fort at that time. In 1716 Thomas McCliesh reported 'here has been plenty of Martins this winter about the factory, in such plenty that several drowned themselves in our pickle cask.'[1] Since marten were plentiful in the vicinity of the post, McCliesh sent company men out to trap them, and during the winter of

TABLE 24 cont'd.

'The Standard of Trade by Which I [Richard Staunton] have Traded By, to ye Best of my Knowledge Alby Fort July ye 25th 1716'	Official standard of trade, 1715	
Hawks Bells 12 pr. Beaver	16	pr beaver
Ice Chissels 1 pr Beaver	2	pr beaver
Scrappers 2 pr Beaver	2	pr beaver
Leather Looking Glasses 1 pr Beaver & 2 pr 4 Martin		(not listed)
Borad Cloth 1¾ Yd pr 5 Beaver & 2 Yds pr 20 Martins	1	yd pr 2 beaver
Baies & Flannel 1 Yard pr Beaver		(not listed)
Duffles 1 yd pr 2 Beaver	1½	yd pr. beaver
Blankets 7 Beaver pr Blanket	1	pr 6 beaver
Brandy 1½ pint pr Beaver & 1 Quart pr 4 Martins	1	gal. pr 4 beaver

All which gives good satisfaction to ye Indians at Present

(signed) Richard Staunton

'It is to be noted I have traded, the rest of ye Small furrs as follows, by reason, our next Door Neighbours, ye French gives great Encouragement for Small Furrs, to what they give for Beaver; Notwithstanding all ye Indians that came here; that traded with ye French Last winter up this river Told me that we given near Double the value for Small Furrs to what they give, Catts excepted; & three times the Value for Beaver, to what they give, And for their future Encouragement, I have promised to trade our 10 Skin Gunns pr 6 Catts p Gunn & ye eight Skinn Guns for 5 Catts pr Gunn.'

Staunton's comparative	Official comparative
1 Catt as 2 Beaver	1 cat as 1 beaver
1 Quaquatch [Wolverine] as 1½ Beaver	2 quaquatches as 1 beaver
1 Fox as 1 Beaver	(not listed)
1 Otter as 1 Beaver	2 otter as 1 beaver
1 Bear as 2 Beaver	1 bear as 2 beaver
1 Cubb [bear] as 1 Beaver	1 cub as 1 beaver
1 lb Castorum as 1 Beaver	1 lb. castorum as 1 beaver
10 lbs. Feathers as 1 Beaver	10 lbs. feathers as 1 beaver

SOURCE: PAC HBC B 3/d/23, pp. 3-4, 21-42

1715–16, they brought in 1100 marten. Given that marten could be readily obtained locally in 1715, there would have been little reason to encourage the Indians to bring them in.

Table 29 lists the top twenty trade goods in order of their importance as sources for overplus.

TABLE 25

Goods traded at Fort Albany, 1715

Goods	Quantity		Official value in MB
Powder	3016	lbs.	2010.66
Shot	9284	lbs.	1856.80
Brazil Tobacco	931	lbs.	931
Virginia Tobacco	0		0
English Roll Tobacco	182	lbs.	121.33
Beads	131.5	lbs.	175.33
Vermilion	16	lbs.	170.66
Black lead	0		0
White lead	0		0
Thread	11.75	lbs.	23.50
Kettles (290)	804	lbs.	804
Guns	271		2250
Pistols	6		24
Twine	1307	scaines	1307
Hawks Bells	936		58.50
Awls	774		64.50
Needles	332		27.66
Shirts	40		40
Stockins	8	pr	8
Shoes	0		0
Yarn gloves	2		2
Cargo breeches	0		0
Pewter buttons	576		4
Blottin buttons	216		3
Ice chissels	181		90.50

TABLE 25 cont'd.

Goods	Quantity	Official value in MB
Hatchets	473	236.50
Wormes	112	28
Scrapers	15	7.50
Net lines	160	80
Steeles	407	101.75
Flints	3500	175
Knives	3365	420.62
Combs	0	0
Scissors	12	6
Spoons	27	6.75
Egg boxes (colored)	29	7.25
Hand cuffs	11	11
Laced hats	4	16
Mocotogans	15	7.50
Sword blades	0	0
Powder horns	8	4
Files	69	69
Blankets	49	294
Baggonets	97	48.50
Brandy	145⅜ gals.	581.50
Flannell	13	13
Cotton	28 yds.	28
Broad cloth	1324 yds.	2648
Duffels	205 yds.	307.50
		15,186 Total value
		[15,069.81]

SOURCE: PAC HBC B 3/d/23, p. 11

TABLE 26

'Furrs and other Commodites Received In ye Trade of Ye aforesaid Goods'

14447	Whole Parcht Beaver
3844	Coate Beaver
1752	In 3504 Half Parcht [beaver]
1244½	In 4978 Martins
2½	In 5 Foxes
7	In 7 Woolfes
175	In 175 Cats
93½	In 187 Otters
20	In 40 Quequachatchs
60	In 30 Black Bears
11	In 11 Cubbs
96	In 48 Moose
304	In 304 lb. Castorum
51	In 510 lb. Feathers
106½	In 1704 Moose Hoofes

22214	[MB]
	From which Deducting the Value of ye Goods Perr Standard theire are over Plus gain'd on this Trade
15186³⁷⁄₄₆	

7027⁹⁄₄₆ [overplus]

SOURCE: PAC HBC B 3/d/23, p. 11

TABLE 27

Fort Albany, 1715: the official comparative standard and Richard Staunton's standard

Commodity	Official price in MB	Staunton's price in MB	Percentage change	Quantity traded	Value of Trade official	actual	Gain/ loss*
Whole parchment beaver	1 = 1	1 = 1	0	14,447	14,447	14,447	0
Coat beaver	1 = 1	1 = 1	0	3,844	3,844	3,844	0
Half parchment beaver	1 = 1½	1 = 1½	0	3,504	1,752	1,752	0
Marten	4 = 1	4 = 1	0	4,978	1,244½	1,244½	0
Fox	1 = ½	1 = 1	100	5	2½	5	−2½
Wolf	1 = 1	1 = 1	0	7	7	7	0
Cat	1 = 1	1 = 2	100	175	175	350	−175
Otter	1 = ½	1 = 1	100	187	93½	187	−93½
Wolverine	1 = ½	1 = 1½	200	40	20	60	−40
Black bear	1 = 2	1 = 2	0	30	60	60	0
Cub bear	1 = 1	1 = 1	0	11	11	11	0
Moose	1 = 2	1 = 2	0	48	96	96	0
Castorum (lb.)	1 = 1	1 = 1	0	304	304	304	0
Feathers (lb.)	10 = 1	10 = 1	0	510	51	51	0
Moose hoves	16 = 1	16 = 1	0	1,704	106½	106½	0
					22,214	21,903	−311

SOURCE: Tables 24, 25 and 26
* Relative to the official value

TABLE 28

Fort Albany, 1715: the official standard and Richard Staunton's standard

Item	Price (MB)			Qty traded	Value of trade (MB)		Overplus gained (MB)	
	Official	Staunton's	Percentage increase		Official Value	Staunton's Value	A	B (if paid in marten)
Gun Powder, lb.	.666	1.00	+51.51	3016	2010.66	3016	1005.34	
or	.666	3.20	+380.4	3016	2010.66	(9651)	—	7640.54
Shot, lb.	.200	.307	+53.50	9284	1856.80	2850	993.20	
Brazil Tobacco, lb.	1.000	2.00	+100.00	931	931.00	1862	931.00	
Kettles, lb.	1.000	1.33	+33.00	804	804.00	1069	265.32	
or	1.000	4.00	+300.00	804	804.00	(3216)	—	2412.00
English Roll Tobacco, lb.	.666	1.000	+51.51	182	121.33	182	60.67	
Beads, lb.	1.333	2.000	+50.37	131.5	175.33	263	87.67	
or	1.333	5.333	+300.00	131.5	175.33	(701.28)	—	525.95
Vermillion, Oz.	.666	1.333	+100.15	256 oz	170.66	341.2	170.58	
or	.666	.735	+10.36	256 oz	170.66	(188.16)	—	17.50
Red Lead, lb.	1.333	1.333	0	0	0	0	0	
Black Lead, lb.	1.000	1.000	0	0	0	0	0	
Thread, lb.	2.00	2.00	0	11.75	23.50	23.50	0	
Guns, each	8.13*	8.40	+3	271.00	2250.00	2279.00	29.00	
or	8.13*	28.67	+252.64	271.00	2250.00	(7769.57)	—	5519.57
Flints, each	.050	.066	+32	3500	175.00	231.00	56.00	
Baggonets, one pair	.500	1.000	+100	97	48.50	97.00	48.50	
or	.500	2.000	+300	97	48.50	(194.00)	—	145.50
Fire Steels, each	.250	.500	+100	407	101.75	203.50	101.75	
or	.250	1.333	+433	407	101.75	(541.31)	—	439.56
Files	1.000	1.000	0	69	69.00	69.00	0	
Worms (Gun), each	.250	.250	0	112	28.00	28.00	0	
or	.250	.666	−12	112	28.00	(166.40)	—	138.40

TABLE 28 cont'd.

Item	Price (MB) Official	Staunton's	Percentage increase	Qty traded	Value of trade (MB) Official Value	Staunton's Value	Overplus gained (MB) A	B (if paid in marten)
Net lines, each	.500	1.000	+100.0	160	80.0	160	80	160
Awl blades	.083	.125	+50.0	774	64.5	96.75	32.25	
Twine, scaine	1.000	1.000	0.0	1307	1307.0	1307.00	0	
or	1.000	4.000	+300.0	1307	1307.0	(5228.00)	—	3921.00
Spoons, each	.250	.500	+100.0	27	6.7	13.50	6.8	
Stockings, pair	1.000	1.000	0.0	8	8.0	8.0	0	
Powder horn, each	.500	1.000	+100.0	8	4.00	8.0	4	
or	.500	2.00	+300.0	8	4.00	(16.00)		12.00
Hatchet, each	.500	1.000	+100.0	473	236.50	473.00	236.50	
Painted Box, each	.250	.500	+100.0	29	7.25	14.50	7.25	
or	.250	1.333	+433.0	29	7.25	(38.57)		31.32
Shirts, each	1.000	1.000	0.0	40	40.00	40.00	0	
Combs	.500	1.000	+100.0	0	—	—	—	
Tobacco tongs, pair	—	1.000	—	0	—	—	—	
or	—	.660	—	0	—	—	—	—
Pewter buttons, each	.0069	.016	—	576	4.00	9.21	5.21	
Blottin buttons, each	.013	—	—	0	—	—	—	
Rings	—	.166	—	0	—	—	—	
Hawks bells, each	.0625	.083	+33.8	936	58.5	77.68	19.18	
Ice chissels	.500	1.000	+100.0	181	90.5	181.00	90.50	
Scrappers	.500	.500	0.0	15	7.5	7.50	0	
Leather looking glasses	—	1.000	—	0	—	—	—	
or	—	.665	—	0	—	—	—	—
Broad Cloth, yd.	2.00	2.85	+42.5	1324	2648.0	3773.4	1125.4	
or	2.00	10.00	400.0	1324	2648.0	(13,240.00)	—	10,592.0
Duffles, yd.	1.50	2.00	33.33	205	307.5	410.0	102.5	

TABLE 28 cont'd.

Item	Price (MB) Official	Staunton's	Percentage increase	Qty traded	Value of trade (MB) Official Value	Staunton's Value	Overplus gained (MB) A	B (if paid in marten)
Blanket	6.00	7.000	+16	49.0	294	343	49	—
Flannel, 1 yd.	1.00	1.000	0	13.0	13	13	0	
Brandy, gal.	4.00	5.333	+33	145.0	581.50	772.8	191.35	
Knives	.125	.125	0	3365.0	420.62	420.62	0	
or	.125	2.66	+2028	3365.0	420.62	(8950.9)	—	8530.28
Pistols	4.00	4.00	0	6.0	24.00	24.00	—	
Needles	.08	.08	0	332.0	27.66	27.66	—	
Yarn Gloves, pair	1.00	1.00	0	2.0	2.00	2.00	—	
Scissors	.50	.50	0	12.0	6.00	6.00	—	
Hand cuffs	1.00	1.00	0	11.0	11.00	11.00	—	
Laced hats	4.00	4.00	0	4.0	16.00	16.00	—	
Mocotogans	.50	.50	0	15.0	7.50	7.50	—	
Cottons, yd.	1.00	1.00	0	28.0	28.00	28.00	—	
					15,066.25†	20,765.32‡	5,698.97	

* Average price
† This figure was calculated by multiplying quantity by price. It differs slightly from the amount recorded in Table 25 due to rounding of MB prices.
‡ Excluding values in parentheses
SOURCE: Tables 24 and 25.

TABLE 29

Fort Albany, 1715: sources of overplus

Rank	Item	Estimated overplus*	Percentage of total estimated overplus	Cumulative percentage
1	Broadcloth	1125.40	19.74	19.74
2	Gun powder	1005.34	17.64	37.38
3	Shot	993.20	17.42	54.80
4	Brazil tobacco	931.00	16.33	71.13
5	Kettles	265.00	4.64	75.77
6	Hatchets	236.00	4.14	79.91
7	Brandy	191.00	3.35	83.26
8	Vermilion	170.58	2.99	86.25
9	Duffles	102.50	1.79	88.04
10	Fire steels	101.75	1.78	89.82
11	Ice chisels	90.50	1.58	91.40
12	Beads	87.67	1.53	92.93
13	Net lines	80.00	1.40	94.33
14	English tobacco	60.67	1.06	95.39
15	Flints	56.00	.98	96.37
16	Blankets	49.00	.85	97.22
17	Baggonets	48.50	.85	98.07
18	Awl blades	32.25	.56	98.63
19	Guns	29.00	.50	99.13
20	Hawks bells	19.18	.33	99.46

* Column A, Table 28

Notes

1 Probably the most insightful over-all studies of the Hudson's Bay Company's trading system in Canada are those of E.E. Rich: *The Fur Trade and the Northwest to 1857* and *The Hudson's Bay Company, 1660–1870*.

2 This literature is particularly extensive and biographies have been written of many of the key European traders.

3 Among the more notable and relevant of these studies are: H.P. Biggar, *The Early Trading Companies of New France*; L.R. Masson, *Les Bourgeois de la Compagnie du Nord-Ouest*; Rich, *The Hudson's Bay Company*; and W. Wallace, *Documents Relating to the North West Company*.

4 Rich's *The Fur Trade* is an example as is J. Galbraith, *The Hudson's Bay Company as an Imperial Factor, 1821–69*.

5 The North West Company, for example, consisted of a series of partnerships of different firms, each of which kept a set of books dealing with its aspects of operations. The lack of a good set of account books dealing with all aspects of the company made final settlement of its accounts difficult after it merged with the Hudson's Bay Company in 1821. The confused state of North West Company affairs led to extensive litigation, but many cases could not be resolved because of the lack of adequate records.

6 Harold A. Innis, *The Fur Trade in Canada*

7 Ibid., 401–2

8 Ibid., 383

9 Rich, *The Fur Trade*, 9–14. For a good discussion of the French–Huron alliance and the Iroquois, see C. Heidenreich, *Huronia*, 237–80.

10 Rich, 'Trade Habits and Economic Motivation Among the Indians of North America,' 38, 46–9

11 Ibid., 42ff

12 A. Rotstein, 'Fur Trade and Empire: An Institutional Analysis,' 18
13 Ibid., 13–14
14 Ibid., 16
15 Ibid.
16 Heidenreich, *Huronia*, 219–80
17 Ibid., 225–6
18 Ibid., 226
19 Ibid., 230
20 Ibid., 229, 247–8
21 C.A. Bishop, *The Northern Ojibwa and the Fur Trade*, ix
22 Ibid., 308–35. See also Heidenreich, *Huronia*, Map 24
23 Ibid., 206–20 and C.A. Bishop, 'The Emergence of Hunting Territories Among the Northern Ojibwa,' 1–15. For a discussion of the hunting range system see E.S. Rogers, *The Hunting Group–Hunting Territory Complex Among the Mistassini Indians*.
24 A.J. Ray, *Indians in the Fur Trade*
25 Ibid., 61–8, 137–43, 195–6

CHAPTER 2

1 Karl Polanyi, 'Our Obsolete Market Mentality,' 66–7
2 C.P. Lucas, *The Beginnings of English Overseas Enterprise*, 16
3 T.K. Rabb, *Enterprise and Empire*, 1
4 Ibid., 1, and G. Cawston and A. H. Keane, *The Early Chartered Companies*, 1–9
5 Rabb, *Enterprise and Empire*, 1; and Cawston and Keane, *Early Chartered Companies*, 20–31.
6 Cawston and Keane, *Early Chartered Companies*, 8–9
7 Rabb, *Enterprise and Empire*, 2
8 Cawston and Keane, *Early Chartered Companies*, 9–11
9 Ibid., 9–10. For an in-depth history of the evolution of the English stock companies see W.R. Scott's classic study, *The Constitution & Finance of English, Scottish & Irish Joint-Stock Companies to 1720*.
10 Chester Martin, 'The Royal Charter'
11 Cawston and Keane, *Early Chartered Companies*, 160
12 For a discussion of these concepts by a 'substantivist scholar,' see M.D. Sahlins, *Tribesmen*, 20–1.
13 C.E. Heidenreich, *Huronia*, 81, 276, 280
14 C.A. Bishop, *The Northern Ojibwa and The Fur Trade*, 7
15 A.J. Ray, *Indians in The Fur Trade*, 177
16 Bishop, *Northern Ojibwa*, 341–4

17 G. Williams, *Andrew Graham's Observations on Hudson's Bay, 1767–91*, 169–70
18 For a good discussion of this subject, see Bishop, 'The Emergence of Hunting Territories Among the Northern Ojibwa.'
19 Ray, *Indians in the Fur Trade*, 203
20 Ibid., 203
21 For a discussion of this tenure system, see E.S. Rogers, *The Hunting Group-Hunting Territory Complex Among the Mistassini Indians*, 82
22 C.E. Heidenreich and A.J. Ray, *The Early Fur Trades*, 15–18

CHAPTER 3

1 H.P. Biggar, *The Early Trading Companies of New France*, 18–32; and A.G. Bailey, *The Conflict of European and Eastern Algonkian Cultures, 1504–1700*, 4–8
2 Bailey, *European and Eastern Algonkian Cultures*, 6–7
3 H.A. Innis, *The Fur Trade in Canada*, 11–12
4 Ibid., 12
5 For a more detailed discussion on coat and parchment beaver see chapter 4.
6 Innis, *Fur Trade*, 9–10
7 Ibid., 16
8 Biggar, *Early Trading Companies*, 32
9 Ibid., 18–28
10 Ibid., 34
11 Innis, *Fur Trade*, 15
12 Biggar, *Early Trading Companies*, 79–82
13 R.G. Thwaites, *The Jesuit Relations and Allied Documents*, VI: 297–9
14 Biggar, *Early Trading Companies*, 66
15 Ibid., 67–8
16 C.E. Heidenreich, *Huronia*, 87–8 and Map 22
17 Biggar, *Early Trading Companies*, 70–1
18 Ibid., 80–4; and Heidenreich, *Huronia*, 233–4
19 Heidenreich, *Huronia*, 264–75; and Heidenreich and A.J. Ray, *The Early Fur Trades*, 20–31
20 Heidenreich, *Huronia*, 276; and Heidenreich and Ray, *Early Fur Trades*, 22
21 Innis, *Fur Trade*, 37
22 E.E. Rich, *The Fur Trade and the Northwest to 1857*, 19
23 Ibid., 20
24 Ibid.
25 Arthur T. Adams, *The Explorations of Pierre Esprit Radisson*, xxiii
26 Rich, *Fur Trade*, 23; and Adams, *Radisson*, xxiii–xxiv
27 Rich, *Fur Trade*, 28–9

CHAPTER 4

1 E. E. Rich, *The Fur Trade and The Northwest to 1857*, 27–33
2 Ibid., 35–6
3 Ibid., 36
4 Ibid., 37
5 Ibid., 40
6 W.J. Eccles, *The Canadian Frontier, 1534–1760*, 109–11; and Rich, *Fur Trade*, 40
7 Rich, *Fur Trade*, 41–2; and A.S. Morton, *The Canadian West to 1870–71*, 81–4
8 Eccles, *Canadian Frontier*, 104
9 Ibid., 115
10 Ibid., 107–9
11 Rich, *Fur Trade*, 44
12 Ibid., 45–6
13 Ibid., 46
14 Ibid., 42
15 For a detailed discussion of this period of fur trade history see Morton, *Canadian West*, 53–124; and Rich, *Fur Trade*, 45–68.
16 Eccles, *Canadian Frontier*, 109–10; and Arthur J. Ray, *Indians in the Fur Trade*, 4–14
17 Rich, *Fur Trade*, 83
18 Ray, *Indians in the Fur Trade*, 51–3
19 Glyndwr Williams, *Andrew Graham's Observations on Hudson's Bay, 1767–91*, 263
20 Quoted in E.E. Rich, *Cumberland House Journals and Inland Journal 1775–82*, First Series, 1775–9, xix
21 Ibid., xix–xx
22 Hudson's Bay Company, Correspondence Outward (from London), Official, Public Archives of Canada, Hudson's Bay Company Microfilm Collection (hereinafter PAC HBC) A 6/8, 118d
23 Ibid., A 6/10, 18d
24 Williams, *Graham's Observations*, 261

CHAPTER 5

1 Arthur J. Ray, *Indians in the Fur Trade*, 72–91
2 Ibid., 27–32
3 For a thorough discussion of Ojibwa expansion, see C.A. Bishop, *The Northern Ojibwa and the Fur Trade*, 308–32.
4 Bishop, *Northern Ojibwa*, 325; and Ray, *Indians in the Fur Trade*, 12–23
5 Bishop, *Norhtern Ojibwa*, 309–10

6 Ray, *Indians in the Fur Trade*, 11–13
7 Bishop, *Northern Ojibwa*, 310–11; and Ray, *Indians in the Fur Trade*, 9–11
8 Bishop, *Northern Ojibwa*, 310–11
9 Ray, *Indians in the Fur Trade*, 11
10 Ibid., 1–12
11 E.E. Rich, *Minutes of the Hudson's Bay Company, 1679–1684, 1st Part 1679–82*, 254–5
12 Ray, *Indians in the Fur Trade*, 4–6 and 14
13 Ibid., 14–16
14 Ibid., 18
15 Ibid., 51–9
16 Ibid., 55
17 For example, in 1716, the ship did not arrive on time and Indians who waited for it were said to have suffered terrible losses on their return home as a consequence. Ibid., 60
18 The inability to use canoes and the great distances were the reasons cited by the Blackfoot for not undertaking a voyage to York Factory in 1772. L.J. Burpee, '... The Journal of Matthew Cocking, Second at York Factory, In Order to Take a View of the Inland Country, and to Promote the Hudson's Bay Company's Interest ... 1772–1773,' 111. Yet, some Blood and Blackfoot had come to York Factory prior to Cocking's trip. See, Ray, *Indians in the Fur Trade*, 20, 55–9
19 Burpee, 'Journal of a Journey Performed by Anthony Hendry: to Explore the Country inland and to Increase the Hudson's Bay Company's Trade, A.D. 1754–55,' 338
20 Ray, *Indians in the Fur Trade*, 59
21 E.E. Rich, *The Fur Trade and the Northwest to 1857*, 97–8; and Fort Churchill Post Journals, 1718–53, B 42/a/2–40
22 Ray, *Indians in the Fur Trade*, 90
23 For an explanation of the made beaver unit of value (MB) see chapter 6, p. 54. A full discussion of the overplus, or the difference between the total MB of furs received and the value in MB of goods bartered in exchange, is provided in chapter 9.

CHAPTER 6

1 For a useful discussion of this facet of the trade see, E.E. Rich, *History of the Hudson's Bay Company*, vol. 1, 44–51.
2 Ibid., 46 and 258f
3 Karl Polanyi, 'The Semantics of Money Uses,' 175–201

4 E.E. Rich, 'Trade Habits and Economic Motivation Among the Indians of North America,' 43–5. It should be noted that there is no evidence that wampum was used as a medium of exchange in the subarctic.

5 G. Williams, ed., *Andrew Graham's Observations on Hudson's Bay 1767–91*, 316

6 Ibid., 317. James Isham provides a similar but less detailed account of this sequence of events. See E.E. Rich, ed., *James Isham's Observations on Hudson's Bay, 1743*, 82–5.

7 Williams, *Graham's Observations*, 317

8 Ibid., 318

9 Ibid., 319

10 Ibid., 319. See also Rich, *Isham's Observations*, 82–5.

11 Williams, *Graham's Observations*, 318. Edward Umfreville, who served under Graham, provides an account of the trading ceremony that is very similar to that of Isham and Graham. Indeed, he may have used the accounts of these two men to draft his own observations. See Edward Umfreville, *The Present State of Hudson's Bay*, 28–32.

12 Williams, *Graham's Observations*, 319

13 Umfreville, *Present State*, 19

14 Rich, 'Trade Habits,' 44. An added reason for employing the 'hole-in-the-wall' was that the Indians believed they had the right to ask for and receive any item they saw regardless of whether or not they had furs to exchange for it.

15 Williams, *Graham's Observations*, 320

16 Ibid., 320–1

17 Ibid., 321

18 Rich, 'Trade Habits,' 42–3, and A. Rotstein, 'Fur Trade and Empire,' 53–61

19 Rotstein, 'Fur Trade and Empire,' 73–9

20 Ibid., 73

21 For example, Rotstein said: 'there were important differences [between Europeans and Indians], more when it came to trade than to politics. European traders were oriented on profits, on fluctuating prices for their staples, in Europe, and tended to regard economic transactions as arm's length and impersonal activities. None of this is true for the Indian tribes whom they encountered. Trade was a highly personal activity, an encounter of two political groups or their representatives (not of individuals) and followed established political patterns.' Ibid., 46–7

22 E.E. Rich, *Copy Book of Letters Outward*, 9

23 Ibid., 12–13

24 Ibid., 196–200

25 E.E. Rich, *Minutes of the Hudson's Bay Company, 1679–1684, 1st Part 1679–82*, 253–7

CHAPTER 7

1 G. Williams, ed., *Andrew Graham's Observations on Hudson's Bay, 1767–91*, 169–70; and Edward Umfreville, *The Present State of Hudson's Bay*, 22–3
2 Williams, *Graham's Observations*, 323–4. See also Rich, *Isham's Observations on Hudson's Bay, 1743*, 85–6.
3 K.G. Davies, ed., *Letters From Hudson Bay, 1703–40*, 136–7
4 Williams, *Graham's Observations*, 324
5 Ibid., 320
6 Rich, *Isham's Observations*, 49–58
7 Williams, *Graham's Observations*, 322
8 Ibid.
9 I. Cowie, *The Company of Adventurers*, 276
10 Williams, *Graham's Observations*, 322
11 R. Glover, ed., *A Journey from Prince of Wales Fort in Hudson's Bay to the Northern Ocean...by Samuel Hearne*, 186–7
12 Williams, *Graham's Observations*, 316
13 Ibid., 320
14 Ibid., 321
15 E.E. Rich, ed., *Hudson's Bay Copy Booke of Letters Commissions Instructions Outward, 1688–96*, 185
16 A.J. Ray, *Indians in the Fur Trade*, 67–8
17 Davies, *Letters from Hudson Bay*, 295
18 Williams, *Graham's Observations*, 322
19 Davies, *Letters from Hudson Bay*, 82, 121n
20 Ibid., 121n

CHAPTER 9

1 The most significant gap is in the York Factory record for the period from 1694 to 1714 when the French held control of the post. Also, there are a few gaps in the accounts of Eastmain before 1714.
2 One of the authors has published a guide to these records, and the present chapter draws heavily on that source. See Arthur J. Ray, 'The Early Hudson's Bay Company Account Books as Sources for Historical Research: An Analysis and Assessment.'
3 E.E. Rich, *Hudson's Bay Copy Booke of Letters Commissions Instructions Outward*, 12
4 Ibid., 88
5 Ibid., 120
6 Ibid., 122–3

7 Ibid., 27
8 Fort Albany Account Books, 1698, PAC HBC B 3/d/8
9 Rich, *Copy Booke*, 124. In a letter written to Pierre Esprit Radisson on 20 May 1686 the governor and committee wrote: 'We will also that you be permitted by the Governor & every one else to dispose such presents as you shall thinke fitting to the Captaines of the Nations to further our Trade & oblige them to bring their Families Downe.' 198
10 Ibid., 124
11 Ibid., 127
12 K. Davies, *Letters From Hudson Bay, 1703–40*, 255
13 Ibid.
14 Rich, *Copy Booke*, 126–7
15 G. Williams, *Andrew Graham's Observations on Hudson's Bay, 1767–91*, 277–80
16 See, for example, Fort Churchill Account Books, 1724–25, PAC HBC B 42/d/5.
17 Fort Albany Account Books, 1698, PAC HBC B 3/d/8
18 Ibid.
19 Correspondence Outward, PAC HBC A 6/4, p. 51
20 Ibid., A 6/6, pp. 50–1
21 Davies, *Letters from Hudson Bay*, 295
22 Correspondence Outward, PAC HBC A 6/5, p. 93
23 Ibid., A 6/5, pp. 10–11
24 Ibid., A 6/6, p. 6
25 Ibid., Letter of 1 May 1740, A 6/6, p. 69
26 Ibid., A 6/7, p. 26
27 For instance, in their 4 June 1719 letter to Kelsey and the council at York Factory, the governor and committee wrote: '... wee have Certain Information that a very Great Quantity of Martins as well as other sorts of Furrs ..., were Brought home as Private Trade, in our Shipps, The last Year and sold to Several Furriers from some Hundred pounds ...' Ibid., A 6/7, pp. 28–9.

CHAPTER 10

1 The distortion of the picture is not as serious as it might have been, however, because marten was undervalued in the company's comparative standard. Thus, while marten fetched a higher price on the European market than beaver, it was valued at one-third of a beaver according to the comparative standard.
2 Norman Nie et al., *Statistical Package for the Social Sciences*

CHAPTER 11

1 York Factory Account Books, 1688, PAC HBC B 239/d/1, p. 54. See also, Arthur Ray, 'Higgling and Haggling at Ye Bay,' *Beaver*, Summer, 1977

2 See page 67.

3 For example, in their 6 June 1698 letter of general instructions, the governor and committee wrote: '... make it yor Endeavr to rise the Standard for the Trade in generall, because of the lowe prices Beavor is Sold for here, and the greate Advance here is on all sorts of English goods.' London Correspondence Book Outwards, 1695–1715, PAC HBC A 6/3, p. 39

4 York Factory Account Books, 1691, PAC HBC B 239/d/4, p. 48

5 K.G. Davies, *Letters From Hudson Bay, 1703–40*, 268

6 Ibid., 263

7 E.E. Rich, *The Fur Trade and the Northwest to 1857*, 43. For a more extensive discussion of the use of alcohol, see A. Ray, 'The Hudson's Bay Company in the Eighteenth Century: A Comparative Economic Study.'

8 Davies, *Letters from Hudson Bay*, 43

9 E.E. Rich, 'Trade Habits and Economic Motivation among the Indians of North America.'

10 Davies, *Letters from Hudson Bay*, 268

11 Ibid., 263

12 It must be pointed out, however, that relationships between price and fur volume cannot be fully analysed on the basis of Hudson's Bay Company data alone, since, at the height of French competition in the eighteenth century, a considerable volume of furs was diverted away from the bayside posts. It cannot therefore be ascertained whether high fur prices simply diverted trade or affected its over-all volume. Some evidence exists for a negative response of fur volume to higher prices: i.e., as prices increased, fewer furs were brought to the posts by the Indians on a per capita basis. This is discussed further in chapter 14.

13 London Correspondence Book Outwards, 1695–1715, PAC HBC A 6/3, p. 29

14 Ibid., 31

15 Ibid., 32

16 Ibid., 43–4

17 Ibid., 31, 39. In 1697 the governor and committee also suggested that the traders show the Indians the stocks of coat beaver piled in the post warehouse so that the latter might realize that the company had no further need for additional supplies of this commodity.

18 Innis approached the question of the effect of competition on fur prices with

caution commenting that: 'the exent to which this practice [meeting competition by reducing prices] was followed is difficult to determine.' Since he lacked detailed information concerning variations in the standards of trade, Innis was similarly hesitant about undertaking a discussion of these standards although he was clearly aware that such variations existed. See: H.A. Innis, *The Fur Trade in Canada*, 139–42

19 G. Williams, *Andrew Graham's Observations on Hudson's Bay, 1767–1791*, 275

CHAPTER 12

1 E.E. Rich, ed., *Hudson's Bay Copy-Booke of Letters Commissions Instructions Outward, 1688–1696*, 14–15
2 Ibid., 205. In the general letter to the posts in 1738, the governor and committee asked what the watering ratios were at the various posts. The response from James Isham was that they added slightly less than one-third water to the brandy and it was principally from the trade of brandy, beads, and paint that they derived their overplus. Letter 68, York Fort, August 1738, in *Letters from Hudson Bay, 1703–40*, edited by K.G. Davies, 263
3 Hinterland boundaries shown in Figure 36 are approximate, and do not imply that inter-post competition was completely absent at all times. Indeed, such competition was a problem at various times.
4 Davies, *Letters from Hudson Bay*, 172
5 For a detailed discussion of the military and policial developments affecting the fur trade during this period see E.E. Rich, *The Fur Trade and the Northwest to 1857*.
6 Evidence previously examined suggests that the absence of competition, rather than the increasing volumes of furs *per se*, was the primary reason the factors could tighten their standards.
7 Davies, *Letters from Hudson Bay*, 331
8 Ibid., 42
9 Ibid., 82
10 Ibid., 88
11 Ibid., 114
12 Ibid., 114 n2
13 Ibid., 122
14 Ibid., 145
15 Ibid., 167
16 Ibid., 136. This would place them on the Winnipeg River, probably in the vicinity of its confluence with the English River. See 136, n1

17 Ibid., 136
18 Ibid., 157
19 Ibid., 168–9, 198, 220, and 259
20 Ibid., 211–12
21 Ibid., 153, n2
22 Ibid., 173, 196
23 Ibid., 196
24 Hudson's Bay Company Correspondence Inward, PAC HBC A 11/43, pp. 47–8
25 Ibid., 49
26 Ibid., 58
27 Ibid., 74–8
28 Arthur J. Ray, *Indians in the Fur Trade*, 138
29 Correspondence Inward, PAC HBC A 11/43 pp. 99–102
30 In fact, some of this debt was subsequently paid, as revealed by entries in the account books of this post. Hudson's Bay Company account books, PAC HBC B 135/d/27, p. 13
31 Correspondence Inward, PAC HBC A 11/43, p. 99
32 Rich, *Fur Trade*, 106
33 Ibid., 106
34 Davies, *Letters from Hudson Bay*, 313
35 Correspondence Inward, PAC HBC A 11/43, pp. 120–5
36 Ibid., 152
37 York Factory Correspondence Books, 1754, PAC HBC B 239/b/11, p. 16. Letter from Ferdinand Jacobs, Prince of Wales (Fort Churchill), 23 August 1754
38 Correspondence Inward, PAC HBC A 11/43, pp. 120–5
39 Ibid.
40 Correspondence Inward, PAC HBC A 11/115, p. 116
41 Correspondence Inward, PAC HBC A 11/3, pp. 128–49
42 The data for Fort Severn (Figure 30) are difficult to interpret in this context because the post was opened only in the 1760s and so there are no records of earlier years for comparison.
43 Correspondence Inward, PAC HBC A 11/115, pp. 124–5
44 Correspondence Inward, PAC HBC A 11/43, pp. 144–8

CHAPTER 13

1 H.A. Innis, *The Fur Trade in Canada*, 15–16
2 I.M. Biss[Spry], 'Overhead Costs, Time Problems, and Prices'
3 Beckles Willson, *The Great Company*, 295–7. See also, E.E. Rich, ed., *Copy-Booke of Letters Commissions Instructions Outward 1688–1696*, xxxvi–xlviii

4 These expenses were further increased by the Indians' insistence on top quality trade goods for which they were reluctant to pay a premium.

5 Arthur J. Ray, *Indians in the Fur Trade*, 67

6 R. Glover, ed., *A Journey from Prince of Wales Fort in Hudson's Bay to the Northern Ocean ... by Samuel Hearne*, 285n

7 K.G. Davies, ed., *Letters From Hudson Bay, 1703–40*, 331

8 Ibid., 331, 355–61

9 Ibid., 331

10 Karl Polanyi and A. Rotstein, *Dahomey and the Slave Trade*, 156–7

11 J. Robson, *An Account of Six Years Residence in Hudson's Bay from 1733 to 1736, and From 1744 to 1747*, London, 1752, pp. 39–40.

CHAPTER 14

1 Arthur Dobbs, *An Account of the Countries Adjoining to Hudson's Bay in the Northwest Part of America*, 39

2 G. Williams, *Andrew Graham's Observations on Hudson's Bay*, 263, 275

3 L.J. Burpee, 'Journal of a Journey Performed by Anthony Hendry [Henday], to Explore the Country Inland, and to Endeavour to Increase the Hudson's Bay Company's Trade, A.D. 1754–1755,' 352

4 Offsetting this, and further complicating our efforts to obtain a clear picture of individual responses of Indians to prices, is the fact that many of the Indians who proceeded beyond the French posts carried the furs of others who did not. For example, when Henday left Fort Poskoyac for York Factory, he observed: 'Several Asinepoet Natives distributed their heavy Furs and Pelts, that the French have refused, amongst our Indians with directions what to trade them for.' Thus, while Indians trading at York parted with some of their furs at the French posts while en route, they also obtained additional furs to trade on behalf of their fellows who no longer made the trip. Ibid., 353

5 Many of the middlemen of York Factory and Fort Churchill visited the posts only every two or three years. Those who traded at the other posts were more frequent visitors.

6 It should be stressed that the cheaper price was not the reason for the innovation's acceptance, but rather, the greater ease of handling of the shorter gun. These guns could be carried more easily in canoes and used in bush country. K. G. Davies, *Letters From Hudson Bay, 1703–1740*, 9

7 Ibid., 136

CHAPTER 15

1 Marshall Sahlins, *Stone Age Economics*, 185–6 n1
2 A. Rotstein, 'Fur Trade and Empire'
3 A. Rotstein, 'Karl Polanyi's Concept of Non-Market Trade,' 118
4 Colin Renfrew, 'Trade as Action at a Distance: Questions of Integration and Communication,' 18
5 Richard Gray and David Birmingham, *Pre-Colonial African Trade*, 2
6 Rotstein, 'Polanyi's Concept,' 118–21

CHAPTER 16

1 H.K. Schneider, *Economic Man*, 5–9
2 See, for example, Jan S. Prybyla, *Comparative Economic Systems*.
3 Irene M. Spry, personal communication, 1973
4 A.S. Morton, *A History of the Canadian West to 1870–71*, 240–1
5 E.E. Rich interpreted such fixed official exchange rates as evidence that market mechanisms were absent from the fur trade. He states: 'There was no escaping the conclusion that in trade with Indians the price mechanism did not work.' However, as R.A. Mundell observes, the setting of fixed prices does not render the laws of supply and demand inapplicable. See Rich, 'Trade Habits and Economic Motivation Among the Indians of North America,' 49; and also see R.A. Mundell, *Man and Economics*, 63–72.
6 M. Sahlins, *Stone Age Economics*, 195
7 Richard Glover, *A Journey From Prince of Wales Fort in Hudson's Bay to the Northern Ocean, 1769, 1770, 1771, 1772 by Samuel Hearne*, 51–2
8 K. Polanyi, 'The Economy as Instituted Process,' 243–70
9 George Dalton, 'Karl Polanyi's Analysis of Long-Distance Trade and his Wider Paradigm,' 73

CHAPTER 17

1 Central-place theory relates the size, location, spacing, and interrelationships of market centres or similar nodes of commercial activity with the functions performed by centres and the spatial behaviour of consumers. The classical statement of central-place theory is by Walter Christaller. See W. Christaller, *The Central Places of Southern Germany*.
2 In studying trade between early state societies, Renfrew noted the organizing effect on trade of the spatial arrangement of market centres or other urban

foci and hence the applicability of central-place theory. See Colin Renfrew, 'Trade as Action at a Distance,' 3–60.

3 B.J.L. Berry, *Geography of Market Centers and Retail Distribution*

4 A good example of such a geographic study is that by Marvin Mikesell, who examines the role of the market in the context of North African culture. Mikesell draws attention to the sharp economic–spatial duality which exists in countries such as Morocco, and which is reflected in such institutions as market centres. 'Westernized' towns such as Casablanca and Rabat stand in marked contrast to the 'traditional suq,' which is the tribal equivalent of a market and a social and political gathering place. The 'suq' began essentially as a form of periodic market: merchants followed a more or less established circuit of marketing places, which were often simply trail junctions or points along a boundary between areas specializing in different forms of agricultural or pastoral activity. The 'suq' therefore had definite spatial and temporal regularity, and essentially fulfilled the various roles which 'western' central places perform. Recently, development of road transportation and the establishment of more tranquil relations among tribal groups have led to changes in the 'suq' which portend the development of permanent market centres on a more westernized pattern. See Marvin W. Mikesell, 'The Role of Tribal Markets in Morocco.'

5 R.J. Bromley, 'Markets in the Developing Countries'

6 Polly Hill and R.H.T. Smith, 'The Spatial and Temporal Synchronization of Periodic Markets'

7 Thomas Eighmy, 'Rural Periodic Markets and the Extension of an Urban System'

8 Hill and Smith, 'Spatial Synchronization,' 354

9 Berry, *Geography*, 59–88

10 The posts were, however, linked by an information system involving Indian messengers.

11 In spite of these assurances, the traders at York Factory continued to maintain that any furs traded at Fort Churchill '... is only a robbing of this place ...' See, Thomas McCliesh's letter from York Fort, 23 August 1723, in K.G. Davies, *Letters From Hudson Bay, 1703–40*, 94.

12 Moose Factory, Correspondence Inward to London, PAC HBC A 11/43, pp. 53–6

13 Ibid., 149–54

14 Fort Albany, Correspondence Inward to London, PAC HBC A 11/3, p. 153

15 L. Burpee, 'Journal of a Journey Performed by Anthony Hendry, to Explore the Country Inland, and to Endeavour to Increase the Hudson's Bay Company's Trade, A.D. 1754–1755,' 353

16 James E. Vance, Jr, *The Merchants' World*
17 Harold Hotelling, 'Stability in Competition'
18 Edward L. Ullman, 'Geography as Spatial Interaction'
19 Donald B. Freeman, *International Trade, Migration, and Capital Flows*
20 See quotation on p. 25
21 Gunnar Olsson, *Distance and Human Interaction*
22 Arthur J. Ray, 'History and Archaeology of the Northern Fur Trade'
23 The difficulties of developing 'traditional' enclaves in contemporary third world countries using 'western' concepts of regional development, and the need to focus on existing systems of interaction between disparate 'traditional' and 'modern' sectors in formulating growth policies, are explored in D.B. Freeman, 'Development Strategies in Dual Economies'
24 It should be noted that a kindred problem has been discussed by Brian J.L. Berry in connection with the development of comparative factorial ecology as a subfield of urban geography. Although defending the major objective of 'comparative' studies (i.e., the search for general frameworks that yield insights into specific phenomena in cross-cultural settings), Berry notes the 'relativist' criticisms leveled at such studies: i.e., the dangers of superficial comparison, and of ethnocentrism. See B.J.L. Berry, 'Comparative Factorial Ecology,' 218–19.
25 Robert A. Murdie, 'Cultural Differences in Consumer Travel'
26 See P.R. Gould, 'Tanzania 1920–1963.'
27 Forthright statements of opposing viewpoints in this debate are found in George Dalton, 'Economic Theory and Primitive Society'; and in Edward Le Clair, Jr, 'Economic Theory and Economic Anthropology.'
28 George Dalton, 'Karl Polanyi's Analysis of Long-Distance Trade and his Wider Paradigm,' 73–4

APPENDIX

1 K.G. Davies, ed., *Letters From Hudson Bay 1703–40*, 42

WALLACE, W.S., ed. *Documents Relating to the North West Company.* Toronto: Champlain Society, 1934

WILLIAMS, G., ed. *Andrew Graham's Observations on Hudson's Bay, 1767–91.* London: Hudson's Bay Record Society, 1969

THWAITES, R.G., ed. *The Jesuit Relations and Allied Documents, VI.* Cleveland: Burrows Bros. Co., 1899

SECONDARY SOURCES

BAILEY, A.G. *The Conflict of European and Eastern Algonkian Cultures, 1504–1700.* Toronto: University of Toronto Press, 2nd edition, 1969

BERRY, B.J.L., ed. 'Comparative Factorial Ecology,' *Economic Geography* 47 (1971): Supplement

– *Geography of Market Centers and Retail Distribution.* Englewood Cliffs: Prentice-Hall, 1967

BIGGAR, H.P. *The Early Trading Companies of New France* [1901]. Reprinted edition. New York: Argonaut Press, 1965

BISHOP, C.A. 'The Emergence of Hunting Territories Among the Northern Ojibwa,' *Ethnology* 9(1970): 1–15

– *The Northern Ojibwa and the Fur Trade.* Toronto: Holt, Rinehart and Winston of Canada, 1974

BISS [SPRY], I.M., 'Overhead Costs, Time Problems, and Prices,' in *Essays in Political Economy,* edited by H.A. Innis. Toronto: University of Toronto Press, 1938

BROMLEY, R.J., 'Markets in the Developing Countries: A Review,' *Geography* 56(1971): 124–31

CAWSTON, G. and A.H. KEANE. *The Early Chartered Companies* [1896]. Reprinted New York: Franklin, 1968

CHRISTALLER, WALTER. *The Central Places of Southern Germany.* Translated by C. Baskin. Englewood Cliffs: Prentice Hall, 1966

DALTON, GEORGE. 'Economic Theory and Primitive Society,' *American Anthropologist* 63(1961): 1–25

– 'Karl Polanyi's Analysis of Long-Distance Trade and his Wider Paradigm,' in *Ancient Civilization and Trade,* edited by J.A. Sabloff and C. Lamberg-Karlovsky. Albuquerque: University of New Mexico Press, 1975

– *Primitive, Archaic and Modern Economies: Essays of Karl Polanyi.* Garden City: Anchor Books, 1968

ECCLES, W.J. *The Canadian Frontier, 1534–1760.* Albuquerque: University of New Mexico Press, 1974

EIGHMY, THOMAS. 'Rural Periodic Markets and the Extension of an Urban System: A Western Nigerian Example,' *Economic Geography* 48(1972): 299–315

FREEMAN, D.B., 'Development Strategies in Dual Economies: A Kenyan Example,'
  African Studies Review 18(1975): 17–33
– *International Trade, Migration, and Capital Flows: A Quantitiative Analysis of Spatial
  Economic Interaction.* Chicago: University of Chicago Department of Geography
  Research Series No. 146, 1973
GALBRAITH, J. *The Hudson's Bay Company as an Imperial Factor, 1821–69.* Berkeley:
  University of California Press, 1957
GOULD, P.R., 'Tanzania 1920–1963: The Spatial Impress of the Modernization
  Process,' *World Politics* 22(1970): 149–70
GRAY, RICHARD and DAVID BIRMINGHAM, eds. *Pre-Colonial African Trade: Essays on
  Trade in Central and Eastern Africa Before 1900.* London: Oxford University
  Press, 1970
HEIDENREICH, C.E. *Huronia: A History and Geography of the Huron Indians,
  1600–1650.* Toronto: McClelland and Stewart, 1971
HEIDENREICH, C.E. and A.J. RAY. *The Early Fur Trades: A Study in Cultural Interaction.*
  Toronto: McClelland and Stewart, 1976
HILL, POLLY and R.H.T. SMITH. 'The Spatial and Temporal Synchronization of
  Periodic Markets: Evidence from Four Emirates in Northern Nigeria,'
  Economic Geography 48(1972): 345–55
HOTELLING, HAROLD. 'Stability in Competition,' *The Economic Journal* 39(1929):
  41–57
INNIS, H.A. *Essays in Political Economy.* Toronto: University of Toronto Press,
  1938
– *The Fur Trade in Canada.* Rev. ed. Toronto: University of Toronto Press, 1962
LE CLAIR, JR, EDWARD. 'Economic Theory and Economic Anthropology,' *American
  Anthropologist* 64(1962): 1179–1203
LE CLAIR, JR, EDWARD and HAROLD K. SCHNIEDER, eds. *Economic Anthropolgy:
  Readings in Theory and Analysis.* New York: Holt, Rinehart and Winston, 1968
LUCAS, C.P. *The Beginnings of English Overseas Enterprise.* Oxford: The Clarendon
  Press, 1917
MIKESELL, MARVIN W. 'The Role of Tribal Markets in Morocco,' *Geographical Review*
  48(1958): 494–511
MORTON, A.S. *The Canadian West to 1870–71.* 2nd ed. Toronto: University of
  Toronto Press, 1973
MUNDELL, R.A. *Man and Economics.* New York: McGraw-Hill, 1968
MURDIE, ROBERT A. 'Cultural Differences in Consumer Travel,' *Economic Geography*
  41(1965): 211–33
NIE, NORMAN H., C. HADLAI HULL, JEAN G. JENKINS, KARIN STEINBRENNER, and DALE
  BENT. *Statistical Package for the Social Sciences,* 2nd ed. Toronto: McGraw-Hill,
  1975

OLSSON, GUNNAR. *Distance and Human Interaction: A Review and Bibliography.* Philadelphia: Regional Science Research Institute, 1965

POLANYI, KARL. 'The Economy as Instituted Process,' in *Trade and Market in the Early Empires*, edited by Karl Polanyi, C.M. Arensberg, and H.W. Pearson. Glencoe: Free Press, 1957

– 'Our Obsolete Market Mentality,' *Commentary* 3 (1947): 109–17. Reprinted in *Primitive, Archaic and Modern Economies: Essays of Karl Polanyi*, edited by George Dalton. Garden City: Anchor Books, 1968

– 'The Semantics of Money Uses,' *Primitive Archaic and Modern Economies*, edited by George Dalton. Garden City: Anchor Books, 1968

POLANYI, KARL and A. ROTSTEIN. *Dahomey and the Slave Trade.* Seattle: University of Washington Press, 1966

PRYBYLA, JAN S. *Comparative Economic Systems.* New York: Appleton Century Crofts, 1969

RABB, T.K. *Enterprise and Empire.* Cambridge: Harvard University Press, 1967

RAY, ARTHUR J. 'The Factor and the Trading Captain in the Hudson's Bay Company Fur Trade before 1763,' National Museum of Man, Mercury Series, Canadian Ethnology Service, Paper 28(1975): 586–602

– 'The Early Hudson's Bay Company Account Books as Sources for Historical Research: An Analysis and Assessment,' *Archivaria* 1(1976): 3–38

– 'Higgling and Haggling at ye Bay,' *The Beaver* (Summer 1977)

– 'History and Archaeology of the Northern Fur Trade,' *American Antiquity* 43(1978): 26–34

– 'The Hudson's Bay Company Fur Trade in the Eighteenth Century: A Comparative Economic Study,' in *European Settlement and Development in North America: Essays on Geographical Change in Honour and Memory of Andrew Hill Clark*, edited by James R. Gibson. Toronto: University of Toronto Press, 1978

– 'The Hudson's Bay Company Account Books as Sources for Comparative Economic Analyses of the Fur Trade: An Examination of Exchange Rate Data,' *Western Canadian Journal of Anthropology* VI(1976): 30–51

– *Indians in the Fur Trade: Their Role as Hunters, Trappers and Middlemen in the Lands Southwest of Hudson Bay, 1660–1870.* Toronto: University of Toronto Press, 1974

RENFREW, COLIN. 'Trade as Action at a Distance: Questions of Integration and Communication,' in *Ancient Civilization and Trade*, edited by J.A. Sabloff and C. Lamberg-Karlovsky. Albuquerque: University of New Mexico Press, 1975

RICH, E.E. *The Fur Trade and the Northwest to 1857.* Toronto: McClelland and Stewart, 1967

– *The Hudson's Bay Company, 1670–1870* [1958]. Reprinted, Toronto: McClelland and Stewart, 3 vols., 1960

– 'Trade Habits and Economic Motivation among the Indians of North America,' *Canadian Journal of Economics and Political Science* 26(1960): 35–53

ROGERS, E.S. 'The Hunting Group – Hunting Territory Complex Among the Mistassini Indians.' *National Museum of Canada Bulletin No. 195*, Ottawa, 1963

ROTSTEIN, A. 'Fur Trade and Empire: An Institutional Analysis.' PH D dissertation, University of Toronto, 1967

– 'Karl Polanyi's Concept of Non-Market Trade,' *Journal of Economic History* 30(1970): 118–20

SABLOFF, J.A. and C. LAMBERG-KARLOVSKY, eds. *Ancient Civilization and Trade*. Albuquerque: University of New Mexico Press, 1975

SAHLINS, M.D. *Stone Age Economics*. Chicago: Aldine, 1972

– *The Tribesmen*. Englewood-Cliffs: Prentice Hall, 1968

SCHNEIDER, H.K. *Economic Man: The Anthropology of Economics*. New York: The Free Press, 1974

SCOTT, W.R. *The Constitution and Finance of English, Scottish and Irish Joint-Stock Companies to 1720*. London: Cambridge University Press, 3 vols., 1910–12

ULLMAN, EDWARD L. 'Geography as Spatial Interaction,' *Annals of the Association of American Geographers* 14(1954): 283–4

VANCE, J.E. *The Merchants' World: The Geography of Wholesaling*. Englewood Cliffs: Prentice Hall, 1970

WILLSON, BECKLES. *The Great Company*. Toronto: Copp Clark, 1899

Index

Account book data: comparability of
121–2; reliability of 113–19
Account books: procedures used in,
97–109; structure of 82–3
Actual standard of trade, *see* standards
of trade
Adams, Joseph 179
Administered trade, *see* trade
Albanel, Father 29
Alcohol 48, 72, 128–44, 194–6
Algonkin 16, 42
Alliances 22–3, 62, 232–3
Alternative trading opportunities 221,
223
Arms, *see* firearms
Assiniboine 16, 42–5, 47–9, 69, 182,
232
Athabascan-speaking Indians 45, 47,
49
Attikameque 16

Backward sloping supply curve
219–21
Balance remaining inventory 82–7, 95
Barter trade, *see* trade
Basques 20–1
Beale, Anthony 176, 211

Beaver: coat beaver 19–20, 31, 35,
159–161; parchment beaver 20,
159–61
Beaver account 97, 101–3
Beothuk, 19
Berry, Brian J. L. 247
Bevan, William 183, 217
Bishop, C. A. 7
Bishop, Nathaniel 210
Blackfoot 16, 45–9, 191–2
Blood 45–9
Brandy 128–44, 201–2; *see also* alcohol
Brazil tobacco 181, 252
Bridgar, John 85
Bromley, R. J. 247

Captain's coat 56, 70
Cartier, Jacques 19, 21
Castor gras, *see* beaver (coat)
Castor sec, *see* beaver (parchment)
Central place theory 246, 248–53
Ceremonial exchange, *see* gift ex-
change
Champlain, Samuel de 20–3
Chipewyan 16
Colbert, Jean Baptiste 30–1
Comparative economic analysis 80

Comparative Standard: *see* standards of trade (comparative)

Competition: analysis of 80; on Hudson Bay 29–32; in the interior 32–6, 39, 44–5, 48–9, 163–217

Complementarity 254–5

Consumer behaviour: Indian 129, 161–2, 224–5; *see also* economic behaviour (Indian)

Country produce 41, 49

Coureurs de bois 30, 32–3, 44, 51, 129, 177–9, 188–90, 251

Credit 55, 186–7

Cree 8, 15–16, 23–4, 42–5, 47–9, 62, 182, 232

Cumberland House 197

Dakota, *see* Sioux

Debts, *see* credit

Demonstration effect 225

De Noyon, Jacques 32

Dobbs, Arthur 222

Dulhut (Duluth), Daniel Greysolon 32–3, 43

Eastmain 28, 34, 50, 167

Economic behaviour 218–27; Indian 5–6, 20, 22, 58, 60, 79, 162, 185, 196–200, 227; *see also* consumer behaviour

Economic indices 122

Exchange: modes of 80; *see also* trade

Economic theories 6

Eighmy, Thomas 247

Expenses 72–3, 121, 198–217

Expenses account 107

Factor (Hudson's Bay Company) 66, 69, 74–5

Factors' Standard, *see* standards of trade (factors')

Factory system 30

Favell, John 197, 251

Felt hat 19

Firearms 33, 41, 43, 62, 87

Fixed costs 198

Formal economic theory 163

Fort Albany 28, 32, 34, 45, 49, 50–1, 87, 165–6, 177–8, 187, 189, 192–4, 196, 201, 213, 215, 250–2

Fort Charles 29

Fort Churchill (Prince of Wales) 28, 34, 47, 50–1, 109–13, 175–6, 182, 191–2, 201, 210–11, 213, 217

Fort Rupert 28–9

Fort Severn 28, 50

French Standards, *see* Standards of Trade (French)

French traders 7, 10, 13, 21, 23–5; *see also coureurs de bois*

French trading network 27

Frontenac, Governor General Louis de Buade, Comte de 30–2

Fur auctions 52

Fur markets 31–2, 53–4, 71

General charge 87–9, 97

General reciprocity, *see* reciprocity (general)

Geyer, George 163

Gift exchange: general 5–8, 52, 55–9, 61–3, 68–9, 73, 166–7, 191–2, 227–8, 242–3; description of 56–7; effect of competition on 199–201; expenses of 89–91, 199–201; purpose of 62

Gift giving, *see* gift exchange

Goods traded: account of 91–3; value of 120–1

Graham, Andrew 35–6, 57–9, 66, 128, 216

Gray and Birmingham 235

Groseilliers, Médard Chouart, Sieur des 23–4
Gros Ventre 16
Guns, see firearms

Haggling 93–5, 233, 239–40; see also trade (market)
Hearne, Samuel 199–200, 241
Heidenreich, C.E. 6–7
Henday, Anthony 191–2, 223, 252
Henley House 189
Hill, Poly 247
Hole-in-the-wall 57–8, 166
Home guard Cree 41
Hopkins, Theodore 195
Hudson Bay lowlands 39–41
Hudson's Bay Company charter 12–14
Huron 5–7, 14, 42, 62
Indian: dependence on Europeans 41; socio-political organization 14–17; see also individual tribal groups
Indirect trade area 48–51
Innis, H.A. 4–5, 20, 161, 198
Iroquois 5, 7, 14, 16, 21–3, 44, 62
Isham, James 66, 124, 139

Jacobs, Ferdinand 192, 195–6
Joint-stock companies 11–12

Kelsey, Henry 159–61
Knight, James 85, 103, 249

La Chesnaye, Charles Aubert de 32
Lake Nipigon 32, 42–3, 166, 177
Lake of the Woods 33
Lake Superior 42
Land tenure 8, 14, 17–18, 61
Laurentian shield 40–3
La Vérendrye, Pierre Gaultier de Varennes, Sieur de 33, 44–5, 190

Lawson, John 125–6
Local trade area 48–9
Long-distance trade, see trade (long-distance)

Made Beaver 54
Mandan 16, 45–9
Market trade, see trade (market)
Marten, Humphrey 194, 252
Matanabbee 199–200
Men's Debts account, 88–9, 91, 107
Mercantile model 253–4
Michipicoten 33, 177
Micmac 19
Middlemen 7–8, 20, 23, 42–51, 48–9, 52, 60, 224, 240–1
Montagnais 16, 19–22, 42
Moose Factory 28, 34, 50, 143, 183–6, 189, 193, 197, 201, 206–13, 215, 250
Myatt, Joseph 177–9, 217
McCliesh, Thomas 177, 226–7, 262

Neutral 7, 16
Nipissing 7, 16
Nixon, John 30, 44, 83–4, 87
Norton, Richard 72–3, 107, 115–17, 175–6, 210–11, 217
Nor'Westers 192–7

Ojibwa 7–8, 15, 16, 42, 44–5
Ottawa 7, 16
Out-of-pocket costs, see expenses
Overplus 52, 66, 73, 80, 101, 107, 121, 125–8, 182–3, 186, 203–17, 240; calculation of 93–4
Parchment beaver, see beaver (parchment)
Peddlers, see Nor'Westers
Periodic markets 247
Petun 7, 10
Polanyi, Karl 242

Politics and trade 60–2, 231–36
Pollexsen, Henry 193–4
Prices, *see* standards of trade
Private trade 117–19, 184–5
Profit and loss accounts 107
Property rights 58–9
Provisions, *see* country produce

Radisson, Pierre Esprit 23–4
Rainy Lake 166
Rainy River 45
Ray, Arthur J. 6, 8
Reciprocity: general 58, 243–4; balanced 244; negative 240, 244
Redistribution 243–5
Regulated companies 11
Renfrew, Colin 235, 247
Rich, E.E. 5, 8, 53, 60, 189, 232
Robson, Joseph 215
Rotstein, Abraham 5, 6, 8, 60, 232

Sahlins, Marshall 14
Saskatchewan River 33, 36, 46
Sergeant, Henry 85, 89–91
Shipping invoice 86–7
Short-distance trade, *see* trade (short-distance)
Sioux (Dakota) 16, 42, 44, 49, 182, 232
Smith, R.H.T. 247
Standards of trade: French 179, 183, 188; comparative (Hudson's Bay Company) 20, 52, 54, 63, 89, 93–5; factors' standards (Hudson's Bay Company) 62, 63, 70–1, 73, 79, 95, 121, 144, 147–55, 165–98,

203–219; standard of trade (official Hudson's Bay Company) 5, 52–4, 63, 66, 71–2, 89, 93–5, 240; Nor'Westers 192–4
Staunton, Richard 128, 177–8
Stores accounts 109–13

Tadoussac 20–3, 29, 51, 233
Talon, Intendant Jean 29
Terms of trade, *see* standards of trade
Tobacco 195–6
Trade: administered 6, 232–6, 243; barter 57, 67, 74; long-distance 234–5; market 6, 10–11, 53–4, 231–2, 237–40, 247; short-distance 234–5
Trade goods 7, 19, 33, 41, 43, 54, 87, 181, 226–7
Trade goods accounts 101
Trade goods–overplus ratio 144–55
Trading captains 15–17, 55, 58–9, 63, 67–70, 73–5, 233, 241–2
Trading routes 26–9, 42–3
Transferability 255
Treaty trade, *see* administered trade
Treaty of Utrecht 32–3

Vance, James 253

Warfare 42–4, 167, 181–2
White, Thomas 250

York Factory 28, 34, 45–6, 50–1, 55, 72–3, 142–3, 165–6, 180–1, 190, 196, 201, 217, 227